No Fixed Address

How to Run Away from It All

D0890495

A Memoir

Eileen Maley

ISBN-13: 978-1-941334-25-6
ISBN-10: 1-941334-25-3

Published by Second Wind Publications

Cover & book design by Amelia Smith

Cover snapshot by Timothy Maley, 1973, Beirut

Author photo by Annabelle Brothers

Disclaimer:

This is a memoir and these stories are as factual as my memory allows. Anyone I meant to offend is no longer alive. Most people I write about are identified by their real names, sometimes just first names. I used made-up names for two people because I can't remember everyone I met so long ago. Conditions, cultures, prices and people have most certainly changed since I experienced them and I hope they are all thriving.

For Timothy

Table of Contents

The Old Country

No Fixed Address

Finding My Way Home

Part One:

The Old Country

Coddiwomple (v.): to travel purposefully toward an as-yet-unknown destination

English slang

VANCOUVER, B.C
1971

The first snow meandered silently down as I walked home from the bus stop on Halloween night. I should have enjoyed the flakes' delicate pirouettes, dissolving before they hit the sidewalk, but I was in a vinegar mood. For one thing, it's not supposed to snow before the end of the year in Vancouver, Canada's only temperate little corner. For another, I was heading home from a retirement party held in a rented reception hall, a sendoff thrown by the corporation for a colleague who didn't want to retire.

The retiree, until that day, had been a deskman at *The Vancouver Sun,* a rewrite man, a copy editor who had first crack at reading reporters' articles. He tidied up the story, correcting the grammar and spelling and often the facts. The reports he scanned were double-spaced, typed on half-size sheets of pulpy paper, a paragraph or two per page. Articles ended with the number 30; I never knew why. People don't seem to do that any more. In those days deskmen were always men. They decided whether an article deserved a byline. They wrote a headline for a piece, rolled it up, stuck it into a pneumatic tube, and blasted it up and away to be set in hot type.

But this Halloween day's forced retirement reminded me of an occurrence I had read about and filed in my head in case I ever needed it. There's this man who was fired from his job. Being an imaginative fellow, he stuffed a jelly donut into the pneumatic cylinder and launched it while he was on his way out the door. Journalists learn to be cynical; it's in the job description.

The retirement bash was a gloomy event, as it turned out. In the honoree's mind, the party was a bitter hoax to toast him, roast him and haul him away screaming. "I don't want to retire," he said in his farewell speech, after an hour of leaning on the open bar. "I've had this same job for twenty-six years, since being discharged from the army. I have nothing else to do. I have no desire to travel to Europe or to write the great Canadian novel." He paused. "I like my job, I like going to work. In fact, I'm pissed off about this whole business and I want to be sure all of you know how I feel, especially the editors, the publisher, and the corporate people who decided to end my working life because I'm sixty-five." He tipped his head back for a final gulp of his drink, and he sat down.

The room was silent. Some well-groomed gray heads wore gray faces. The party broke up. Nobody had the appetite to keep smiling.

This day had been his last shift. If he'd had one more day, I would have brought him a jelly donut.

On my way home, a plan sprung fully formed into my alcohol-fizzled brain. I loved my job at the *Sun*, but I didn't want to keep doing it until I was nudged or pushed out the door at sixty-five. I felt in my heart that a newsroom full of working reporters and editors was a boneyard of broken dreams, of wishing for so much more. I had one of the sweetest jobs in journalism. It involved no toil. I wrote a daily column reviewing television programs, and writing about the industry locally and its people, whose efforts were beginning to gain in strength and visibility here. I had been a fan of television since Howdy Doody wore a onesie.

All of this predated technology as we know it now. This was back when the pistachios on the coffee table were magenta. The paper provided me with the latest state-of-the-art equipment, before we used terms like "state of the art." The "latest" meant a color TV set, a handful of channels, and I spent my evenings at home watching the same programs that you were watching. There were no advance viewings.

Then I traveled across the living room, sat at my desk and typed out my opinions in so many words. Then I called a taxi, which came and took my thoughts in a brown envelope to the newsroom, and then I watched clever Dick Cavett, in color, just for my own pleasure, then I went to bed. I could sleep late if I wanted to.

It was, in fact, too cozy. While everybody else I knew was working during the day, I had little to do. Hose out the apartment once in a while, read good books. I spent too many afternoons aimlessly wandering around the second floor of the Hudson's Bay Company store admiring the fashions. I began to feel that I was being watched, I was so familiar around the store. Or is that a symptom of paranoia?

The job didn't balance with the rest of my life. My divorce papers were finally official. My ex-husband, who was always hard to find, was found living in Rome. My best woman friend had moved to Hong Kong. My family was thousands of miles away back east and I had no interest in backtracking. I felt suspended without supports, floundering around, making questionable decisions. I was about to make another. The idea of leaving the country had been tickling the back of my brain for a while.

I didn't sleep much that night; I was too busy thinking, planning. The United States, half an hour from Vancouver by car, was out of the running. There was this iniquitous war the Americans were waging in faraway Vietnam. U.S. immigration policy was complicated and time-consuming and I no longer had the desire or the patience to break through this wall. I don't mean to be sentimental, but ever since the assassination of John F. Kennedy, the country had gone to hell. England was out: too damp and smelly and rude, in my experience as a tourist. It had to be an English-speaking country where I could find work, and it had to be warm enough to imagine that snow was a design for a whimsical Christmas card. Aha, there's Australia. Beyond that, a good friend in Hong Kong, a long way around, and no reason to hurry back.

How could I leave this magnificent city? Vancouver is where other Canadians want to go when they die. My most precious memory of the sight of Vancouver had come some months earlier. I was flying home from a family visit back east. It must have been early summer when the sun doesn't disappear from street level until ten o'clock. My flight was coming in to land, the eleven o'clock sky was exceptionally clear, a dark but transparent blue. From the porthole window I could see it all. Ahead, the Pacific, sleek sapphire jelly at the shore, then black. To the north, the ragged mountains, a blue-black wilderness with snow on top, then black. Here and there, a few lights on the mountains. Below, the city itself spreading through the rest of the picture, a flat tray of diamonds, lit up and sparkling, the way cities look so magical from the air at night. At ground level it was dark, but up here, still a blush of a sunset.

Yet, this late October evening, I was determined to leave it behind. Screw it.

In the morning I would call P&O and book a leisurely boat ride on the next ship across the Pacific to Australia. P&O was the biggest and best-known Pacific boat line on the west coast, and had a busy office in Vancouver. Its original name was the Peninsular and Oriental Steam Navigation Company. As the company merged and remerged, added and subtracted ports of call, its name changed as well. By the 1960s it was redundantly called Pacific and Oriental Orient Lines, or P&O Orient Lines, but we Vancouverites knew it simply as P&O.

Halloween that year was on a Friday night, and the P&O office was closed Saturdays. I spent the weekend refining my plans, deciding what to keep and store, what to take with me, what to sell, what to toss, and how to go about each of these tasks. I'd been squirreling away a chunk of my paycheck for some months now, with vague thoughts of buying a house. I was a self-made thousandaire and I could afford to take off.

I was on the phone as soon as the P&O office opened Monday morning. The SS *Iberia*, the next outbound ship, was sailing from Vancouver December 1, just the right amount of time to get my affairs in order. The ship would arrive in Sydney a few days before Christmas. The trouble was, there were no beds left in tourist class, and only one in first class. Could I fly to Hawaii, assuming some passengers disembarked there, and sail from Honolulu south and westward? No space. So I gulped and signed on for first class. Lucky for me, the one and only double cabin with an available bunk was already promised to a woman, not a man.

I bought two steamer trunks, navy-blue-painted tin chests with silver-tone corners. The one holding my life's treasures would go back to southern Ontario to be stored in my parents' basement. The other trunk would come with me to Sydney, ballast in the ship's hold. This one carried an important pair of wispy-thin suede boots with two-yard-long shoelaces and enough holes to consume fifteen minutes of lace-up time. One boot had a tiny leather star high on the left calf. Along with the boots, my workaday wardrobe, a few important books—little else. For my three weeks on board the ship, I stuffed my faithful two-piece set of old gray Samsonite luggage. Everything else was sold, some to colleagues at the paper, the rest to a newly minted doctor who was moving to the city and needed furniture, dishes, vacuum cleaner, blankets, vegetable peeler, everything. I suggested she just move into my vacated apartment, but she had already chosen a place across town near the hospital where she would be working.

It was another undeveloped, incomplete dream of mine, boldly or stupidly quitting a great job, canceling my address and expecting to land on my feet. I counted on this journey to fulfill my poorly organized expectations, whatever they turned out to be.

§

*We don't get much of a spring or fall
up here; for ten months a year, the
weather has teeth in it.*

Marcel Theroux

OTTER RAPIDS, ONTARIO
1960

In Canada, the word "north" means anywhere more than an hour's drive north of wherever you are. Most Canadians live near the U.S. boundary, hugging it for warmth. Chances are that sixty or seventy-five miles north of Anyville is wild country, where single-engine airplanes crash in the woods and are never found. That space on the top three-quarters of the big map is vacant. Very few Canadians have met an Inuit or a polar bear. To paraphrase comedian David Steinberg, Canada is a four-thousand-mile-long clothesline of thirty-six million pairs of frozen mittens.

Otter Rapids wasn't really a place, but a northern wilderness construction site where a hydroelectric power plant was in the late stages of construction. There were no roads in or out. I had moved there in January to recover after breaking up with my longtime high school boyfriend, and quitting a dead-end office job in a very small town called Morrisburg. I was almost twenty-one years old. I had no place else to go and I knew this was a short-term solution, as the construction project would be finished by the end of summer and we would all have to board the train on its southbound run.

My name, from scratch, is Eileen Augusta Popescue Jackle McGregor Johnson Maley. Let me explain. My father was Alex Popescue, who was a son of a bitch, according to my grandmother, but I never met him so I don't really know. The grandparents who raised me were named Jackle. My mother, Alma Jackle Popescue Jackle McGregor, reverted to her maiden name after she divorced Alex Popescue and informally changed my name to Jackle too, to make life less complicated. McGregor was my mother's second husband, my stepfather, and again my name was spontaneously changed to match the rest of the family. In those days a divorced woman was a pariah and having a child with a different surname waved a red flag, a cause for curiosity and inquiry. Each time my name was changed, we happened to be moving to a different part of the country. I walked away from my old friends and never told my new friends about the name changes. I was as embarrassed as my mother by all of this.

Johnson was a regrettable 1960s marriage; Maley is a good marriage. Maley is my name to keep. In the mid-1970s someone asked me why I hadn't kept my former name. Which one, I wondered. My name when I fled to Otter Rapids was McGregor. I didn't have a lot of baggage or knowledge about the world, or even curiosity.

§

The nearest road, dirt or otherwise, was eighty-five miles to the south through the bush. To get there from Morrisburg, I rode a cross-country train west from nearby Ottawa to Cochrane, Ontario. Cochrane was considered pretty far north, a onetime stopping place for fur traders, and was generally considered to be unpolished. The ladies' room in the Cochrane train station had a sign saying "No spitting." It gave me pause.

From there I switched to the northbound train, the Polar Bear Express, which runs from Cochrane to Moosonee on James Bay, itself a gulf of Hudson Bay. Otter Rapids was more than halfway up the line, hour after hour of evergreen trees. Then suddenly we were in a clearing, with one gigantic metal saucer in the middle of nowhere, its face upturned to the eastern sky, frighteningly futuristic, probably a radio transmitter, though nobody on the train seemed to know what sort of signals it transmitted or received.

The train was notorious for its insouciant schedule—stopping to allow moose to cross the tracks, or for the crew's lunch breaks and fishing diversions, if the weather allowed. Track conditions and mechanical breakdowns added to the gamble of the train's arrival times. Even now, it is known as a flag-stop train, like hailing a cab in the big city. Most of the flag stoppers who hailed the Express were Moose Cree First Nation people in invisible settlements tucked among the spruce and pines. Or, seldom, other isolation seekers who had needed to get out of town. They also used the rail service to mail a letter or order canned peas and rounds of ammo.

My stepfather was a civil engineer in charge of generation—the process of producing electric power at the dam-building site. To my mother and me and close friends, he was Mac. Most people at the camp were called by their first names. But my stepfather was Mr. McGregor, which was strange when we were all at a neighborhood party. The party guests were Bill and Margaret, Fran and George, Betty and Henry, Mr. McGregor and Alma, my mom. My parents and three little half-sisters had lived in this isolated site for about three years when I decided to move in with them, to seek some comfort while I made plans for a more satisfying life.

The massive Ontario Hydro project on the Abitibi River was near completion, but there was a job for me in the warehouse—more typing. The most memorable parts of the job were my bathroom breaks. With no facilities at the warehouse, one of the warehousemen was called upon to drive me home in a warehouse truck, then bring me back to work. I felt humored. It had to be an indulgence for some favored warehouse driver-of-the-month as well, a short trip, a cigarette break, then back to work.
It was all kind of silly since I walked to work in the morning, and walked home again at the end of the day.

The other perk, probably offered to me because the rest of my job consisted of filling out forms, was that I got to choose the movies that would be shown each month in the recreation hall. It was my duty to pick one or two from the A list, a handful from the B list. The only one I remember was *The Old Man and the Sea*, certainly from the A list. The movies drew good crowds, including maybe twenty or thirty Cree who arrived on foot from the surrounding woods. They sat up front in the folding chairs that screeched as they were opened on the concrete floor. The native women wrapped their heads in kerchiefs. They never spoke to anyone; they didn't look around the room. They remained still and silent when the rest of us laughed at the celluloid antics, and their shoulders shook with laughter when tragedy filled the screen. I would have liked an interpretation.

Because I had arrived in winter, I didn't wander too far from home, mostly because the snow was deep, the air was cold, and it was dark out there. I took our family dog, Penny, for walks around the edges of the camp, but I avoided the dump, where, I was warned, the wolves and bears went for lunch, not on the same shift.

The January air had a savage scent and a flavor—I used to think it was ozone but nobody else ever said so. To notice the odor, you need to have snow on the ground, frozen air in the sky and no breeze. This air is sharp and crisp, of course, and makes your breathing shallow. If you breathe deeply the cold hurts your insides. There's a reason it's called bitter. My mother told people she wouldn't let my little sisters go to Sunday school if the temperature was lower than twenty-five below, Fahrenheit. I don't know if that was true. We dressed in layers. I wore so much clothing that my arms were out to here and I waddled across the tamped-down road, hearing the snow squeak like those folding chairs in the rec hall.

We, meaning ordinary Canadians, didn't spay or neuter our pets in those days and there weren't any vet services in Otter Rapids anyway. So Penny, an English bulldog, regularly went into estrus, and for a week at a time, the house was surrounded by horny half-dog, half-wolf critters that snuck out of the woods from their Cree settlements. We were careful to keep our dog indoors, and to watch our step outside, as we didn't want to disturb any of the visitors. These half-wolves gathered in a circle around the house, and stood there, grinning at us, panting at us, alertly waiting for Penny to show an interest. This was as close as I came into contact with a living wild animal in the north.

The winter finally melted away and I marveled at seeing the midnight sun in late June. Wild purple roses bloomed, vegetable gardens began to produce generous harvests, mostly carrots and cabbage as I recall. The long daylight sun prompted rapid growth, nature making up for a brief summer. Plenty of bugs as well. So many mosquitoes and gnats and black flies in the air that a noisy poison-spray machine was hauled by tractor every day at seven a.m.

11

and again at seven p.m. Up and down our little streets, choking blasts of yellowish mist that visually blocked the far side of the street. We called our pets and the children inside, closed our windows and doors, and held our breath.

One sunny July day I took Penny and my three sisters for a walk north up the railroad tracks. The bush landscape didn't change for the first mile or so, but then we saw a little homemade house a stone's throw into the woods, and we went to explore. The occupant of the cottage was a white man, in his forties or fifties, who was glad to see us. He didn't get much company. He invited us inside and asked us to sit down while he brewed some tea, sugar but no milk. He never stopped smiling. We admired his rough-hewn walls, covered with animal skins he had shot, skinned, stretched, splayed and nailed to his walls. My sisters, aged eight, six and four, enjoyed the treat, as tea was something only the grown-ups were allowed to drink at home. The dead animals on the walls didn't impress the girls. Our host had a cat, which jumped excitedly on and off the furniture, unafraid of the dog or the kids. The man didn't tell me much about himself, except that he liked to hunt, and sometimes he rode the train down to Cochrane to stock up and to see the bright light.

When we arrived back home I was pleased to announce my discovery, but everyone else knew about him, a solitary but friendly and harmless civilian. I hate it when I announce a provocative bit of news, then learn that everyone already knows about it. Plus, I'd been hoping for a more compelling story and was disappointed, somehow, to learn that he was respectable.

There was no television, barely any radio reception, but we weren't limited to reading books and playing records. I learned to play bridge, like my parents, but forgot how later. I was invited by other young adults, mostly married couples, to join them on weenie roasts with roaring fires. Darkness came late but the sky glittered with cold starlight as we sat on the ground around the flames, faces flushed pink in the glow. We ate and drank beer and lustily sang "Good Night, Irene" and "This Land Is Your Land," the Canadian version, which goes ". . . from Bonavista to Vancouver Island . . . from the Arctic Circle, to the Great Lakes waters . . ."

My best friend, Pat, invited me to go with her for a weekend visit to Abitibi Canyon, another Hydro generating station down the tracks. She had a friend who lived there with her husband and baby. This site was smaller than Otter and had been in operation since the late 1930s. We had to switch from the Polar Bear Express to a little spur line that carried necessities to this outpost and didn't provide service for passengers, except in the ambulance car. So we made the arrangements, tucked our skirts under our legs, lay down on a shelf and rode, feet first, to our weekend destination. We stayed with her friends. The isolated outpost housed fewer than two hundred people, there to run and maintain the power plant. A number of families with children lived in regular houses, but the place was a giant candy store for the likes of Pat and me. Half the population was made up of young single men who hovered around the Saturday night dances, their testosterone palpable in the rec hall, not one of them subject to a boss called Mister. These guys actually, politely, stood in line waiting to dance with the two of us. Pat and I were as excited as they were. One guy even proposed marriage before he told me his name as we cozily danced to "Moments to Remember" by the Four Lads. I like to imagine I threw back my head and laughed like a paperback vixen. I was never so desirable. It was a one-night Cinderella story which came to nothing. Pat and I returned with

13

her friends directly to their house for the night. And it ended the next morning with us stretched out on a shelf in the ambulance car heading home. No doubt there were such dances at Otter Rapids, but it appears I was being sheltered from temptations.

In late August the headpond, the reservoir behind the dam, was ready to be filled and, from below, I watched the powerful Abitibi drain away as the faucets in the powerhouse above were turned off. The downstream flow slowed to a dribble, fish floundered, gasping against the air in the remaining puddles on the river's rocky bottom. At the time it was okay to marvel at mankind's ability to manipulate nature, and it was a guiltless wonder to observe. On the far side of the dam the deep-set river basin began to fill with water, a gigantic bathtub holding the flow, creating the pressure to turn the turbines into making electricity, to heat and light many thousands of homes and factories somewhere to the south.

People were leaving as well, almost all of us. Some were headed for another Hydro project, and others found opportunities elsewhere. I left with my parents and sisters, who were moving back to Niagara Falls, where I had grown up, and where another Hydro undertaking was about to begin.

But me, I was moving on. I had decided to study interior design at a school in New York City, of all things. I wanted to do something artsy but commercial at the same time—not the "starve in your atelier" kind of artsy: I needed to make a living. As for big cities, I had already visited both Buffalo and Toronto, so I had no concerns about concrete jungles and crossing busy streets.

§

No-one should come to New York to
live unless he's willing to be lucky

E. B. White

NEW YORK
1960-1961

I was ready for New York. I had received the necessary student visa documents and figured out how to transfer my savings. I packed my two-piece set of gray Samsonite and carried my mother's castoff Persian lamb coat on my arm. It weighed more than any known sheep, Persian or domestic. In my baggage was a paperback copy of *New York on Five Dollars a Day*. In my purse I stashed a train ticket, a street map, and the address of a hotel where I had booked a room, in a neighborhood near the school, also marked on the map. The New York School of Interior Design soon would be my alma mater. I had memorized the map—I knew where I was going.

The overnight train arrived on schedule Saturday morning, Labor Day weekend, and I took a taxi from Grand Central uptown, eyes popping with delight at the recognizable sights along Madison Avenue, on the way to the hotel. I got out and watched the driver unload my luggage from the trunk. But no: it was somebody else's matched set of gray suitcases, a different brand, sleeker lines. I remained calm. I decided to deal with that later, after I arranged for my room. I don't suppose I tipped the driver.

I had never before checked in to a hotel without my parents. This modest hotel was on a list of recommended lodgings for students of the school. I had written ahead to book a room, figured it was a done deal. It hadn't occurred to me that there had been no response. The pleasant woman at the front desk shuffled stacks of paper, testing the patience of the other guests in the line. I could hear sighs and scraping feet behind me. Finally she admitted that the hotel had never heard of me, and had no rooms available. Now what? I asked permission to leave my heavy fur coat behind the desk on this warm summer day and figured I could think about options as I carried the stranger's luggage and walked the straight line back to Grand Central to claim my own.

I unloaded the unfamiliar bags at the terminal's Lost and Found, but my own suitcases had not showed up. I stood there at the counter looking with disbelief at the man who barely glanced at me. "Next," he said, and I was shunted aside. I walked back to the hotel, the only place in the world I could go. I decided to sit in the lobby and think.

Think, think. I thought about calling the school but it was Labor Day Saturday and I didn't expect anyone to be there. I considered contacting the YWCA to see if they rented rooms or had any other ideas. I had never heard of Travelers' Aid, and I still don't know if it existed at the time. I tried to think as bellboys pushed carts of luggage around me through the lobby. Guests dressed in their late-summer cottons strode between the elevators and the revolving front door. But I didn't know anyone in New York, and couldn't drum up a remote contact. No point in calling home. My copy of *New York on Five Dollars a Day* was in my lost luggage. I thought about phoning other hotels, but didn't know where to begin and besides, I had budgeted for this place and knew I couldn't afford the Waldorf Astoria, the only other hotel I could think of. Neither had I realized that Labor Day weekend might be a time when New York hotels would be filled. It would soon be getting dark. Maybe I should call the police.

All this cogitation and angst in the lobby caught the attention of the front desk; it probably wouldn't improve their reputation to have me sitting there, forlorn, abashed. Especially if I decided to call the police. The desk clerk tiptoed over and asked how long I expected to stay and I improvised a number: six months. I guess that was the right answer, as she said they'd found a room for me after all. Half my troubles were over.

I moved into this closet of a room, its single bed tucked against the wall like Van Gogh's bedroom in Arles. The little room, the little bed, looked as safe as a mother's womb. The window overlooked an alley, but if I stretched my neck I could see the United Nations building. Nearby, through the whooshing traffic and keening from the fire station a block away, I heard a soprano practicing her scales. They didn't have sopranos in Otter Rapids. This woman had a strong voice, up a chord, down a chord, and she put me to sleep.

Next morning I walked back to Grand Central to collect my missing luggage, but it still hadn't turned up and nobody seemed to care. I bought myself a fresh change of underwear and a toothbrush while walking around the Upper East Side, trying not to look like a wrinkled rube as I gazed up at the heights. I was still too excited to worry about lost luggage, and I did, after all, have a snug place to sleep.

First day of school, that Tuesday, one of the administrators called me to her office to tell me that my bags were there. A Samaritan had opened them, seen brand-new textbooks from the school with my name inscribed but no address, and kindly delivered the two suitcases to the school. See, I knew it would work out.

§

Not surprisingly, almost all the students at the New York School of Interior Design were young women. Some led glamorous lives, like the one whose sister was a cast member on Dave Garroway's *Today* show. Another already had a contract with an uptown upscale client, but wanted to study the finer points. One who invited me to her apartment had a Picasso reproduction on her sophisticated living room wall and she laughed—the bitch—when I didn't recognize the artist. (I'd already admired it, hadn't I?)

I was the only Canadian student that year, and the one with the least cachet. When setting up a bank account nearby, I told the clerk I was in town to attend school. He guessed out loud that I was going to Bible school. I wanted to kick him under his desk. It was essential to disabuse him, and to begin working on looking more bewitching, less like I'd come out of the north woods.

I knew before I started classes that I was supposed to peel the cellophane wrappers off new lampshades, but I didn't know much else about my chosen vocation. At school I learned to say "chaise longue" instead of "chaise lounge"; "sofa" instead of "couch" or the Canadian favorite, "chesterfield." We mustn't say "drapes," we were to say "curtains," unless they were *draperies.* We were to cringe at French Provincial unless the piece was crafted hundreds of years ago in the provinces. We blanched at all that was faux. No plastic shower curtains, please. Clearly, we wouldn't be allowing clients to buy furniture in a furniture store, only from a design studio whose access was restricted to the likes of us real designers who dressed in suits by Dior and carried embossed business cards. I studied hard and learned what I was taught. I even got an A in taste, which I brag about whenever it's appropriate, but that isn't often.

I learned about architecture and architects from classical Greek to Mies van der Rohe. Art from the caves of Lascaux to Robert Rauschenberg. Antique furnishings, Sheraton, Chippendale, all those guys. I once knew the proper proportions of a Corinthian column. I could go on.

I didn't realize until much later that I wasn't cut out for this life. I liked knowing these things, but it's unlikely I could have bonded with the type of person who would pay me to create an *Architectural Digest* lifestyle home. Could some millionaire homeowner trust a woman with hips this wide and social skills this reticent, to spend her millions? I don't think so, but I wasn't ready to know that yet.

After a couple of weeks in my budget hotel room, I decided to move into one of those women's residence hotels for some companionship. I still didn't have any friends and it was against my nature to go looking; I was bred and raised to be reserved. The women's hotel was located on East 68th Street near Madison, a block east of Central Park, and a block west of Hunter College, with the Russian Embassy on the corner. My new address was an elegantly shabby old mansion, with a dithering antique elevator. No guests were allowed above the ground floor. We were housed two to a room, fed breakfast and dinner in the basement dining room. Sundays we were on our own. The food was pretty good except for Tuesday's vegetable, some dark green slop called collard greens, which I don't believe— thank you, Lord—grew in Canada.

A Monday off and a parade surprised me early in October. I'd never heard of Columbus Day. I thought I already knew a lot about

19

American culture, but here was an excuse for a holiday out of the blue. The connection between Columbus and all those Italian floats, bands and costumery took a while to sink in. The possibility that the holiday would be offensive to native American Indians would have boggled me at the time. New York hosted a lot of parades; brass bands, spirited people, amusing floats, horses that clopped in time to the music, on a level so appealing, they exuded a sense of joy about the city—all's well with the world. Columbus Day seemed like a great way to celebrate a holiday; no gifts to buy or exchange, no special meals to prepare, no cards to mail. Just a day off, and if you're lucky enough, a parade.

I was in for a couple of other surprises about Americans. They didn't know what a butter tart was, or a plastic bag of cheese curds. I was proud to defend all things Canadian—Freud called it "the narcissism of small differences." On meeting new people—and weren't they all?—I was invariably asked where I'd come from. When I said "Canada," the next question was "Where in Canada?" And I was stumped. Did they mean where did I grow up, where was I born? Where did I go to school? Where did I live before coming here? Whichever answer I decided on, the next question was "Do you know So-and-So?" and I never did. Canada is not that small, I swear.

For several weeks that early fall, I watched the filming of street scenes in our neighborhood for *Breakfast at Tiffany's* with Audrey Hepburn. My, she was thin. One day I stood on a Park Avenue corner and saw the shiny new President Kennedy being driven uptown. He sat in the back seat of his open limo. He didn't wave, and I didn't mind. I was living large in New York.

Our next-door neighbor, Dorothy Kilgallen, the investigative journalist and panelist on *What's My Line?*, often swept past in a chauffeured car, brazenly sitting in the front seat with her uniformed driver. I saw Paul Newman and Joanne Woodward pushing a baby carriage up the avenue. This was more than I expected; not just the recognizable buildings and ambiance of New York, but all those famous people walking around, just like us.

The young women living at the residence hotel during my stay were working actors, models and dancers, some wannabes; some were students of the arts. My assigned roommate was a stunning blonde, not very bright, who borrowed my Persian lamb coat without permission, leaving behind a few long blonde hairs adrift on the black lamb curls of the coat's surface. And who, at the time, claimed she was having an affair with President Kennedy's brother-in-law. She never introduced me to him but still a shiver ran down my spine. Oh New York, so chic, so shameless. I had become a mid-century modern. I knew I was right in the middle of . . . something.

There was less bitchiness among us than I had expected. We formed little cliques, of course, but in general were all friendly with one another. One of the dancers living there introduced me to a male dancer who asked me if I could dance. Practicing in front of my mirror in my teens, jiving at school hops and attending square dances on Friday nights, made me say something like "Sure I can." He invited me to go with him to a big noisy hall uptown in Manhattan's old German neighborhood. The place really rocked. I quickly learned that this guy was a pro on Broadway, not just off-, and on his free evenings he expected a lithe and limber partner who had a soupçon of rhythm. I let him down. The only time he looked amused was when the music turned to the Twist. What fresh hell is this, I wondered to myself, mentally quoting Dorothy Parker. People from Otter Rapids didn't twist. Everybody else on the floor was contorting and grinding their lower torsos in sync with the beat. I needed to become more acclimated, rehearsing in the privacy of my full-length mirror. My dancer date was polite and I was flustered; I was not the type of partner he was looking for. I later figured out that he was probably gay. But in those years, in my life, there were only two sexes.

There were other dates, nothing that could have progressed, and some good memories with the women who lived in the hotel. Four was a good number for exploring, especially at night. We were all brand-new in the city, two short and two taller. I thought of us as a cross-section, with one shared characteristic: the pleasure of being young, healthy and happy in this inspiring city. The taller ones were me and a lovely blue-eyed belle from South Carolina, who came to New York to be a fashion model. We coached her when she practiced slinky-walking on a runway, hips thrust forward. The slink was funny because she was pink-cheeked and innocent looking, the cover girl on a calendar from the A&P. One short friend, a perky buckaroo cowgirl, came from a ranch in Idaho. She showed us pictures of her horse, and of herself on a horse, sometimes herself on skis, heading downhill. Sally from Houston was quiet and thoughtful. She was impressed that I could look out the window and say, "I think it's going to snow." She told people I could "conjure up snow"—her Texas-flavored words. No, I just felt the chill and looked at the heavy sky. Sally was always freezing, and I assumed she just wasn't used to northern winters. Then we discovered her winter coat was a Houston winter coat, a thin covering of wool-like material that weighed itself in grams, wasn't even lined. We hustled her off to get a proper coat and a scarf.

We went everywhere we'd heard of, and a few places we hadn't. Together we explored the brightest and the darkest corners of

Manhattan. In my mind we danced and sang up and down the streets, pirouetting along the sidewalks, popping into galleries and department stores, museums and movies, churches and nightclubs. Some evenings we ended up at the White Horse Tavern in the West Village, having a drink next to the beats, poets and folk singers, dangerous degenerates for certain. I can't remember if they were called Beatniks or if that came later. How titillating to sneak-peek through the fog of cigarette smoke at all these strange men with straggly hair and beards, black turtlenecks and sunglasses in the dark. We never actually dared to talk to any of them or respond to their overtures. It seemed too risky in the pre-dawn of this soon-to-be tumultuous decade. After all, this was the bar where Dylan Thomas downed seventeen whiskeys before he was rushed off to a hospital and pronounced dead. I wondered if anyone paid his tab.

Soon enough, graduation was in sight. My Texas friend Sally and I decided we should look for work in San Francisco. I hadn't forgotten I was an uninvited guest on a student visa and couldn't simply stay. But I hoped that having spent all this time in the country already, and living most of my life in Niagara Falls, right on the river, within a spitball's throw of the border, where I could see America from the front porch, I might be a little more entitled. Despite hours of filling out forms and waiting for interviews while applying for permanent resident status, I was sent to the end of the line. The application process took several afternoons at the immigration office in Lower Manhattan, always while mingling and jostling with other hopeful people, all shapes and all ages, in a wondrous array of costumes, babbling a confusion of tongues, in the chaos of this undisciplined space. But it was not to be. They sent me back.

"Where shall I begin, please, your majesty, sir," he asked. "Begin at the beginning," the king said, gravely, "and go on till you come to the end; then stop."

Lewis Carroll

TORONTO
1961–1964

Lucky for me, the receptionist at *Canadian Homes and Gardens* magazine dyed her hair turquoise one day, and so was sent packing. This was a time, mind you, when demonstrations of sassiness like teal-colored hair could get you fired, and when job application forms could ask the date of your last period. I was lucky because I had just moved to Toronto to seek my fortune as an interior designer and stumbled upon this interesting alternative. I got the job.

Hardly anyone needed to be received by a receptionist at our high-floor editorial offices in the Maclean-Hunter building on the redundantly named Avenue Road. There was no waiting area for visitors who were early for appointments. There were seldom any appointments. Staff writers usually went to see their subjects; subjects didn't come to us. Most people who came in the door worked there, knew where they were going. So the staff gave me little jobs to make sure I didn't have extra time to sit around and read other publishers' magazines. It was a foot-in-the-door job but I was happy to type and proofread, move a floral display or hold a light for a photo shoot, and graciously answer the phone for the writers and editors of the country's only gracious living magazine.

The writing staff took me with them to lunch in Chinatown, around the corner from the towering building. They were friendly, delightfully witty lunch companions, always a bit intimidating. They taught me how to use chopsticks.

Extra-timorous at that age, I seldom spoke to my superiors, unless I was spoken to first. People said I was a good listener. Back when I first started dating, I fared best by going out with boys who talked a lot. Otherwise we would both sit there like two clams and I could hear myself swallowing every ten seconds or so. Still new on the job, one morning I shared the elevator all the way up to our office floor with one of the senior editors. I looked all around my empty brain but I couldn't think of a thing to say. I could have said "How about those Maple Leafs," and "Do you say Leafs or Leaves?" But I didn't, I thought of that later. Of course, he hadn't spoken either. But when we arrived at our destination, he turned to me and snidely said, "This has been a most enlightening conversation."

I'd gone directly to Canada's commercial capital that spring and stayed at the YWCA while looking for suitable employment. Standing in line at the Y cafeteria, I met a woman named Iris who worked in advertising. She had just moved from Edmonton and was hoping to find a copywriting job at a national agency. After a few breakfasts together we decided to share an apartment.

Iris found the work she coveted at a major ad agency. I thought of her when I watched *Mad Men*, as the show's early seasons matched Iris's career somewhat closely, although she wasn't stuck in the typing pool—she was writing and developing ads for clients. At home Iris used the adjective "groovy" long before anyone else I knew. She called certain people "rounders," as opposed, I guess, to "squares." Iris had long been a jazz fan and cool words like "cool" were staples in her vocabulary.

The two of us enjoyed decorating our empty apartment. It was my first shot at using my new interior design skills, although we had no money. We toured a neighborhood where cheap and garish furniture was sold, only stopping to look at the price tags of the plainest models. We bought a brand-new fifty-dollar black chesterfield (sofa) that looked suitably unobtrusive. It was rigid, insufferably so, and tilted so far forward it wanted to drop you onto the floor. It never did get much wear; nobody could snuggle into its iron-hard recesses. We spent a lot of time sitting on the floor, on our new rug, listening to Iris's Bossa Nova LPs on her record player.

Comfort didn't matter; we were going for gracious living. In a carpet store, we bought twelve one-yard square samples of discontinued broadloom, six in mustard and six off-white, stitched them together in a checkerboard pattern and, while sitting on the floor, framed them with black carpet fringe for an area rug. Sewing sections of rug required the most treacherous carpet needles. They were disturbingly long and slender; good thing Iris and I got along so well.

We phoned a lumberyard and ordered nine decorative concrete blocks and three pine boards, each a different length, which we had measured for our pyramid-style bookshelves. The lumber salesman was amused, but our order was delivered as promised to our fifth-floor city apartment. We painted the boards and bricks in mustard yellow, the *au courant* color, to match the carpet.

We sewed covers for toss cushions and an oversized floor cushion. We had copies of Toulouse Lautrec posters, and a print of Adolf Dehn's *Central Park*, framed in black, for our white walls. We even bought a large stretched empty canvas and painted it, one of us at either end, in wild freeform swirls and blobs. We learned that when someone says "I could make a painting as good as that," it isn't true, and we ended up junking our own abstract art project.

Iris was and is very engaging, and attracted some intriguing male companions. It didn't hurt to have blue eyes, chestnut hair, a pretty face. One breezy Sunday afternoon, a new friend with a famous corporate name showed up to take her for a ride in his open sports car. I asked Iris, "Do you have a babushka?" Famous name turned to me and said, "No, I have a Ferrari."

Before I left the city, Iris and I had moved into our own apartments, but we remained friends. She has since written and published several books, usually about artists, and I've enjoyed keeping an eye on her through her work.

Downtown Toronto was just beginning to emerge from its sardonic reputation as "Toronto the good." Richard Benner, a film director and screenwriter who had moved from the U.S. to Toronto, made a comment that "the country is so square that even the female impersonators are women." Back in the early 1960s, a walk downtown on a Sunday afternoon did not include shopping, even window-shopping. Canada's major department store, the T. Eaton Company, had installed heavy, opaque draperies across its flagship store's windows, drawn closed on Sundays, to prevent peeking. Mr. Benner was joking; Eaton's was not.

One day I got a phone call from my stepfather. He wanted to buy my mother a mink coat and asked me to go shopping for him, as Niagara Falls was no Toronto when it came to buying furs. (Rather, Niagara Falls was the place to shop for snow globes and felt wall banners.) I happily agreed, and took an officemate with me for a couple of lunch hours to scrutinize the mink selection at the Hudson's Bay store and the city's other premier furriers. The salespeople had seen the likes of us before: young women who came in at lunchtime to try on mink and fox and chinchilla wraps just for fun. The stores' surveillance staff was on alert as we caressed the kitten-soft skins sheathing our arms and torsos, tickling our chins, their softness and warmth as decadent as nature's most forbidden transgressions. Now of course it is a sin. This was before I or anyone else was enlightened about wearing the coats of dead animals. After explaining my mission in the most congenial store, I found just the right coat and astonished the salesclerk by announcing, "I'll take it."

As Toronto slowly awakened from stuffy Victorian to artsy multicultural, magazines in Canada struggled to survive. The products consumed by Canadians are the same ones that Americans buy. Canadians read magazines that are produced in the U.S., so advertisers feel no need to peddle their wares in Canada. I don't know if a lifestyle magazine like *Canadian Homes* was more vulnerable than other categories, but the advertising revenue was not rolling in, and *Canadian Homes* faltered in the summer of 1963. It didn't exactly fold, but it was badly bent. The magazine was sold to a newspaper chain to become a glossy monthly insert in its weekend papers, sort of like *Parade* but with a residential focus. Being on the bottom rung of the editorial department, I was the lowest paid, and the first one hired for the new publication.

I was happy for the move, not only because it meant my job, but also because I had fallen, calamitously as it turned out, for one of the staff writers, Barry Johnson, whom I would later marry. I didn't know much about men at the time, but I liked the looks of this one. One weekend, I took him to Niagara Falls to meet my parents, who took an immediate, visceral dislike to him. Well, what did they know?

All I knew was that he looked like Cary Grant. Or maybe George Clooney, who was barely born at the time. Or so I thought until after the fracas, when I looked at my old photographs and Barry seemed so ordinary. As for my parents' reading of him: at the time he had an ex-wife and two young children whom he was obliged to support. It hadn't sunk in how attractive he looked to other women. And he didn't have the attributes of a good provider. His paycheck seldom lasted until the end of the month. But nobody's perfect, eh?

The editor of the new iteration of the *Canadian Homes* insert was young, inexperienced and inept when it came to dealing with people, at least with me. I felt ill one day and threw up en route to a photo shoot, and he accused me of being pregnant. Just because I was sleeping with one of his staff and it was his car I had soiled, didn't mean I was carrying a child. I certainly was not, and I was duly insulted. After a short stint in the new version of my old job, I quit and went looking for a new one. I was lucky to find a slot with dear old *Liberty* magazine, also published in downtown Toronto. You have to be pretty elderly to remember *Liberty.*

Liberty was fresh and hot from the mid-1920s to the late '40s, when it began to cool off and finally ceased publication in 1950 in the U.S. In its good days it described itself as "the most daring, exciting, sensational and popular general interest magazine." It said "it charted the moods, attitudes, lifestyles, fads and fortunes of middle America for three decades." Although *Liberty* fizzled in the U.S., it continued to publish in Canada for another fifteen years. I found my job there during its fifteenth year.

My first week on staff, Peter Jennings, the boy wonder news anchor of a Canadian television network (later the anchor of ABC's *World News Tonight*), walked in the door to be interviewed and photographed for the cover. I was impressed. This was more fun than furniture.

My job title was assistant editor. I was expected to write articles. I knew nothing about writing for a magazine, or journalism on any level. I brought my early assignments home and Barry helped me learn the basics. For a feature article, I needed a catchy lede (which I always thought was "lead," silly me), followed by facts, interspersed with more catchy comments, alternating dull facts with frills, more or less. For a hard news story, if I were to write for a newspaper, the most important literal facts came first, followed by the details in descending order of importance. Keep it clean and simple. One memorable example I was given: A reporter was sent to the scene of an avalanche. The lede he filed read, "God sat on a hillside and watched as four people were killed by an avalanche on a nearby mountain." His editor wired back, "Forget avalanche. Interview God."

I sweated over an article praising disposable dinnerware called Dixie cups. The company that made Dixie cups paid the costs of photographing the cover that month, a family having a picnic. I wrote a series of articles about some of Canada's smaller cities, none of which I'd ever visited. It was all from local Chamber of Commerce materials. I rewrote a first-person article about landing on a Normandy beach on D-Day. (I was heroic but modest.) For the Christmas issue I was asked to describe how to tie a bow. It sounds easy but it wasn't; my hovering fingers wove circles and knots in the air above the keyboard as I typed.

After a few weeks in the city offices, we were told that the magazine was moving to the suburbs, at the end of the bus line. At least I would be traveling against the traffic. The rental space was in a cinder-block industrial building, barely big enough to hold us all. We published a couple of dismal issues before we were told that the magazine was folding, forever this time.

Unsure what to do next, I signed on as a temp for a giant insurance company. So many people worked in the building that we were each given off-beat arrival and departure times. The high-rise building swarmed with hordes any time of the day. Neither the cafeteria nor the elevators could have handled all of us otherwise. I was scheduled to begin at 8:23, break for lunch at 12:09, return from lunch at 12:49 and leave for the day at 4:47. Or something like that.

My job was to type handwritten information for new insurance policies onto company forms. I was sent to a spacious room, bigger than any classroom I had ever sat in, but set up much the same way, with lines of desks in neat long rows. At the back of the room, where she could keep an eye on us, was the room's supervisor, who mostly made sure we were typing nonstop, and that we sat down and rose up at the juggled appointed hours. There was no talking allowed. Just the clicking of fifty or sixty typewriters. On our lunch breaks I learned that many of the women working there had never had a different job experience. Quite a few were near retirement age. The prospect was chilling. As women had retired or otherwise moved on over the past few months, they were supplanted by us temps. Before long, the whole room would be empty. The department was going to be replaced by a computer—one of those refrigerator-shaped black behemoths with blinking red lights, like the mainframe in the window of the IBM store down the street. It felt like a segment of Rod Serling's program, *Twilight Zone.* Creepy. Time to move on.

§

When God sneezed, I didn't know
what to say.

Groucho Marx

VANCOUVER
1964-1971

On assignment from the *Vancouver Sun*, where I was employed, I joined a new art therapy group at the distinguished Vancouver Art Gallery. Sounded respectable enough. A dozen or more people were seated at drafting tables, given paper and colored pencils. The instructor began by asking us to "make a mark." That was her word, "mark." To me a mark was a simple Nike swoosh or an extended dot, one color. As I recall, there was no introduction; we weren't told what art therapy was or did or proved or maybe even improved.

When we were asked to show our marks, I saw that the others had drawn elaborate multicolored pictures, with curly-topped trees, square box houses, smiling suns with bright golden spokes radiating outward. I guess many of these people knew what art therapy was supposed to be.

When I flashed my feeble yellow squiggle, one of my fellow participants shouted to me, "What are you trying to hide?" I think she was gunning for me. The instructor didn't say a word. Then the shouter added that she had been "under Fritz," and I knew what she was talking about. I didn't go back for the rest of the course. The psychiatrist Fritz Perls was the Fritz being tapped here, and we all knew who he was—the founder of Gestalt therapy, an influential force in the 1960s, especially on the west coast. The shouter was quite right; no way was I about to confess my darkest feelings, even unconsciously, even the disregard I had for this woman. I had plenty to hide. (Around this time, I wanted to shoot my husband.) Next time, if I ever chose to do this again, I would draw a cute little house with a red door, daisies all around. A double arch in the sky to depict a bird in flight.

One of the counterculture trends that inundated the west coast of the U.S. and Canada in the late 1960s was self-help pseudo-psychotherapy sensitivity training in novel forms, especially for groups who sat in circles. My own self-help rendition meant reading Alan Watts, the guru philosopher who wrote so well, who explained the peaceful happiness of living in the moment. You dig? I kept trying to enjoy the moment when I cleaned the oven. I tried. But I drew the line at the group gatherings. They had seemed desperate and sad. The period and Vancouver are remembered for a younger, freer life force, for the spirit and vitality of hippies and their drugs, but a strong factor in the culture was psychobabble for people who were more mature and gainfully employed.

These approaches have fizzled out, especially here in the Northeast, but at the time, group therapies such as Fritz Perls' Gestalt, primal scream and Werner Erhard's EST thrived. Some group leaders encouraged the participants to be blatantly honest, express their anger, insult the person in the next chair, say what they really thought. "Why are you so fat?" or "Why do you still live with your mother?" were jettisoned around the room, along with "What are you trying to hide?"

One Californian I know attended an anger management session and was handed a bataka, a bat made out of foam rubber.

She was instructed to recall something that made her angry, then beat on her neighbor with the harmless toy, to rid her system of her wrath. But in arousing the right frame of mind, she got so mad she said "Fuck the bataka," removed her high-heeled shoe and tried to pummel the poor guy with the pointy end before the instructor stepped in. This was supposed to help the psyche. All sorts of therapies were acceptable, and were popular. Everybody was under somebody. "What's your sign?" was a popular pickup line.

Barry and I had decided to move to Vancouver in 1964. He had lived there before, and traveled west ahead of me. I loved going alone on the three-day train ride, through the evergreen forests and lakes of northern Ontario, the long stretch of open prairie, the spectacle of the Rockies, and finally the west coast in all its mountainous glory.

He found a regular reporting job on the morning paper, *The Province*, and I was hired by the *Vancouver Sun*, the afternoon daily.

I was hired as a reporter for the women's pages, once known as the society pages, and now called Life or Style. This was Canada's second-largest newspaper, bulked up with ads, a daily with a fine reputation. The building was then a round brick tower on the edge of downtown, located just downwind from a place that processed coffee. The smell of raw coffee at the crack of daylight was not appealing, but it might have been enough to pre-caffeinate us journalist/junkies.

The women's pages' corner of the newsroom floor housed our editor, dear little Thelma, plus a fashion editor, a food editor, two reporters and two society columnists. (Why two—I don't know. Did Vancouver's high society have its own Hatfields and McCoys?

Could be—there were enough lumber barons and shipping and mining tycoons who entertained us press people on their yachts.) Our role was to cover general news for and about women. Our own department's bathroom in the corner had an alcove with a fainting couch, which must have been left over from the days of swooning society page ladies. When we moved to a new building a couple of years later, the chaise longue did not come with us.

A woman who called herself Penny Wise wrote a shopping column. That wasn't her real name but we called her Penny anyway. Our daily advice came by wire from Ann Landers. My first interview was with Patti Page, who popularized "Old Cape Cod." (An omen?) I interviewed plenty of women singers, women actors, women doctors, women scientists, the woman school bus driver of the year, and women who had exceptional stories to tell. Not much about the struggles—abortion, rape, equal pay, spousal abuse, child abuse, sexual abuse— nothing strenuous, and I was not one to question the wisdom. Protest didn't occur to me until I heard about it later in the decade.

Because I was the new guy, I was designated the early riser, had to be at the paper before sunrise to work on another floor in the composing room. There the atmosphere changed dramatically. Rows of Linotype machines discharged heat, clanging noises and a sour smell of hot lead as operators transferred typewritten words into neat rows of metal type, each bar the width of a newspaper column. It was my daybreak job to proofread the women's pages, and make sure everything fit where it was supposed to go. It meant being able to read lines of metal type backwards and inside out. I also shortened or lengthened headlines to fit; cut stories to conform to the space or found fillers to plug the vacancies. It was a parlor game and I enjoyed it. The number one rule of the composing room was Do Not Touch. Because of union concerns about protecting the rights of the compositors, no editorial people were allowed to handle any type. It was a good rule for me; otherwise I'd have had ink all over my hands and my clothes for the rest of the day, every day. I was finished there before nine. The remainder of my shift was spent being a reporter. Who's today's lucky interviewee?

After work each afternoon I walked to the corner and met a number of colleagues in a pub and drank draft beer and smoked cigarettes until we broke for dinner. We gossiped about the ones who weren't there, bragged about our assignments and our well-chosen verbs, and played word games, often until the last call of the beer parlors, as they were quaintly named. This so-called holy hour, from six to seven, was a government requirement intended to eject the afternoon slackers from the pub, so we would go home and eat something. The pubs reopened later, but we didn't go back.

To live in Vancouver in the 1960s was as desirable as living anywhere in Canada could be. The climate is kinder, the mountains and the Pacific beaches are spectacular, and day-to-day living itself was more casual. The city even had its own jester, a merry fool in booties with curly pointed toes, and a cap that sprouted colorful felt petals from its peak, jingle bells attached to the tips. He had received a grant from the Canada Council to amuse people by walking around downtown, and cheering up the passersby.

Some people called Vancouver "Edge City." This was Canada's answer to San Francisco. You couldn't move any farther west. Vancouver was edgy before "edgy" came to mean "fashionable." When someone famous was due to fly into town for the first time, reporters from all the media rushed to greet the visitor as he disembarked from the plane and ask him, "How do you like Vancouver?" Sometimes the important visitor rolled his eyes and shook his head, but the crafty ones wisely praised the city's sophistication and sparkling good looks.

Because Vancouver was the major port city on the Pacific coast of North America, it had long had problems with drug use and abuse. We heard about old sailors who struggled and lost their way because of opium or heroin. But mostly, when we moved to Vancouver early in 1964, drug use was still a rumor. One day we ran into a couple of acquaintances who said they had just come from seeing the movie *Mary Poppins* after smoking a joint. Their amusement and enjoyment of the movie seemed excessive. They were adults, giggling and grinning like pussycats. A joint? Never heard of it.

But within a short time, Vancouver's counterculture had detonated, beatniks morphed into hippies, and the whole world knew about LSD and pot and hashish. Demonstrations and sit-ins and be-ins flourished. The radical *Georgia Straight* newspaper thrived. People began living in large groups in funky old houses they called communes. Rock and roll grew louder. Protesters and peace-lovers grew long hair and made love—free love, they said. Stoners danced in the streets. Nudity paraded on the beaches. For some in the city, the world had gone to hell.

I was getting married to Barry Johnson. I should have paid attention to what Providence had foreordained about this union. I generally don't listen to fateful warnings, but this was one time when there were so many bolts of lightning hurled at us— including a real fire—that we were surely asking for trouble.

It was November in Vancouver. I skidded on an icy patch on a friend's front step and twisted my foot. The bone was broken and I was cemented into a cast, just days before our scheduled wedding. I collected congratulatory messages on my cast. A day before the ceremony, my doctor removed the plaster and replaced it with a snug wrap of bandages, which I tried to keep clean and pure. And, I noticed in the photographs, to keep hidden behind my other leg.

That same afternoon we visited the Department of Vital Statistics to pick up the license, but because of a technicality it couldn't be issued that day. There was a waiting period and we were short by one day. Neither of us was good at arithmetic. Barry got on the phone to plead long-distance with British Columbia's deputy minister of health, who relented and granted the license.

A friend was supposed to pick up the wedding party and drive us to the church on time. But she got delayed with a client and in the rush to pick us up smashed her car into a pole. We arrived late, shaken, and resolutely ignoring the omens directed our way.

Then we learned that nobody had remembered to bring any money. Luckily our photographer had some cash and anted up.

So we got married and then a bunch of us headed for our West End apartment to celebrate. The festivities were barely under way when the fire alarms rang and our twenty guests were forced to flee down sixteen flights of stairs while firemen extinguished a blaze in the building's garbage chute. I clutched my wilting bouquet and juggled a rented champagne flute as I hobbled round and round, down the stairwell in my three-inch heels. Neighbors known and unknown toasted us outside on the sidewalk and shivered in the drizzly rain for an hour or so. Finally the elevator took us back up, but the marriage never truly got off the ground. Barry and I attempted to work out our differences, generally involving other women who thought he looked like Cary Grant, and we didn't get legally unmarried for three years, but it was a rough and ragged time, living through the detritus of broken promises. He and I had spent a number of trials getting back together, then separating again, then again. Sometimes we were at my place, sometimes not. I was miserable whether I was alone or thrashing it out with him in his or my or our apartment.

We had been married a few weeks when I had a dream that I still remember. Barry and I were walking in the park when we ran into someone I knew. I went to introduce my new husband but I couldn't remember his name. I don't generally look for meaning in my dreams, but this one was hard to ignore. I know it takes two to make a marriage, and both sides share the blame when it fails. I admit I was naïve and featherbrained and I didn't know the difference between libidos and real life. Since this is my story, I'll just say it was all his fault. Train-wreck memories need not be wrapped in a pink ribbon and stored away in a Valentine box. These are the memories that are best forgotten and long gone from my psyche.

Throughout my years in Vancouver, I had one solid woman friend, my matron of honor who banged up her car taking us, the bridal couple, to our wedding. She was Kayce White. I met her when she lived in Vancouver and I was still in Toronto, working for *Liberty*. She had submitted a piece of fiction which I can't remember except for a reference to a crooked card game. We ran her piece, and Kayce and I became pen pals, and still are, if only semi-annually, via email. She was a blond, but not too blonde, with a divorce, an adolescent daughter, an imagination and the wit to keep herself afloat by freelance writing. For years the two of us shared good books and holiday meals; we laughed together and cried our hearts out together over our love lives. She taught me to add a cup of coffee and fresh dill when making a pot of beef stew. We often stopped by the Hotel Georgia, whose basement was home to the Vancouver Press Club. There we knew we could find good company and buy a drink though we weren't allowed to be members. We cajoled, threatened and demanded that women be allowed to join. Our pleas and complaints to the club's officers made some of them wince, and some of them shrug, but our finger-wagging saber-rattling wasn't effective. They weren't ready to let us join.

Pleasant memories persist, in part because Vancouver is such a lovely city. Many Sundays I loved to go alone on the bus out to the campus of the University of British Columbia at Point Grey Peninsula, and walk home the few miles along the narrow beach. I'd skid down a steep wooded ravine to the shore. The water's edge was lined with logs that had drifted away from rafts made up of logs roped together, all being floated down the coast from logging operations up north. Much of the walk meant hopping from log to log. Across the harbor entrance I could see suburbs scaling the mountains, which are snow-capped part of the year. Brisk Pacific winds diluted the halitosis of seaport and fish, rotting greenery, tar and pitch. I admired the cargo ships entering or slipping out of the harbor, many of them named the something *Maru*, which is a Japanese suffix commonly applied to names of merchant ships. It doesn't translate easily; *maru* can literally mean anything that is truly pleasant, beautiful, lucky, or beloved.

Those walks were attempts to wash away the chaos of the past week, and somehow helped to make my career dance along nicely. I'd moved from the *Sun* to write for a new city magazine called *Vancouver Life*, working long days, evenings and holidays. I especially remember trying to phone people at their offices, while I'd forgotten it was Thanksgiving Day. My marriage was permanently asunder by now and I tried my hand at payback, blundering through, renting one apartment after another, partying too much, serially smitten with . . . whomever.

Never truly comfortable at the magazine, I went back to work for *The Vancouver Sun*, writing features of all sorts for the Leisure supplement, along with regular interior design articles and advice. Then I was named travel editor and book editor and, a year or two later, television columnist. It all happened fast. When I applied for the travel editor's job, I was living alone. I must have charmed my editor by saying I had no responsibilities, no spouse, no kids, no cats. My passport was up to date, and I was free to leave at any time. But when I was given the job, it hurt to be told the paper's change in policy: Free travel junkets were no longer sanctioned, as they had been until I came along. Instead we would use material from freelancers and wire services. Blah. It wasn't quite legit, my superiors said, to accept such generous hospitality and maybe have to find fault with the host country or the airline or the free hotel. But the airlines who organized the trips weren't ready for the change. The airline people kept calling and urging me to go to a number of exotic destinations, all expenses paid. It pained me to say no. After these phone calls, I'd go visit my editor and request an exception.

As a one-time-only concession, the paper allowed me to go on a trip to Czechoslovakia in the spring of 1969, not long after the failure of Prague Spring. In April 1968 reformer Alexander Dubček became the country's leader and attempted to introduce a few scraps of democracy and personal freedom. It was too much for the USSR. In August, the Warsaw Pact nations, primarily

Russia, invaded Czechoslovakia, tanks rolled in the streets, and the Soviets took back strict control of their wayward satellite nation. But we were sent as travel writers and tourism promoters. If there were any spies in our midst, they disguised themselves well enough.

A plane full of revved-up press people and travel agents from all over Canada boarded the Czech airline's inaugural flight out of Montreal. It was a novel experience for the airline as well as for us. The plane's bathrooms stung our eyes with powerful blasts of disinfectant, the stewardesses flaunted hairy legs beneath their miniskirts. When we arrived in Prague, armed Soviet soldiers who looked like boys patrolled the streets. Despite them, and despite a phone call waking me in the middle of the night demanding to know if I had a man in my room (I didn't), the trip was invigorating good fun. We not only toured the sights, we inspected the light fixtures and telephones in our rooms, looking for hidden cameras and microphones. We'd been inspired by James Bond, though I wouldn't have recognized a wiretap if it bit me.

Then there was the call from Canadian Pacific Airlines offering a trip to Fiji. Press junkets were a great way to travel. We were housed in first-class hotels, fed the country's finest dishes; we met the most colorful local people and were treated as if we were important. I was able to accept the Fiji trip because I was a union member and the paper was in the midst of a serious labor dispute. I was locked out of my job. There was no paper. Of course I could go. There was nobody to say no.

One fragment of the Fiji trip: We were driven to a primitive native village, bogus or otherwise. Our hosts greeted us in straw huts, wearing sarongs, bare feet, hibiscus behind their ears. We were seated on the bare tamped-down earth to observe a feast being barbecued for us on an open fire at ground level. The pork and its accessories were distributed by bare hands, and we savored every dripping bit of it with our own sticky hands. Then we returned to our hotel, where the bathroom's toilet seat was wrapped with a paper belt proclaiming its high standards of sanitation.

Technically we weren't on strike; we had been locked out after some weeks and months of negotiating behind closed doors. I don't remember the issues, but I was faithful to the American Newspaper Guild. Being an editor didn't mean being management in this business. Holding up a placard, I marched around and around the newspaper building with my brothers and sisters. What surprised me was the disloyalty of Vancouver's citizens, our readers, who honked rather rudely and booed and yelled at us as they drove past. Hey, we were the victims here.

The various unions were well organized, efficient and savvy. Within a couple of days, the unions had a substitute newspaper, the *Vancouver Express*, up and running. A newsroom was set up in a hired dance hall, with rented picnic tables in rows, telephones and typewriters in place of table settings. Newfangled offset presses rolled somewhere in town and distribution somehow continued. All the actors were in play, and we continued to cover the city and its environs. Our attitude was "We don't need you guys. We can do this without editors and publishers and managers. Our public needs us."

And so it went. The twelve-page *Vancouver Express* was published three times a week for three months before the dispute was settled. What went missing were wire service news, a lot of advertising and, curiously, obituaries. We even continued to receive paychecks from the unions, although their totals had shrunk by about a third. When our readers complained, it was because of the lack of obituaries.

Three months later, back at the actual office, my responsibilities resumed. My job was not only travel editor, but also book review editor. A truly delicious pair of assignments. As such, I found my desk each morning covered with cartons of new offerings from publishers, hoping for some attention and praying it would be positive. New books smelled so good, felt so clean, snapped open so crisply. A handful of reporters, who inevitably were readers, clustered around my desk as I stood, wielding my X-Acto knife to unpack the day's cartons of treasures. I kept the best books for myself. And I soon had my reviewers lined up. One deskman read a book a day, I swear, and promptly churned out a review for each one. Some people took books home and never wrote a word. I scratched them from my list. I felt the power.

Same with book authors. Some adored me if they were treated to positive reviews. Some cut me off or complained bitterly about being misunderstood if the reviews were less kind. One author even called and offered to review his own book, as he explained he was the world's leading authority on the subject. I said no. It was also our policy to ignore the vanity press.

But it was my next assignment and promotion, television reviewing, that got to me. Not the labor of it, of course not, but life itself. I worked at home, usually at night. The lack of fellow employees to mingle with, the shortage of a daytime friend to canoodle with, the long afternoons of looking for something to do —not for me.

Along the way I met a group of globe-circling British travelers who had stopped for a while in Vancouver. They told exotic tales of seeing the world, hiking the Himalayas, encountering primitive tribes in darkest Africa. They headed east when they left England, had nearly completed the circuit, and most of them ended up back home. But some of them are still in Vancouver.

Kayce, my buddy, had moved to Hong Kong, of all places. Barry, no longer my husband, accepted an offer of a travel junket to London, but he was broke. I gave him some money if he promised to stay away. I figured it was a good bet, as he would soon be broke again and his return ticket would have expired. In time, he moved to Rome, and it was while he lived in Italy that I filed the divorce papers and set myself free.

Seeing the world while I still had enough vitality was one of those fantasies that began to seem logical inside the spongy corners of my mind. No commitments, no cats, no debts.

A Halloween snowstorm and a retirement party for a colleague who didn't want to retire were the events that pushed me over the precipice. So, the first Monday in November, 1971, I called the world's biggest ocean liner company and booked passage to Australia.

§

*The danger is that, in this move
toward new horizons and far
directions, that I may lose what have
now, and can't find anything but
loneliness.*

Sylvia Plath

NO NEED TO HURRY BACK
December 1, 1971

I woke up before daylight in a strange bed in an empty apartment. It took a second or two. I'd been sleeping in a chair that unfolded to become a single bed. I'd had it for years, sat in it hundreds of times, but never pulled it open for sleeping. I'm not big on overnight guests. There was no other furniture in the living room this morning. The walls were blank, the curtains gone and the corners were swept clean of *oose*, as the Scots called dust bunnies. The bedroom was bare too, looking destitute. If the apartment had been any bigger, my sighs would have echoed.

Later that day, the building's super would take the chair, which she had already paid for, and collect the sheets, blanket, pillow and a towel as a bonus, an unexpected gift. Everything else from the hollow apartment was either packed up or sold and gone. I looked out the windows across to Vancouver's inner harbor. My ship had come in overnight, as promised. The SS *Iberia* had docked seven floors below me and a couple of blocks beyond. I noticed as I looked around that December 1st was a fine clear day. The apartment did have a wonderful panorama. Today I could see the mountains lined up behind the inlet. It was said that if you could see the mountains, it was going to rain. And if you couldn't see the mountains, it was already raining. I had often watched passenger ships glide past, coming and going. I realized I wouldn't see this exact view again. Ever.

I had been packed for days. A pair of matching suitcases waited by the door. Next to the carry-on luggage was the traveling trunk that would be stashed somewhere in the ship's hold until the trunk and the suitcases and I disembarked in Australia.

I was ready to go by seven thirty, but passengers were not allowed to board before four. I'd been efficient, but I hadn't planned how to fritter away this long morning and most of the afternoon. I had partied, wept and hugged a bunch of friends good-bye the night before. Now they were back at work. I served myself breakfast, a muffin and orange juice in the bright glare of the empty fridge. Now what. I walked to the corner store for a newspaper and coffee to go. I read every word in that edition of *The Province*, breaking up the sections with walks to the window, to see if my ship was still there. It was, with no outward signs of activity. The stillness and the blankness of my confined space had made me jumpy.

A couple of years earlier, when my newspaper colleagues and I were worrying about an impending strike, three of us women decided to go see a fortune-teller who had a sterling reputation, and find out, without telling her the true purpose of our visit, whether our paychecks were in jeopardy. She wasn't aware of our employment connections or concerns, but she did tell me a couple of harbingers which seemed far-fetched at the time, and which did come back later to poke me in the eye.

One was the highly unlikely premise that I would change my life by traveling west. West was the Pacific Ocean. At the time I was already in Edge City, as far west as I figured I could go.

The other portent she divulged, with a whisper of reverence in her voice: "I see a star over your head." How could that mean anything but fame and glory, a red carpet under my glass slippers? Then she moved her eyes from her crystal ball, examined me closely, up and down, and predicted," I think you will work in a jewelry store." So humbling. But a decade or so later, there I was, managing an art gallery which sold jewelry as well as fine art. All I can say is "Huh."

Back to the corner store for a mass-produced ham sandwich and a 7-Up. At home again, I paced, I smoked, I sat on my bed-chair and imagined a handful of misgivings. I pretended to read a book, reading the same paragraph over and over again. I kept checking the time. I kept looking out the window. The hour finally arrived. I called a taxi, the super's husband dragged my trunk and I carried my on-board luggage to the elevator, down to the lobby. The cab took me the short hop to the pier. A few friends had come to the dock to see me off. I wondered if I would ever see them again.

§

Part Two:
No Fixed Address

*Throw off the bowlines. Sail away
from the safe harbors. Catch trade
winds in your sails. Explore. Dream.
Discover.*

Mark Twain

ABOARD THE SS *IBERIA*
December 1971

At the dock I presented my ticket to a man in a white nautical uniform, other crew members disappeared with my bags, and a woman who introduced herself as the social director escorted me to my cabin.

My roommate was an older woman from California going to visit her daughter in Australia. She was stretched out on her bed, head raised against her pillow, reading a book. She had declined the sightseeing tour of Vancouver. I barely saw her during our voyage; she ate at an earlier sitting and hung out in our little room. She was pleasant and quiet, easy to live with. The cabin, not anyone's idea of a stateroom, was called first class, but would not have qualified for that rank on a modern ship. My roommate slept down in the lower berth, I slept up. The shower in our bathroom splatted down from directly overhead. The space was too tiny to allow a bit of an arcing fountain; otherwise the water would have landed on my roommate's narrow bunk.

Down the hall was a bathroom in the literal sense. It was a big room full of cubicles, all with oversized bathtubs. At least one of the tubs offered hot saltwater baths. I tried it once; very unpleasant and itchy to sit in hot seawater. The soap couldn't work itself into a lather, but neither could I—I'd been given the choice of salted or unsalted, like peanuts. I decided these old British ships added the salted tubs for the expat wives who needed to punish themselves because they were going to live in a torrid clime with a houseful of servants and the dubious luxury of time to drink gin and quinine all day.

The SS *Iberia* was blinding white, handsome on the outside, not so much on the inside. The décor was postwar frumpy. When it rained, buckets were placed in strategic spots on the floors to collect the drips and spatters. This was, it turned out, the last voyage of the ship. I seemed to be very good at connecting with things as they draw their last gasps. The *Iberia* wasn't so old, only eighteen when she was withdrawn from service at the end of this round trip: from Britain across the Atlantic to the Panama Canal, north along the Pacific coast to Vancouver, down and across to Australia, then back through the Suez Canal to England. She would arrive in her home port in April 1972 and then, without passengers and lifeboats, sail to Taiwan to be demolished.

After I'd settled into my modest sleeping quarters and freshened up, switching from streetwear to glitzy, as I figured I should, I went to the dining salon, which looked resplendent in starched linens and silver. Before our sailing date, P&O had thoughtfully mailed out pamphlets illustrating the table settings, telling us which fork to use, so that we simple folk wouldn't be humiliated. And there on the tables was a dazzle of polished silver on the snowy cloths. P&O must have had a crew hidden away who just ironed all day and another group who polished silver.

A place setting went like this, from left to right: fish fork, dinner fork, salad fork, plate, dinner knife, salad knife, soup spoon, cocktail fork. Above the plate, the dessert spoon and dessert fork. Above all those the forks, there on the left, a bread plate with a butter knife. I can't remember how the wine glasses were aligned. Somewhere in there, a napkin so stiff that it might have cracked if it were opened too vigorously.

And there were courses, with choices, for each set of instruments. Appetizer, soup, fish, meat, salad, dessert and savory. The *Titanic*, so I've read, served ten-course meals, and it is tempting to say something about sinking. A savory, which has different names in other cultures, and was probably spelled "savoury" on the P&O menus, is a wee bite of palate-cleansing piquancy after dessert. In *Iberia*'s case, it was a single cracker with nippy cheese, or a bite-sized pizza, or a lone cocktail sausage.

My table mates for the voyage were the ship's purser and two silver-plated, recently retired English couples. One was a Harley Street doctor and his wife. He had a soft voice, a BBC accent, and immaculately manicured fingernails. The other pair lived in the Bahamas, to avoid British taxes, as he made quite clear. This guy had his meds all lined up in front of his silver arsenal, disrupting the symmetry of the table's centerpiece. He had gout, he explained.

The purser was the source of offbeat information about the ship's business, dinner table *bon mots*. He told us there were elderly people on board who circled round and round the world, not bothering to disembark while in port. The elders were well cared for, with plenty of partners for bridge and books to read.

They were served multi-course meals which they barely touched, clean bedding and towels, mildly amusing entertainment, medical staff on board and a watchful crew who kept an eye out. Sailing the seas kept them off the roads and out of trouble. And when the end came, they were honored with a respectful ceremony on the deck at dawn, wrapped in a cloth shroud and slipped gently over the side. It saved the heirs the costs of caskets and funeral plots, floral wreaths and catered lunches.

I reported this juicy concept to friends I had made on board. We were all fascinated. We slyly glanced at the old-timers who stayed in their deck chairs while the rest of us lined up to go ashore to see the sights. We assumed these lucky folks had toured these ports enough times in the past. The people sitting near the exit ramp, who had equipped themselves with lap robes and buried their noses in books, became subjects of our discreet inspection. We were curious to see who might be so comfortably well off, and who might qualify for burial at sea.

The purser also told us that during that first night out of Vancouver, a couple of stowaways were discovered on board. The ship paused outside of Victoria, on Vancouver Island, where the uninvited visitors were transported by launch to shore. Years later I found out that the stowaways were colleagues of mine from *The Vancouver Sun* who had come aboard to see me off, then decided on their own to tour the engine room and missed the calls to go ashore. I was also told that their adventure cost them plenty.

No mingling was allowed between us and the many hundreds on the decks below us. Over the years in Vancouver I had sometimes gone to say farewell to friends who were heading elsewhere by ship. On these occasions, my friends were usually booked in tourist class or the equivalent of steerage, at least four people to a cabin; in one case there were eight or more bunks. Well-wishing friends were welcome to come on board to see our friends' new quarters, have a look around. In the heady milieu of *Iberia*'s first class, however, sturdy gates and tall fences kept us in our proper places. No fraternizing.

After the Second World War, Australia launched a campaign to attract immigrants from Britain and, shortly after, from other European countries. P&O became the carrier which delivered the newcomers, who were called "ten pound Poms." The ship's fare was ten pounds for English migrants, and their children traveled free. More than a million people traveled this way to their new home. Pom—or, more often, "bloody Pom"—is the nickname Australians use for Anglos who arrived on their shores. It stands for "prisoner of bloody England," or sometimes "pomegranate," the skin color that a British newcomer turns in the hot southern sun.

Dinner had been the first opportunity for a panoramic view of my fellow travelers. Later that evening, at a sing-along in the main lounge, a large number showed up. Two seatings were needed to feed all the first-class passengers so I'd seen only half the group at dinner. I admit I wasn't as eager to burst into song as I was to note who else was on board. I wasn't the only one. This good-natured event was the largest gathering of fellow voyagers during the three-week journey. The majority was a concentration of Greatest Generation globe-trotters. Of the almost seven hundred people in first class, only a handful were under forty. The rest were decidedly retired, elegant, well-mannered, with hair of polished silver. At the same time, some in our gang, the minority group, had survived San Francisco in the '60s and looked like it.

One of the younger passengers moved quietly through the entertainment lounge as we sang, whispering invitations to those of us in his age category to meet later in a bar and get to know each other. Meanwhile, as we hesitantly warbled along through "On Top of Old Smoky" and "Down in the Valley," a crew member walked around with a microphone to amplify individual voices. He paused in front of a tenor with a strong clear voice, to capture the man's melodic performance of "The Drunken Sailor." The singer, brawny and ornery-haired, showed up later at the under-forty gathering at the bar.

He was Timothy Maley. I sat in the empty chair at the table where Tim had joined four or five others, all of us learning a little about our fellow travelers. As individuals left the table to circulate, Tim and I stayed in place, and spent the next hour or so chatting. He had boarded the ship in San Francisco and was heading to Australia to teach school.

Throughout the days at sea, Tim and I spent a lot of time together. We watched relatively new movies in the ship's little theater, washed and sometimes mingled our laundry. He asked me to teach him how to iron, and he produced a few perfectly pressed, wrinkle-free handkerchiefs. Neither he nor I have ironed a handkerchief since then. We had plenty of days and evenings to just talk. Unlike anyone else I knew, Tim read poetry, and I'm relieved to report that he never recited any of it to me.

After graduating from Boston University, Tim had worked as a social worker for the Massachusetts Department of Child Guardianship, in the days when the agency was more casual about limiting the number of clients per social worker. Including the children, parents and foster parents, he had ninety-six people whose needs he monitored. Most of his charges were hardened or hardening teenage boys. He also told me about making the rounds to collect a half-dozen infants, strapping them into his car, and taking them all together to a medical clinic for their shots. I pictured him in the examination room with the babies, coping with diapers, bottles, wriggling and wailing. I liked that in a man.

Tim decided to move west and switch to teaching. He enrolled as a post-grad at San Francisco State College. His timing was not good. By the time he qualified to take on a classroom, San Francisco had a surfeit of teachers, and Tim joined the ballooning ranks of substitutes. He was on the phone early in the mornings, getting strings of busy signals before the days of the redial button. He hoped for a job for the day, or the week, or ideally, the rest of the school year. Some months and semesters were better than others, but none was permanent. He still hates the telephone.

Tim heard that Australia needed teachers, and even reimbursed travel expenses for certified American teachers. That is why he was on board the SS *Iberia*.

We didn't do a lot of meeting people that night, but we did get to know our wayfaring colleagues over the next three weeks. Most were American. Unlike the majority of the passengers, hardly any of us was on an extended vacation; these travelers were about moving on, changing our lives, migrating.

Among the lot, there was a fresh-faced honeymoon couple from Oregon, relocating to New Zealand. A pair of bitter Vietnam vets were moving to Australia because of the unnerving hostility they encountered back home in Queens, New York. An English nurse planned to meet up with friends in Sydney, and decide from there where to go next. A hairstylist from Ohio was going to seek her dream in Brisbane, far from home. The man who had invited all of us under-forty passengers to meet was a San Francisco artist and seasoned traveler who planned to settle in northern Australia. One who couldn't wait to get back home, however, was a Wyoming cowboy and dude ranch operator, on a lengthy trip with his wife and in-laws. The family was assigned to Tim's table in the dining room. The rancher, Tim reported, lamented about claustrophobia as he paced around and around the decks.

Early the next morning Tim and I met on the sports deck to play quoits. We were out in the open sea, no land in sight. We had to brace ourselves, feet wide apart, to stay upright. Quoits is a ring-toss game, something like pitching horseshoes, with rings woven out of ship's rope. The wind howled out there in the North Pacific that December day, and the quoits, assuming that quoits were the rings, blew wherever the wind decided. The higher we tossed, the more the wind took control. The rings seldom landed over their designated spikes. Neither of us won, and it didn't matter. As Tim tells people, it was like at first sight.

This was not a shipboard romance. It was a harmonious, friendly relationship for twenty-one days on board the vessel. Each stop meant a day on shore while the ship restocked and refueled. Tim and I stuck together in Hawaii. What I had remembered about seeing the city of Honolulu from my travel editor days was a lot of tall hotels along Waikiki Beach, backed by a commercial strip of shops selling seascaped muumuus and landscaped rayon shirts. Behind all of this, a modern downtown with commercial buildings and a sky-high water tower in the shape of a pineapple, painted yellow and green and rusting at the edges. I understand the water tower is no longer there. Pity.

The sea air smelled like home, only warmer, and we didn't want to leave the inviting shoreline. Instead of taking a bus tour of the environs, Tim and I and another new friend, Anna the nurse, walked away from the center of the city along the beach until we got hungry, then went inside an empty hamburger place and pool hall in a quiet suburb for some lunch and a round of billiards, which we played like the novices we were, and we didn't care. We three giggled easily in this almost vacant restaurant and ate our burgers and fries, our last genuine all-American meal for a long time.

Only three more island stopovers before we arrived in Sydney. That meant long days at sea, and P&O had to come up with ways to keep us entertained and safe. Most books I've read about overseas crossings tell about storms and sickness and huddled masses in the lower decks. One day, probably our second day out, the sea was a little rough and we were advised to hold on to the railings along the corridors as we walked. Dear little wooden fences appeared around the perimeters of our dining tables. Nothing spilled, nobody fell down, there was no hardship. The ship had stabilizers. We were coddled.

One day, somewhere out there in the middle of nowhere, we were informed we would be crossing the international dateline, an occasion for a celebration on the deck by the swimming pool. Wear your bathing suits, the announcement said. The pool water's temperature had by now adjusted to match the warm ocean that surrounded our ship. Tim confessed he'd dived into the pool the first day out of Vancouver, but was jolted upright by the reality of fifty-four-degree water, a number posted next to the pool. It had seemed like a reasonably mild temperature, like a good idea.

The highlight of the summery poolside day was the tossing of virgins into the pool, meaning the drenching of those who hadn't crossed the dateline before. Of course they weren't chucking in the more mature passengers, and there weren't many of us young enough to be safely, inconsequentially dunked by the ship's officers. I protested loudly, squawking that they were breaking the rules, that I'd crossed this line before, on a press junket to Fiji. I believe I was expected to complain. So, as I was being grabbed and lifted by several sets of arms, I argued that there were plenty of other people aboard who must have been new at this. I'm sure I flailed my arms and legs. I got pitched in anyway. Splat.

This reminded me: While flying home from the Fiji junket a few years earlier, the pilot had announced that we were crossing the dateline. A number of passengers stood up, jammed the aisle as they leaned toward the nearest portholes with their cameras and photographed the moment. All we could see out there from thirty-five thousand feet was water. I amused myself on this long flight with a nefarious idea of being the person in the photo lab who developed the pictures, the one who drew a dotted line down the centers of the portholes in their snapshots.

The ship arrived in Fiji a few days later, and we were greeted at the dock by a squad of hula dancers in grass skirts, enthusiastic young women writhing to the pineapple syrup sounds of guitars and ukuleles. I've never been welcomed ashore anywhere else by such a performance. I wondered if this was just for our ship, or a full-time job, as lots of passenger liners and yachts sailed into Suva's harbor. I could imagine these women dancing here day after day, courtesy of the Fiji Tourism Bureau. Nice work, if you've got the moves.

I never longed to live in a hammock suspended from a pair of palm trees in Polynesia. Two cultural experiences in my earlier life must have made an impression. A tiny girl named Nancy in my second grade class invited me to her birthday party. I was greeted at the door by Nancy and her mother, both of them dressed in Hawaiian costumes, grass skirts made of strips of green cellophane, flowered bra tops, bare feet, plastic leis, artificial orchids behind their right ears, lots of lipstick and rouge. All the guests were the girls from Nancy's class. It was winter in Canada.

The party proceeded as they usually do, with pin the tail on the donkey, musical chairs, fishing with sticks and string and clothespins. Right after the cake and ice cream were eaten, Nancy's mother announced that it was time for a very special treat. She clapped her hands, asked us to sit still and pay attention while she stationed herself in the center of the basement rec room. She dropped the needle on a record, all ready to play. As the twang of the slack key guitars and ukuleles slipped into song, Nancy's mother began to dance the hula. Her arms waved from one side to the other, her hips swayed in tune. Her bare feet, toes pointing up, slid from side to side. Her face wore a half-smile, eyes cast shyly downward. I looked over at Nancy, there on the sidelines. Her face was blank, her little arms so thin. I believe she was holding back tears. We were all embarrassed for her. This woman was a mother, not a wahine, but the show went on. The party broke up right afterwards.

The other tropical experience was '50s and '60s restaurant food that called itself Polynesian. Drinks with tiny parasols, entrees called poo-poo platters, tiki torch décor. Much of it was sweet and pink. The fanciest of the lot was Trader Vic's, a chain of upmarket Polynesian restaurants, one of which was popular in Vancouver. Trader Vic invented the mai tai, so it's said. What I remember about the restaurant was a menu item called Chinese gooseberries. They later became popularly known as kiwi fruit, no longer so exotic, and here to stay.

In Pago Pago, pronounced Pango Pango, a handful of American women boarded the ship as soon as we docked, to have lunch on shipboard, take home a bag full of fresh apples, and catch up on the news. The ship's crew had expected the visitors. These people, mostly teachers and health care workers, were hungry for fresh, recognizable food, some fruit, some vegetables. They told us how isolated they were here in Samoa, in the middle of the Pacific, how they depended on ships stopping by, that there was nothing fresh or frozen or refrigerated in Pago Pago's markets, and by the time television news programs arrived, before the days of satellite broadcasting, the information was already old. They were pale and they looked stressed. They should have been laid-back and caramel colored, at least, in this latitude.

Anna the nurse and I walked into the town, passing rows of poinsettia and hibiscus bushes in bloom along the streets, and we were hailed by some local fellows who told us they were Samoan kings and princes and chiefs. Yeah, right. As if we were mere girls. We kept walking around the downtown area and, when we saw a grocery store, went inside to check out the produce. It was unappetizing. Rubber carrots, withered salad greens, shriveled beets, wrinkled shrunken potatoes. No wonder those pale Americans were so eager to grab some fresh food from the ship.

Back out in the bright sunshine, we met up again with the aristocratic dudes, and agreed to join them and their friends, male and female, for a cold drink. The bar had ice. It didn't need air conditioning; the temperature inside and out was perfect. The Samoan gentlemen entertained us with unlikely claims about their high ranking in the community. They didn't provide much detail, and they didn't seem to have jobs. I don't know what they expected from us. So Anna and I spent a light-hearted hour or so studying social anthropology instead of the alternative, a bus tour around this utopian Polynesian jewel of an island. I told Anna that I didn't want to live there; neither did she. Chances are, if we'd had a few days here, with time to wiggle our bare toes in the Pacific and relax in the perfect atmosphere, we might have felt more attracted to the island. But a few hours on a pleasant day wasn't enough to persuade us. We walked around some more, just the two of us, enjoyed getting wet during a brief rain shower, then—dry already—we returned to our ship in the late afternoon and sailed off into the tropical sunset.

Next stop, and next to last, was New Zealand. We arrived in Auckland on a bright Sunday morning. The downtown streets first appeared to be the opening scene of a familiar dystopian movie—empty, no people, no traffic, no parked cars in their designated slots. Typical commercial shops and businesses lined the avenues, but where was everybody?

It was Sunday morning and nothing was open. And Auckland's emptiness was suddenly quite pleasant. Something about the air, the sunshine, the very cleanliness, was so fresh and pure, not a bit begrimed; it felt as though nobody had been here before, as if the city had grown up but was never populated. The remote island nation had an Adam-and-Eve, unspoiled, wholesome, apple-cheeked air, a feeling that grew stronger throughout the day.

This time Tim and I took the bus tour, through the city and into the nearby countryside. In a city park surrounded by tall buildings stood an improbable flock of grazing sheep, not only living an urban life, but also one of the few examples of animate beings we encountered. We were driven out to a small zoo where someone showed us the sleeping kiwis, not the little fruit, but birds the same color, same shape as the Chinese gooseberry. Still, hardly any humans. It appeared that people were allowed to sleep until noon on Sundays—another plus. This might be an excellent place to live.

§

To awaken quite alone in a strange town is one of the pleasantest sensations in the world.

Freya Stark

AUSTRALIA
1971–1972

Just because Canada and Australia both speak English, and are sisterly offspring of our great mother England, doesn't mean it was easy to insinuate myself into the culture of Sydney. The trouble with moving halfway around the world is that there are dumbfounding little surprises around every corner, even when you think you know where you are going. The man in the neighborhood greengrocer, which he called the Fruitateria, looked at me in despair when I asked for broccoli. It was January, midsummer down there. "It's not in season," he explained. I thought that was as unreasonable as saying potatoes were not in season. I asked for skim milk. They couldn't sell it by law, he patiently told me, because milk was meant only for young children, and they needed to drink whole milk, he said.

Then I was puzzled when people were pleased and surprised that I had a telephone in my flat. "Are you on the phone?" people asked. The phrasing of the question threw me at first. At the time, telephones were hard to come by and there was a waiting list. I hadn't appreciated how lucky I was.

I found the apartment within a couple of days of the ship's arrival. I initially stayed in a hotel in the center of town, one which I had booked before I left Canada. My new home was in Sydney's late-night honky-tonk neighborhood, called King's Cross. At that age, I could sleep through anything. My new landlady told me her previous tenant had also been a Canadian, "but not a real Canadian" she said. "She spoke with a French accent."

My one-room home was oddly dark and muted for such a sunny climate. It had a single bed in one corner, other essential furniture scattered around. The focus of the room was an intimidating stove built like a double-wide motorcycle, matte black and curvy cast iron, laced with open spaces between its working parts. The only heat in the room came from a what looked like half a toaster on the floor, with coils that glowed menacing red. When I had to use it, I never took my eyes off it. The stove was so big, the heating system so small, the space had an Alice in Wonderland quality.

The place was no beauty but it was both foreign and exotic and I felt exhilarated having a home abroad, far away from all and any crap I may have left behind. The future was brand-new, whatever it turned out to be.

The apartment came with cockroaches as big as my thumb. I'd heard of them, of course, but they were not native to Canada and I'd never seen one before. As a lone big bruiser approached my bed one evening I whacked it with my nearby shoe, saw it lying still and was certain I'd killed it. But in the morning it was gone, no sign of it. I decided these fiends had learned their behavior from the U.S. military in Vietnam, who were so much in the news. We were told that after a deadly nighttime skirmish in the dark swamps and jungles, the survivors carried away all their dead before daylight to spook the North Vietnamese, and to prevent them from counting the bodies.

I didn't know it then, but King's Cross was the most notorious part of the inner city, with organized crime, nightclubs, prostitution and jiggle joints, as the tabloids call them. Its original name was Woolloomooloo Hills. It's fun to say Woolloomooloo. Accent on the last "loo." The hippies, then the boomers, took over the area later in the century, and I understand it has now been gentrified. An aside: My cousin lost her apartment in New York because of gentrification. "The gentry moved in," Debby explained, "and we were the -fication."

Our ship arrived in Sydney three days before Christmas. Tim and I made sure we stayed in touch. Tim had joined Jim and Nick, the Vietnam vets we got to know on the ship, renting an apartment in a very nice neighborhood called Double Bay. They hosted a holiday party Christmas Day for us single stragglers on *Iberia*'s passenger list. Judy, the Ohio hairstylist, came to the party, but was about to move up the coast to Brisbane. Anna the nurse had disappeared into the crowd, having met with friends as soon as we docked in Sydney. The five of us new immigrants sat cross-legged on the apartment floor and ate takeout fried chicken, with Australian wine out of a box, a novelty that hadn't yet arrived back home. We exchanged hastily bought and wrapped little gifts, and wished each other good luck, which was just as important at the time as saying Merry Christmas.

The first letter I received from my mother told me that her mother, my dear old grandmother, had died. She had been in a nursing home in Saskatchewan, near some of my aunts and uncles and cousins. She was eighty-five, though I would have guessed older, since she had been old all my life. I wrote to her faithfully, but after she moved back to Saskatchewan I never saw her again. I was sorry now I was so far away, and felt a nudge of loneliness and great distance. I also felt guilty, as if my leaving the country made her give up the will to live. Feeling guilty is so self-indulgent, I told myself.

§

It's just a job. Grass grows, birds fly,
waves pound the sand. I beat people
up.

Muhammad Ali

SYDNEY
1972

The few contact names I'd collected were not helpful, so I applied for a writing job I saw in the classified ads. I was hired to write press releases for an American who was starting a public relations business. I loved the little house in Paddington that he used as his office. In this old residential part of the city, the narrow stone houses were decked with intricately spun wrought-iron fences, balcony rails, stair rails and gates, reminiscent of New Orleans. Going to work was an attractive way to start the day. But my employer didn't have a lot of accounts to advocate. And there's only so much you can extol about doors, the Australian Door Manufacturers Association being one of his clients. Plywood was his other client. So I gave it a burl, as they say. I wrote a lot of information about these home-building products, but I never knew where he sent them or if they appeared in print. No new clients seemed to be forthcoming. I sensed that this nice young man's dreams weren't working out, and he seemed relieved when his only employee left for greener pastures a couple of months later.

I landed a reporting job at *The Sunday Australian*, which at the time was Rupert Murdoch's crown jewel. The Sunday had its own staff, separate from the daily paper, including the sharpest reporting and photography staff in the country, as well as a talented art director whose job was fundamental to the appearance of the paper, and whose desk was right there in the newsroom. All seven days, the *Australian* was the country's prestige newspaper, with an elite readership. Physically, the paper was a tablecloth-sized broadsheet, beautifully designed, with lots of white space, artistic photography, a handsome document to wrap Australia's fish and chips and line its budgie cages.

Rupert Murdoch's presses and television networks had not yet overtaken the rest of the English-speaking world. At the time he had inherited and owned a number of newspapers throughout Australia, and had just begun to add to his collection in England. As such, he was very much in evidence in his News Corp building in Sydney. He spent Saturdays at the *Sunday Australian*'s copy editors' table, in a lavender-colored shirt, sleeves rolled up, overseeing the editorial content of his prize paper. He may have been partial to the Sunday edition because he had recently married the paper's fashion editor. That's pure speculation on my part. Maybe he spent lots of time and money on his other publications, but they didn't look like it. There he was in the cafeteria, stirring the soup and poking the meat pies. And there he was again in the composing room, holding, actually clutching clusters of metal type, the very activity that might have caused a walkout and shutdown of any big daily in Canada.

I was assigned to cover a variety of general news topics, but I never had the hard nose needed to become investigative. Neither did I have the contacts to dig into the dirt. I wanted to report, not expose—it wasn't in my nature. A number of times I was asked to find out what really happened—like when a plane skidded off the runway and my editor didn't believe the official story. Who, me? Or find out how much hot money a certain somebody collected and stashed away.

Then there was the foreignness of it all. My editor asked me, out in the open newsroom one of my first days, to interview Sir Don Bradman, and I had to blurt out, "Who's that?" All the typewriters in the newsroom stopped clacking, and every eye in the room was focused on me. Maybe this was a test, perpetrated on all of us alien new hires. Turns out that Sir Don was and is still considered the world's greatest cricketer batsman, but I was out of my hemisphere. Scratch that assignment.

For some reason I wasn't let go; instead I was reassigned and reconsigned. After several months at News Corp, I was transferred to the *Daily Mirror*, just down the hall, to another of Murdoch's dailies, but one with less distinction. Every day, the front page of the tabloid ran a photograph of a woman in a bikini. I guess that's a distinction. The upside of the transfer was my new job title. I was a subeditor, a job that was called copy editor or deskman in Canada, like the fellow at the beginning of my story who was forced into retirement before he wanted to go. Women rarely held this job; I was one of just two in the country, so I was told. I expect I impressed somebody with my catchy headline-writing skills, which was like a word game for me.

I had to remember a lesson I'd been taught about such a job: sometimes copy editors are bored with the material they are reading and let their eyes glaze over without paying attention. A few years earlier, one of the Vancouver papers printed an embarrassing, mortifying mistake. The subject was the monthly meeting of a women's auxiliary group. The freelancer was one of the auxiliary members who volunteered to compose a report. She followed the activities of the meeting in chronological order. The meeting was brought to order, she wrote, listing the names of the group's officers who sat up front. She reported how the last meeting's minutes were received and each agenda item was dealt with, in proper sequence.

About the sixth paragraph down, the reporter wrote that one of the group members in the audience reached into her purse, stood up, cocked her pistol, shot and killed the vice president. The copy editor hadn't read that far down—neither had anyone else at the paper. Not yet. The headline said something like "Women's Auxiliary Holds Monthly Meeting."

Someone at the *Mirror* told me the reason I was chosen to be a subeditor was that I came from a country where women don't blanch when they overhear swear words. Foul language might be spoken here within earshot, because the managing editor and other top-tier editors' offices were right next to the copy desks. And these editors, it seemed, were more stressed than the rest of us, and so they swore. No shit, I should have replied. Australia's other woman subeditor sat next to me, and she looked fine; she didn't seem to suffer from overhearing potty-mouth language.

It's true that at parties or in public, if a man swore in front of a woman he would first blush, then stammer, then apologize. As if it were important. On the other hand, there were tales of women who went on dates with men who left their women stranded alone in the car in the parking lot while the men went inside the pub for a beer or three. Was there a connection here?

I no longer needed to write about subjects I didn't understand, or didn't approve of, but I still agonized because of a tussle between national customs. First, reporters objected to my authority. One bloke complained loudly that he "didn't want a *bird* handling my (his) copy." He got over it. But I still had problems with conventions. What to call an African American in an American wire service story which had been slotted for a one-column headline? I used the word "black," which was the accepted term at home at the time. Australia still used "Negro," which had superseded "coloured" when "black" was still an offensive term in that country. The paper went with "Negro," which made me uncomfortable; it seemed like it had to be an insult.

Meanwhile, Tim was hired to teach fifth grade in a public school in the Sydney suburb of Bankstown. He had problems with the culture too. The kids in their neat uniforms and neckties were perplexed because he refused to strike them with a cane when they misbehaved. Corporal punishment was not in his training, nor in his character. The children adored him, some of them cried when he told them he was leaving, and throughout the school year, his classroom had the best attendance records.

Tim and I continued spending time together. We went to movies and some good live theater, and we dined out on escargot farmed in the nearby Hunter Valley. On my birthday, as we waited for a table in a fancy restaurant in Double Bay, I succumbed to a stomach bug. On our way out the door, I began feeling truly ill. I needed some kind of vessel and luckily there was a potted plant by the doorway, which was not visible to the diners, thank goodness. The poor aspidistra got the shock of its life. I didn't stop to clean up my mess. I was incapacitated. We sat together on a park bench nearby, Tim's coat wrapped protectively around me and his arm around my shoulder. We walked back to his apartment and Tim cooked up a couple of hamburgers, not that I was able to eat. But I felt comforted and cared for. It was a good feeling.

Sensing that Australia would not be our permanent home, the two of us made side trips. We didn't want to leave the country without seeing more of it. He was able to go to Papua New Guinea during a school break, which still makes me jealous. Before starting our new jobs we took a sixty-five-hour, twenty-five-hundred-mile-long train trip to the west coast, to see what the world looked like from the other end. The trip began on a Monday with an hour-long ride through and past Sydney's sprawling pink and baby blue suburbs, followed by formal afternoon tea served on board. Before long we were in the Blue Mountains, steep, green and wet. It was raining heavily, had been raining here for weeks. The rivers were flooded and the willow trees up to their knees in water. We were told the willows were the coolabah trees under whose shade the jolly swagman sat waiting for his billy to boil. Words to live by, altered from the Australian national anthem, "Waltzing Matilda."

Tuesday morning we were in a barren landscape, the Nullarbor Plain. Some early risers boasted that they'd already seen emus and kangaroos hopping across the plain. The flat and featureless view from here made it easy to see kangaroos bounding across the bleak land. Easy for other people, that is. My reflexes were never quick enough. I was the one calling out "Where? Where?" while everyone else on the train was excited and snapping pictures. All I could see was a pipeline parallel to the tracks, carrying water to Broken Hill, seven hundred miles west of Sydney.

The train made a stop in Broken Hill, the center of the Australian outback version of the Wild West, with plenty of cattle ranches, called cattle stations. This is where the cattlemen wear wide-brimmed cowboy hats with beads dangling from strings attached to the edge of the brim. As we disembarked from the train, we understood the reason for those festively fringed hat brims. The station platform was abuzz with swarms of agitated flies. Those frisky dancing beads kept the flies away from the cowpokes' eyes, noses and mouths. Hatless and hapless, we tourists got back on the train. A quarter of a mile away we noticed a pile of bones near the tracks. And ten minutes later, a freshly deceased kangaroo lying in a dried-up river bed. As I looked at the dead animal, I wondered if I'd scored any points in my lifelong quest to spot wildlife. I guessed not.

Later in the afternoon we were at the coast again, in Port Pirie off the Southern Ocean. The next island over is Antarctica. We had an hour here to look around while the train changed engine and crew. A Norwegian ship was tied up next to the grain silos just across from the train station. We were invited aboard. A Port Pirie longshoreman told us the grain was barley and he took us over to peer down into the hold of the ship. The temperature was only ninety-eight today, he told us proudly. He added that it was unseasonably cool for Port Pirie. I think he was making a joke. Barley dust stuck like oatmeal on our damp skins, and flies headed directly for the nose and mouth, just like the ones from Broken Hill.

When we reboarded our air-conditioned train, we were about to ride along the longest stretch of straight railway track in the world, three hundred miles without a single curve. The Nullarbor was once a seabed, with more salt than the sea itself. Its only plant life is saltbush and bluebush, dark and scarce and dry as twigs. There was animal life, lizards, dingoes, rabbits and kangaroos. But all we saw were buzzards on the telegraph wires.

Wednesday morning, we were still cruising through the Nullarbor. The only settlements were clusters of four or five bungalows for railroad employees and their many children playing outside. There were no stores for these families, but a supply train called the Tea and Sugar train plied the line and a train called the Mobile Theatrette came by with movies. Water was piped in from five hundred miles away. At the time, the region was getting some press attention because of a report of a half-naked girl sporting across the desert with a flock of kangaroos. A local bushman snorted at the story. "Any bird go flittin' around here with nothin' on would bloody soon burn off what's bobbin'."

By six we were in Kalgoorlie, where gold has been mined nonstop since 1893. We had time for a bus tour, which took us down wide streets, around a half-dozen mine shafts, past the hospital and the drive-in movie. Highlight of the bus tour was Brookman Street at dusk, the red light district where the city burned honest-no-kidding red light bulbs, the girls waved at the bus going by, and a few passengers hooted and slapped their thighs as if they couldn't believe their eyes. The water was piped in from three hundred and fifty miles away, a million gallons in every mile of pipe.

Early Thursday we arrived in Perth. We were met by my old Canadian friend and fellow journalist Ormond Turner, who was living in the city by the Indian Ocean. He drove us around to see the well-groomed, bright green parks and a little farther to have a look at the ocean. Its very sight quenched our thirst.

Turner told us about his early morning arrival in Australia, flying a red-eye from Hong Kong to Darwin. When his plane landed, Turner went directly to a pub to soothe his red eyes. He also felt a little wonky from the long trip. When he placed his order at the bar, two local mates strode up to him, flexed their biceps, and looked him in the eye. He didn't pay any attention. One of the blokes decided to make contact, glared at Turner and threateningly said, "Hank the Yank who fucked a duck." The remark was intended to make Turner throw the first punch, but instead he burst out laughing, as we all did when he retold the story. Good on ya, mate.

For an evening's entertainment in Perth, Turner, his girlfriend, Tim and I went to a pub with recorded country and western music, lots of white people sitting around drinking lots of pints of beer, talking in English. There was Johnny Cash, singing away, ". . . because you're mine, I walk the line." And I shrugged to myself, "Here I am on the farthest spot of solid ground I can find away from my native soil, and this is what I get to experience." A day later we flew back to Sydney.

We toured all we could of Sydney. The Opera House was under construction, and wonderful to see, even though it was a year away from completion. We swam and sunned ourselves on the city's beaches, on the lookout for sharks as the "Swim at your own risk" warning signs advised. We went horseback riding out in the country, checked out the Southern Hemisphere critters in the city's zoo, as well as the Southern Cross at night, part of an alien sky that again made me realize how far I was from home. Another aside from the Southern Hemisphere: The water draining from bathtubs circulates counterclockwise, opposite the way it circles north of the equator. Don't ask me to explain.

We went to see *The Godfather* with a couple of Australian friends, who confessed they couldn't understand a word that Marlon Brando mumbled. I had trouble sometimes understanding some Australians, especially those from rural outposts. A group of us ate at a Chinese restaurant that featured a Mexican mariachi band who moved from table to table. Tim requested that the band play "Wonton Amera." The others didn't get it; neither did the band. It's said a woman will fall in love with a man who can make her laugh. I'll vouch for that. We visited people in lovely modern homes along the rocky coast. We admired the blooms in the Botanical Gardens, and the art in the local museums and galleries. I loved the little meat pies sold at lunchtime from street corner stalls. I once ate a sandwich made with Vegemite, a spread made of brewer's yeast and other things. Peanut butter is better.

One long weekend we went to Melbourne, about six hundred miles south of Sydney. Travel advice was not encouraging. The city's tourism brochures suggested "Take a look at our contemporary buildings" or visit "the exciting fruit and vegetable market." Billy Graham once said, glowingly, it was the most moral city in the world.

Well, it wasn't that bad. It had that look of contrived English quaintness, with statues of Queen Victoria here and there, and more statues of unfamiliar governors and generals on horseback. And there were such attractions as Captain Cook's cottage, the Carved Fairy Tree and Miniature Village. We toured the National Gallery and then Como, a historic mansion, with grounds and gardens delicately manicured. Indoors, the mansion was flamboyantly overstuffed, lined with spooky old dolls in the nursery and dead birds hanging upside down, mounted on the sitting room walls. We weren't looking for a hot time anyway. That was eons ago, and we hear the city now has a lot more dazzle.

After a few months, Tim and I decided to find a place together. Rents were high, most places wanted long leases, and there weren't many choices. We ended up in a one-room flat in Strathfield, with a shared kitchen and an outdoor shower. Outdoor showers were charming in summer, but Sydney winters were not Sydney summers. Our kitchen-mate was an unhappy middle-aged woman who reluctantly gave up shelf space in the fridge and burners on the stove. She had a right: she had rented her room in this house for decades, poor soul. We sensed we wouldn't be there very long.

At the end of a late shift at the paper, I took the subway to the station a few blocks from our apartment and walked home. I had to walk past a convent which was well guarded by a gang of German shepherd custodians. You'd think the dogs would get used to my walking past the nunnery five nights a week, but no, they didn't. I hated the barking, the growls, the threats, the exposed upper lips, the ambushes out into the empty street, the helplessness of being alone out there.

We tolerated the living situation, knowing we weren't going to stay in Australia. It was a fine country but it wasn't home, and there was a lot of world left to see. When I left Canada the only concrete plan I had was to get this far. I was so relieved to have met a travel companion who had similar daydreams. Now we had some plotting to do. With a world map in front of us, we roughly planned a route that included as much real estate as we could afford to cover.

We agreed to stretch our funds as far as we could by staying in the lowest-priced lodgings we could find, just basic overnight shelter. We would move over land and sea on trains, buses and boats, to see as much terrain as we could. We would make our money and our experiences expand to the breaking point—third class in the third world. We weren't going anywhere just to see the sights, but to try to inhabit places as much as possible.

Once we were ready to leave, we closed our Australian bank accounts in exchange for American Express travelers checks. I spent a very nervous fifteen minutes walking from my bank through the downtown streets to the American Express office with a great wad of Australian cash stuffed and bulging in my handbag. Credit cards were unknown to us. There was Diners Club, and maybe American Express, but they were meant for business executives on three-martini lunches. Some backpackers we met were using Bank of New South Wales traveler's checks, a more obscure and dubious brand by the time they got to the Northern Hemisphere. They sometimes ran into trouble trying to cash them.

We designated our parents at home to oversee the better part of our savings, and send it to us when we ran low. Tim had inherited some money from his grandfather. I was always a faithful saver and became more diligent in Vancouver when I vaguely thought about saving to buy a house. The house turned into a trip around the world. Once we started, Tim and I took turns cashing a hundred-dollar traveler's check, which generally lasted most of a week. Some couples we met on the road squabbled over money: "Your bread was toasted, and it cost five bahts more." Who needed that. Our third-class travel, with second-class privileges, cost us $300 a month each, about the same as it would have cost to stay in one place, modestly but adequately, at home.

We never thought about health insurance. We weren't unhealthy. We didn't fret about something called anti-bacterial food wipes, nowadays touted as a must for travelers. Wi-Fi? Come on.

So in September, when the Australian spring arrived, we boarded a northbound train, heading for the Great Barrier Reef. I hadn't shed enough belongings before leaving Sydney and I was dumbfounded by the weight of my luggage when I climbed aboard the train. This must be why they call it luggage. I couldn't possibly lug all this stuff around the world. On our itinerary I could see no occasion for the high-heeled shoes, the party dress, the thin suede boots, the warm coat. When we arrived in Townsend, I rounded up a collection of firm cardboard boxes and packed up at least three-quarters of the clothes I thought I'd like to have for this long journey. Some things—the boots, for example—were shipped to my parents for safekeeping; the rest were delivered to the local Goodwill or its equivalent. By the end of our travels, a tattered pair of jeans, two shirts and a change of underwear were all I needed to cart around. Somewhere along the route I had to buy a new pair of shoes, and I replaced them with what was available, corduroy sneakers. They were practical, unless it rained. Then they stayed wet for days. A year later a young man struggling with English told us we looked like vagabonds. He meant it as an insult, but I rather liked the image. I hadn't expected to become so feral; it just came with the territory.

In the fabled watery world of the Great Barrier Reef, we saw what we could above the water line. We didn't actually go underwater. It cost more than we expected and we were so new at this, we didn't dare blow our allowance before we left Australia. What I remember most about the area was sitting on an empty beach and cutting Tim's hair so that we could enter the Developing World, which wasn't ready for his irascible tresses. Getting ready to leave Australia, we were both a little lighter.

We made our way west to Darwin. At our small hotel we sat in wicker chairs in a screened porch surrounded on three sides by steamy jungle and a brackish stream. The porch in its jungle setting made me think of a Humphrey Bogart movie set in Africa or some clammy tropical place. A plaque on the wall said that this was the very spot where the world's biggest crocodile had been shot and killed, about a hundred years earlier. It was thirty-some feet long, according to the plaque. I watched for a while through the screen, hoping for some action in the greasy green river. Nothing happened. They don't make crocodiles like that any more.

§

EAST TIMOR
1972

I was eager to visit my first underdeveloped country, one that hadn't been tarnished by Western culture, a region that hardly anybody had ever heard of. Our little plane flew out of Darwin and landed on a dusty airstrip near the village of Baucau, East Timor.

Timor is a crocodile-shaped island about six hundred miles north of Australia, its ownership sliced in two. The western half belonged to Indonesia, the bad guys in this story; our destination was the Portuguese colony at the other end.

Although East Timor had been a Portuguese colony for several centuries, the local people speak Tetum Prasa, Mambai, Makesai, Tetum Terik, Baikenu, Kemak, Bunak, Tokodede or Fataluku. That's about one language per family.

We were lucky. Our plane was met by a local man named Peter, who spoke English and proved to be our helpful innkeeper, concierge and guide. Peter filled his Land Rover with all nine air passengers and drove us into town, to the Pearl of the Orient Hotel, $1.80 a day, a hotel he happened to own. If there were other hotels in Baucau, we didn't notice them. It wasn't luxurious, but it was clean and neat; it had electricity from early morning until midnight, but no hot water. We were to learn that hot water was almost never available in the kind of world we were so keen to explore.

Peter warned us not to travel to the Indonesian half of the island, as those people were barbaric, a terrifying enemy. Under the rule of the brutal despot Suharto, Peter told us, the Indonesians wanted to wipe out East Timor's population and take the land. We had no intention of going there, we assured Peter. We didn't realize how literally true his comments would turn out to be.

We were awakened at dawn our next morning by dogs, chickens, roosters and geese just outside the open window of our room. The sun was shining, the air was warm and dry, another perfect day. We saw women with bananas, cassava melons and yams arranged decoratively on their heads, on their way to the market, which was under a grove of trees next to a cliff overlooking the ocean. Children headed to school with books balanced on their heads. We did not see any beggars, any signs of poverty or broken people. Peter was standing around at the market, doling out wisdom to visitors and locals alike. He showed us where to find the beach, as the trails out of town were not marked.

Following Peter's directions, Tim and I walked down a sloping path of white sugar sand through the palm and jungle growth to an exquisite empty beach overlooking the Banda Sea. Off to our right, fourteen hundred miles away, was New Guinea; to our left a bracelet of Indonesian islands. Straight ahead, facing north, were the tiny islands Alor and Wetar, and a mere six hundred miles beyond that, the equator.

The day remained perfectly balmy, with a gentle breeze, unoppressively summer. The ocean shimmered iridescent turquoise, gently lapping wavelets spilled over the fine sand. There is no place more magical than a sandy beach with no other human beings in sight. This was one of the prettiest. It reminded me of a Disney movie. Happily bobbling orange and white clownfish smiled and waved at us to come on in, and some little mermaids giggled with bubbly mirth, as I prefer to remember that beach.

On our way back up to the village we noticed that we had made the only footprints in the sand, except for some decorative S-curved squiggles crossing the path, this way and that. The writhing arcs were so distinct, they had to be new, at least as recent as our hours-old footprints, which were already beginning to fill in with sand. When we got back, we asked Peter about the island's snakes. Yes, he told us sadly, they're all poisonous, "though just a little bit," he hedged. But the Indonesian end of the island, he warned us, was home to boa constrictors big enough to crush buffaloes and horses to death. We three—Tim, Peter and I—took a moment to shudder.

That evening in Baucau we talked with Portuguese soldiers based in Timor—lonely, bored young men—who were having dinner at the Pearl of the Orient, and who wanted to practice their English with us. They invited us to their mess to listen to Pat Boone records. Literally. We declined. Instead we were curious about the next evening's event that had the community excited. It was a cockfight, of all things.

The arena was built much like a hockey rink at home, with straw on the ground rather than ice. The bleacher seats were filled with excited men and boys with cigarettes dangling from their mouths, gesticulating and talking rapidly in Tetum or Kemak. Their passions were accelerated by the gambling being transacted in the dimly lit, smoky ambiance. The spotlights and the attention switched to the action in the cockpit, as it is called. The word "cocky" must also have come from this sport. Gamecocks, which were bred, conditioned, trained and pumped up on poultry testosterone, were equipped with knife-sharp spurs attached to their heels. They circled each other for a while, heads bobbing, then one attacked, then the other, and soon enough one wounded or killed his opponent as the spectators roared. Why anyone would want to do this to a pin-headed rooster is beyond me. As you would expect, cockfighting is illegal in much of the Western world, although those laws were generally made to prevent gambling, not for the birds' welfare.

It was here in Timor that Tim and I began asking "How was it?" as one or the other came out of the bathroom. This went on for the next year and a half.

The next morning we packed up and left by bus for Dili, the capital of East Timor, and awaited a flight out of the colony's alternate airport. We had booked one way to Bali, a few islands off to the west. We waited and waited. The plane kept not showing up. No explanation. No show. The Zamrud Airline agent shrugged it off. No big deal.

One evening I was grateful for the delay. We attended an outdoor concert in downtown Dili by the beloved Portuguese fado singer Amalia Rodriguez. We bought a tape of her music and still love to listen to her haunting voice. At a restaurant after the concert, we talked to the Australian man who was her manager on this circuit. I asked him what "fado" means. He told me it means "fight." But this was not martial music. It took me a while to realize that it means "fate." You would think by now I would have known how to translate Australian.

So we waited some more. We went to the airport daily to make sure we weren't missing anything. Nobody seemed bothered by the plane that never arrived. Maybe the pilot waited at the Bali end of the run until enough ticket-holders showed up to make the journey worth his while, but nobody said so. After a while we became friends with the airline agent, and he loosened up.

The agent explained that Zamrud Airlines offered the only way out of Timor, unless we went back to Australia by way of the Baucau airport. He told us of impatient travelers being unwittingly stranded for weeks in Dili. Boats seldom stopped at these islands. And now, he finally admitted, Zamrud, an Indonesian company, was recovering from a major crash in Sumbawa just weeks before; the airline had no working planes, no parts, and didn't bother to inform or update East Timor.

The agent added some compelling details to his story. He said some people hired Land Rovers or trucks with drivers, then paid bribes to customs officials because they were not allowed to cross Timor overland. On foot it was a three- to six-week trek across mountain trails to cover the hundred and twenty miles to Kupang, the capital of the Indonesian side of the island. Roads were few and far between. Travel was mostly through rugged jungle and mountain walking trails. Not much of it was accessible by vehicle. The island is roughly the same size and shape as New Jersey.

He told us of one recent group who barely survived. A bridge collapsed under their hired truck and landed in a dry riverbed. One woman had a badly swollen ankle; another was bitten by a scorpion. The truck, unbeknownst to its passengers, was carrying contraband. A second truck came to liberate the contraband, but left the travelers in the jungle for three days without food or water before someone arrived to rescue them. Tim and I agreed we would wait for Zamrud, no matter how long it took.

Finally, eventually, this aerodynamic brute, a well-worn, high-mileage DC-6, aroused the town with its roar. It landed with its nose pointing high in the air. The pilot was American. He helped his disembarking passengers off the plane and waved the new group aboard for the return trip to Bali. When we were all seated, tilted backwards, a steward handed out our lunch, paper bags with sandwiches made of sliced white bread filled with chocolate sprinkles, and the captain welcomed us aboard Zamrud Airlines.

Off and up we soared, making stops in Kupang, Sumba, Sumbawa, and finally Bali. We flew over Komodo, the island where you never want to sleep on the beach, because of the notorious monster killer Komodo dragons. The world's biggest lizard, up to ten feet long and two hundred pounds, has toxic venom and likes to eat anything with flesh. We had seen a dyspeptic Komodo dragon in the Sydney zoo, behind inch-thick plate glass, and I felt the sensation of my blood running cold.

Our last stop before Bali was on the island of Sumbawa, where our plane taxied up to the shack that served as the airport. Alongside the runway was the three-week old wreckage of Zamrud Airlines' most recent crash. But we paid little attention—hell or high water, we were going to Bali.

§

Two years after our visit, Peter's nightmare came true. East Timor was embroiled in a barbaric civil war and invasion by Indonesia, to the tune of wiping out a third of East Timor's population. Through warfare, genocide and starvation, the massacres were so extreme and lasted so long—more than three decades—that news reports sometimes made it into the U.S. press.

All these years later, East Timor is now independent, a democracy, elects its own leaders, belongs to the United Nations and sells its coffee to Starbucks. But it all came at an inconceivable price. I sometimes wonder about Peter. I hope and expect that he was savvy enough to escape the worst of it.

§

I would live all my live in nonchalance and insouciance, were it not for making a living, which is rather a nousiance.

Ogden Nash

JACK RIFE, ADVENTURER
1972

Jack Rife, who lived alone in a cottage on the beach in Bali, was the captain of the Zamrud Airlines DC-6 that flew us to Bali. We were a mile high out of Timor when he put the plane on automatic pilot, wandered back to bum a cigarette and chat with his eight passengers. Our pilot had a Kentucky accent, was dressed in tattered yellow Levi's, a sweatshirt and a baseball cap. A toothpick poked out from the corner of his mouth. He was in his early forties, I guessed, and he had a pleasant face.

"We stop for immigration and customs in Kupang," he said. "They'll want to see your passport, visas, and see your on-going ticket out of the country. And by the way," he drawled, "if you have any grass, put it in your shoes. They don't look there." Nervous titters from the passengers. As he spoke, a slender Indonesian steward handed us our chocolate sandwiches.

At our first stop, Kupang, the capital of Indonesian Timor, a new mattress and box spring from Macy's was slid into the aisle of the plane. We no longer had access to the john. Meanwhile, our pilot told us about the string of islands we would be crossing. The next stop was Sumba, where the natives made intricate handwoven

92

cloths, mostly the size of sarongs, woven in a distinctive warp and woof pattern, often with an occasional silver thread to break up the design. In 1972 they sold for $150 in Australian galleries. In Sumba they cost $10. All these years later they are worth many hundreds more. Jack Rife told us he dealt in them on the side.

"This is it," he announced, "Waingapu Municipal Airport." We looked out the windows at the grass landing strip, one shack made of straw, and Sumba cloths strung like laundry along a sagging clothesline. While the passengers got out to inspect the cloths, Jack strolled up and down the lines of local people who had come to the airport to see him, their eyes following him as if this were a tennis match. He stopped to chat, he congratulated a new father with a hug, he shook hands and handed out candy to the kids, he patted people on the shoulder. In response, his friends beamed at him adoringly.

The next stop was Sumbawa. Another grass landing strip but no souvenir shop. The only interesting item out there was the Zamrud DC-6, beginning to rot and rust in the field. The pilot forgot to lower his landing wheels but nobody was injured. So there it sat, stripped of its workable parts.

"Zamrud had eleven DC-6s," Jack told us. "Three of them are under the sea and the rest are on the ground. This one we're flying today is rented from another airline." We passengers took another spin of gratitude around our worry beads. In Sumbawa we picked up crates of shrieking parrots and cockatoos, another sideline of the pilot, and the containers were placed on top of the mattress. His exotic birds were shipped to American pet shops from the jet base in Bali.

Last stop was Bali, green and paved and neatly laid out in rectangles down there. We landed, heard a heavy sigh from the cockpit, and we the passengers spontaneously broke into applause.

§

Days later, at his bungalow on Kuta Beach, Jack Rife talked about himself. His home town was Turkey Creek, Kentucky, near the West Virginia border. He started flying at age ten in a homemade glider in the back forty, lied about his age and got a flying license at fourteen. After military service in Korea he became the personal pilot for Dr. Wernher von Braun, who designed the V-2 ballistic missile, then became an American hero working for NASA. Satirist Tom Lehrer wrote a song that went "'Once the rockets are up, who cares where they come down? / That's not my department,' says Wernher von Braun."

"All I had to do was fly him around," said Jack. "And my other chore was to follow him wherever he went, pick up his cigarette butts, chewing gum wrappers and little bits of paper he had thrown away, and send them to security, in case they contained some important formulas or theories."

From NASA Jack was recruited to join Air America, the CIA air service in Southeast Asia, flying "medical supplies," he euphemized, between Laos and Vietnam. Other than holidays, Jack hadn't lived at home since 1964. He moved to Bali in 1968, to take over Zamrud operations in eastern Indonesia. "You know, honey, when I came here," he said, "passengers had to bargain and dicker over the price of their airline tickets. That was the first thing that changed."

"In those days, months would go by before I saw another white person," he said. "Hotel rooms in Kuta Beach cost a dime a night then. Now they've skyrocketed to fifty cents." Jack hadn't had a paycheck from Zamrud for five months, but adventurers know how to improvise and make do. "First time I flew into Indonesian New Guinea I saw a man sitting there pulling whiskers out of another man's chin with a crude wooden thing. Next time I flew there I loaded up with cheap Japanese tweezers and mirrors. All I did was saunter out of the plane, sit down in the shade under a wing, and with the mirror and one set of tweezers, pull at my three-day beard. Within a few minutes there were hundreds of people standing there watching me. I didn't say a word. In a few hours I had traded them all for their stone axes, which sell like hotcakes back in the States." He then found another area in New Guinea where the locals preferred tweezers and mirrors over the useless pearls they found in their oysters.

He picked up eggs in Bali and sold them at five times the price on the neighboring island of Lumbok. Passengers never seemed to mind holding baskets of eggs on their laps.

Jack said it was a sort of vacation time for him now. Zamrud's credit with the fuel company had been cut off, and even borrowed aircraft couldn't fly without fuel. "But this has happened before. I'll just go fishing for a while. Zamrud will pay its bills and everything will go back to normal."

Zamrud Airlines ceased operation in 1982. Jack Rife didn't show up on my Internet searches.

§

As I see the world there's one element that's even more corrosive than missionaries: tourists. The very places they patronize are destroyed by their affection.

Tahir Shah

BALI
1972

Our flight from Timor landed just outside of Denpasar, the capital of Bali. My first stop inside the terminal was the ladies' room. It looked like any other tropical public washroom, except for a poster tacked on the wall. There were no words on the placard, just two drawings side by side. The first showed a cartoon silhouette of a person standing on a toilet seat, squatting over the bowl, feet firmly planted on the ring that is the seat. There was a red slash through this picture. The second was an outline of someone sitting on the toilet, Western style, and smiling. The message was clear: plumbing had come to Bali.

I wondered if I was immature enough to remove the thumbtacks and slip the poster into my baggage, to send home for my own future bathroom wall, but I wasn't and I didn't. I later recognized that this was a symbol of a rapidly changing Bali, for good and otherwise.

On advice from fellow travelers, we hightailed it out of Denpasar, the city of the open sewers, where human waste floated publicly, offensively, in trenches alongside the cement curbs of the downtown streets. I expect we had arrived when wastewater treatment was a half-finished project, that installing sewer pipes was next on the to-do list.

We headed for a less modern village called Kuta a few miles away. We rented a room in a guest house called Jesen's, thirty-five U.S. cents a day, which included a breakfast of tea and a hardtack cookie. Our bed was made of straw, smelled farm-sweet, and had a little whisk broom set on top of the batik bedspread. I don't know if it was meant for the morning's cookie crumbs. Its handle was too short to sweep the floor.

Our hosts were a young couple with a baby and the innkeeper's kid brother, also named Jesen, a teenager who liked to hang out with us, practicing English, and telling us his dreams of becoming a tour guide. (People in Indonesia have only one name, I'd been told.) Young Jesen walked with us around the village streets, helping to translate as we went, and asking us endless questions about our lives. He was shocked to hear that we didn't practice any religion, and that we lived thousands of miles away from our parents.

Jesen and most Balinese were Hindu. The rest of Indonesia is Muslim, with a minority of Hindus and Buddhists. More than two hundred million Indonesians are Muslim, making it the world's biggest Islamic country. Occasionally an Indonesian or two would approach us and proudly announce that they were Christians.

In our fragrant straw bed Tim and I fell asleep listening to the gentle chimes of gamelan players nearby outside our open window. Gamelan is the traditional ensemble music of Bali and Java, mostly bamboo flutes and percussive sounds from a type of xylophone beaten with mallets, hand-played drums, gongs, chimes and cymbals. The sound is gentle, echoing, ringing, haunting.

There was no glass or screen in our window. We watched geckos crawling our walls, and counted their chirps. They can't blink, it's said, but they can scale walls and they do talk. If they say "gecko" seven times in a row, it means good luck. I found myself counting each time they opened their little reptilian mouths.

Kuta Beach was becoming a booming center for tourism, mostly Australians at the time, with some Americans and Europeans. The initial attraction was the beach, broad and sandy with a few palm trees popping up here and there. There was one restaurant on the beach, no hotels. Jesen the elder, the owner of our hotel, told us beachfront property had no value because you couldn't grow anything on it.

We noticed another sign of metamorphosis in Bali's culture: sinuous women, naked to the waist, carrying pots on their heads, appeared in many paintings in the shops. Sometimes we saw real live women, also nude from the waist up, carrying pots or baskets on their heads, walking along the footpaths. They tied batik sarongs around their middles; they wore no other clothing that we could see. But we never saw a younger woman so dishabille. Those women under fifty or sixty had abandoned the custom, and covered up. It was their senior, gray-haired grannies who honored the old traditions. Like here only backwards.

In 1972 Kuta had no plumbing, no electricity, no paved streets. Nighttime was illuminated by our personal flashlights, and by the moon and stars, as well as by lanterns casting pale golden light throughout the commercial section, very near our hotel. Many of the establishments sold food grilled outdoors. All of it smelled divine, even the roasted cucumbers, especially in the shadowy darkness.

The odor of grilled meat must have driven the dogs crazy. Lots of dogs, skinny, scrawny, feral and hungry, wandered the streets, noses to the ground, constantly looking for something to eat. Banana peels seemed to be a main source of nutrition. The dogs showed no interest in us and we didn't try to be nice to them. They didn't appear to be pet material.

We met and befriended an American our age who had the distinction of wearing an endless supply of crisply ironed Brooks Brothers oxford cotton shirts, all monogrammed on the cuffs with his initials, JWP-IV. His fashions were decidedly out of place in this culture of cutoff shorts and bikinis. John was living in Bali—more splendidly than we were—and he was about to construct the first luxury hotel on the beach. He offered Tim the job of supervising the construction, saying that all it took to get the necessary permits was a generous greasing of palms. Tim was to supply his own grease. But Tim had other plans.

Since then, I've been told, the beach town has become an overcrowded strip of hotels, fast-food restaurants, neon and nightlife, a carnival strung out on intoxicants, another tacky vacation resort that burned too brightly, too fast. Ruination by tourism, you might say, but at the time Bali was a simple, prosperous and happy place, much more so than the other Indonesian islands we saw along the string. It's easy to feel morally superior about the changes, and I do, but it's difficult to fault the Balinese for enjoying the comforts of abundance.

The shops along Kuta's main streets were supersaturated with art, mostly paintings and sculpture. Much of it depicted classical gods and goddesses, dancers, and half-naked women with clay pots on their heads, surrounded by jungle greenery. Carved wooden figures of happy-go-lucky deities, some tall bossy gods as well as squat chubby fellows, filled the shelves. A few Balinese artists on the streets offered to swap their bare-breasted paintings for sweaters, as it was chilly at night in the hill towns where they lived, and warm clothing was hard to find. We kept our sweaters but sent home a stack of Balinese art, some of which has faded over time.

Art was so essential to life on this island. There is, or was, an intersection of two main roads outside of Kuta. A familiar-looking eight-sided red stop sign was attached to a carved stone monument of a menacing figure with a ferocious scowl, armed with a scimitar, glowering straight at the driver. It was a stop-or-else warning. Now that there's a superhighway system on the island, I suspect the sign is long gone. Or maybe, with any luck at all, a similarly carved traffic god patrols all the intersections.

Every other street housed a tailor who would whip up a bespoke ensemble within a day or two. I ordered a tunic made of flour sacks, a popular fashion among the visitors. I don't know what happened to it. Tim chose a classic sports jacket, three-button, with lapels, in an autumn-colored floral display pattern. I do know what happened to it: He passed it on to his old buddy John Alley.

We signed up for tours around the rest of the island. We admired the gentle hillsides where rice was grown on terraced tiers. Everywhere we were driven, wedges were sliced into the sloping hills to create level paddy fields, which needed to be pancake-flat to hold enough water to make thick mud for seeding the rice plants. The terraces were beautifully groomed, kept pristine by the farmers who believed it was necessary to honor the rice as a gift from the gods.

We checked out the inland art center of Ubud, a village more serious and grown-up than Kuta, where traditional dance performances took place, and the best-known painters and sculptors lived and worked. Active volcanoes belched smoke and ash from time to time, but never seemed to alarm the local people. And art flourished everywhere. No stone was left uncarved.

We went in the evening to a theatrical production staged on the main road to Kuta Beach. No motorized traffic had to be diverted or delayed; there weren't enough cars to bother anybody. We watched as a plain white sheet was strung on a line across the street, to be used as a screen. Then shadow puppets made of goatskin aligned with lantern lights to cast silhouettes on the screen, and puppet masters manipulated long wooden rods attached to the figures. The performances mimicked universal human drama, love and war and betrayal, to the sounds of gamelan music. It played out live in the middle of the road. No fee to attend, no little bowl for suggested contributions. We just sat under the stars, on the sandy road, on the far side of the sheet, and enjoyed the magic.

I was happily surprised to see on the web in 2018 that Kuta has a modern hotel called Jesen's. Swimming pool, rooms as modern as any Western motel, bars and restaurants, free Wi-Fi. The rate has gone up to $17. I can't help but wonder if this was run by our former hosts. I'm glad we went when we did. Free Wi-Fi be damned.

§

I stayed in a really old hotel last night. They sent me a wake-up letter.

Steven Wright

JAVA
1972

After several weeks in Bali, Tim and I boarded a roughed-up little bus. It coughed, it barked, then it rumbled noisily, but it wouldn't budge. Passengers waited patiently with flocks of small children and chickens on their laps. Tim and some of the other passengers got out, leaned on the back end with hands and shoulders, and shoved. But pushing wasn't enough. Finally another bus moved up behind us and rammed our bus out to the main street. Away we went, westward, heading for the big island of Java.

Both islands belong to Indonesia, a mile of water and a ferry ride apart, almost touching. So we were surprised how much their flavors and atmospheres differed. Bali was Hindu and Buddhist, thriving and happy; Java was Muslim and hungry, broke and miserable. From the bus, we could trace the equatorial scenery of Bali; stone temples, green rolling terraced hillsides. On Java it was straw shacks, flat plains studded with triangles of sulfur-spewing volcanoes, beggars who didn't even have bowls, only open palms, sitting on cardboard slabs in doorways or in the streets. Java was agrarian from one end to the other. Patches and rows of green vegetables left not an inch to spare. Mountains were quilted right to the top and over the other side with crops. Rows of food were planted along the railroad right of way, within an inch of the tracks. But there wasn't enough for everyone.

Our bus took us to Surabaja, a seaport and Indonesia's second-largest city. A German couple we met en route had looked forward to seeing this metropolis. Surabaja had been exalted and adored in a popular German song and our German friends were eager to feel the magic. Yet, despite being so big and a standout of German classic hits, the parts of town where we landed in Surabaja seemed unfamiliar with Westerners on their streets. People stood in small groups and stared at us. Sometimes kids and young adults ran up to touch us, gently, on the arm or the shoulder, as if we were ephemeral. We were alien and they were inquisitive. When we walked around Surabaja, gutters of dank water lined both sides of the streets, coated with mosquito larvae. Third world Asia's version of Dogpatch. The air was heady with the stench of overcrowded poverty; people without shoes walked around with handkerchiefs covering their noses.

It seemed everyone was a retail merchant. Portable shops were set up on the sidewalks in front of permanent storefronts. It was necessary to bargain for everything. Some airlines still insisted that passengers haggle for the price of a ticket. Products like newspapers and cigarettes, with prices printed on them, required a certain amount of dickering. I tried to ask a small boy what his yo-yo was called. I couldn't imagine a more appropriate name than "yo-yo." I didn't find out the toy's Javanese name as the child was determined to sell it to me instead.

We went to see a large open-air market, not at all meant for tourists. Among the displays of familiar household objects and food items, live birds and captured wild animals, merchants set up booths offering neatly arranged rows of former toothpaste tubes, metal containers that predated the plastic ones, squeezed empty and tightly coiled. The tubes were made of tin and aluminum. I couldn't imagine what to do with them, but obviously some people could. Others had tables of small empty boxes—sturdy pretty containers for scented soaps or cosmetics, seemingly retrieved from tourists' wastebaskets in the better hotels. Now this I could understand: something sweet and fresh to brighten a lady's boudoir.

In our hotel, which was built long like a motel, the walls between the rooms didn't quite touch the floor. At night mysterious critters raced down the long stretch from room to room to room, squeaking along the way. We secured the mosquito netting tightly around us, closed our eyes and pretended to be asleep.

We happily discovered a spotless and pristine zoo in Surabaya. The zoo had shade trees and cool fresh air, good for the animals as well as the visitors. No candy wrappers, cigarette butts or used gum on the grounds. We learned that many zoo favorites were Indonesian natives; rhinos, tigers and panthers came from Java, elephants from Sumatra. Boys and men at the zoo asked us to take their photographs. They lined up, stiffened into a row and smiled at the camera. Then an Indonesian family asked if they could take our photograph with their camera. We lined up, froze and said cheese.

It's sad, even horrifying, to report that now the Surabaya zoo has become known as the zoo of death. Many of the animals have died, some of them gruesomely; others are ill and virtually starving. Visitor numbers have declined, there is no funding for the facility, staff is overstretched and untrained, and there are calls to close the place and redistribute the suffering animals.

We had been warned not to mail letters through slots in hotel lobbies or any free-standing mailboxes, because an international postage stamp was worth more than the average citizen was carrying around in his pocket. Stamps, we were told, could be removed and returned for cash at the post office, and the letters discarded. We should attach the postage to our letters at the post office and have the postal clerk cancel the stamps in our presence.

A number of years later, I received a puzzling letter from an old friend in Vancouver. He wrote to me via my parents, who then forwarded it to me. He said things like "I didn't know you were traveling again." I realized from the context of his message that he had received a letter I had sent from somewhere a couple of decades previously. "Neither snow nor rain nor heat . . ."

We made our way to the middle of Java to see Borobudur, the ninth-century Buddhist temple cut into the jungle, tucked between twin volcanoes and two rivers. I don't remember if we went by bus or taxi or both, but I know we didn't have to slash through volcanic ash and jungle, as did Stamford Raffles, the early-nineteenth-century British administrator who is credited with finding it. The temple had been abandoned when Java transitioned from Buddhism to Islam, and had been pretty much forgotten. Even after being rediscovered, it didn't attract attention. When we got there, the jungle surrounding the temple had been cleared away, but the square wedding-cake pyramid, nine layers high with each side almost four hundred feet long, had been neglected for decades.

There wasn't another person around. Tim and I, strangely, had the place to ourselves, our Indiana Jones moment. We felt as though we had discovered the temple even though we'd been driven to the site in a modern vehicle. We were alone, yet someone had kept the encroaching jungle cleared away. We climbed the platforms and photographed each other next to the panels of relief carvings, or one of the five-hundred-plus Buddhas. A couple of years after our visit, the Indonesian government, with lots of international support, began a restoration project, and Borobudor is now a World Heritage Site and a favorite of tourists, predominantly Japanese and Chinese.

On to downtown Jakarta, the world's most crowded city on the world's most crowded island, to see the towering white marble monument erected by the previous dictator, Sukarno. His likeness, more than forty stories tall, transcended the city's skyline. A marble museum and a handful of other imperial monuments cast shadows over the modern high-rise buildings and the scurrying crowds on the wide city streets and central square. In lesser parts of the city, people laundered their clothes, bathed and shat in filthy brown streams, ate whatever they could find or beg, and otherwise ignored us interlopers in their territory.

What to do about beggars? The traveler's dilemma. We were a couple of bleeding-heart, yellow dog liberals who couldn't decide on a policy. Do we give a small amount of money to each one of these sad souls? We would run out before we got to the end of the block. Do we have sudden bursts of guilt and pay up, or do we ignore them and continue on our way? Every morning the torso and head of a man was propped up at eye level on top of a barrel on the corner of our street. He had no arms or legs, and he didn't speak. He may have been blind. He didn't miss a day, was gone by evening, presumably carried home by a family member. By the second or third day Tim couldn't stand it any longer, and stuffed a fistful of grubby rupiah banknotes in his begging box. It looked like a lot, but the money had so little value—a thousand rupiahs wouldn't have bought a banana.

We had rented a hotel room in a sprawling building with a dance hall and bar on the ground floor. A Muslim celebration at the end of Ramadan, after a month of fasting and the cleansing of souls, explained why the place was jumping with rock music, Johnnie Walker Black Label, and raucous male laughter. Our room was just upstairs and down a long hall from the bathroom. The partying and hollering had spread upstairs, along the corridor outside our room. Some of these men hooted at us to come out and join the party. But we didn't sense that this was a friendly invitation. I had no intention of shouldering my way through the celebrants to the designated bathroom. But I needed to find a receptacle for peeing. We looked around desperately for a vessel but could not find anything in our luggage or among the hotel room's accoutrements, until Tim reached under the bed and fished out a sticky Fanta bottle. I told Tim not to look (this was vanity, not modesty) as I struggled to be neat during this experiment while the holiday makers banged on our bedroom door. At least nobody was stirring in the hall early the next morning, when I hastened down the hall to the bathroom to rinse the Fanta bottle, and cleanse my own soul. "How was it?" Tim asked me.

§

A ship in harbor is safe, but that is not what ships are built for.

John A. Shedd

TAMPOMAS
1972

The Indonesian government travel brochure advised us, "Travel by sea is not recommendable, especially for punctual tourists." Nonetheless, travel by sea seemed like a charming way to go from Jakarta to Singapore, seven hundred miles north, across the equator, past and around hundreds of little palm-fringed islands. We were in no hurry to arrive.

Finding a way out was not easy, but Jakarta was the kind of city you wanted to escape as soon as possible. Nobody spoke English at the official tourism office. The people spoke Cara Jawa, or Basa Jawa, which I believe were the same thing, but it left us stumped. After some searching, we found a boat line with an English-speaking staff member who explained that they had a ship sail two days earlier, and the next one was two months away.

Then, with wild gestures and a bit of luck, we finally booked a cabin on the good ship *Tampomas*, part of the government's Pelni Lines, scheduled to sail around five that afternoon. Someone in the office told us four o'clock, some signaled six, and some eight. It didn't matter. We were on the dock by two thirty.

No one knew how long the trip would take, maybe two days, maybe four, perhaps six. And the *Tampomas* didn't go all the way to Singapore, but to a small round island called Tandjung Pinang, a four-hour ferry ride, perhaps, from Singapore. The ferry more or less met the ship. Close enough.

The *Tampomas* offered a choice of first class or deck class. First class offered an air-conditioned cabin, private Western plumbing, and a selection of condiments to go with our three bowls of rice per day. (All the time we were in Southeast Asia I grew long fingernails, for which I credited the rice.) Deck class meant sleeping on a hatch cover with at least a thousand other people, lining up at mealtime for a banana leaf of rice scooped from an oil drum. First class cost twenty dollars, deck class was ten bucks. There was one cabin left in first class and we grabbed it. We were frugal but we weren't stupid.

At five in the afternoon the ship did not sail. Boxes and crates and families were still being loaded into the hold. The fog had snuggled in around Jakarta's harbor, the pale orange sun had long since disappeared. Around seven the engines shuddered, a few patient well-wishers waved goodbye from the shore and we glided out to sea.

The next morning the fog was even thicker, the water glassy calm, the air on deck a steam bath. We gave up hope of an equatorial sunbath. We read our books in our air-conditioned stateroom, savoring the luxury of it.

Early in the afternoon we dropped anchor, squinted out through the fog to see why. Shadows of boats with black sails, a hint of an island coastline far off. A launch pulled alongside. Three men in customs uniforms scrambled aboard, sat at a table in the bar shuffling papers for ten minutes, scampered back into the launch and disappeared into the soup. Still we sat there until dark.

At five thirty the next morning a man banged on our cabin door, shouting something we couldn't understand. I assumed he meant breakfast was ready. He didn't. He meant we had arrived just off Tandjung Pinang, although the fog was still opaque, and we couldn't see anything.

We peered over the deck to see a launch bellied up to our ship. A wobbling vertical rope ladder was the umbilical cord between us, way up here, and the launch, way down there. Men in the launch shouted at us and gestured, making big circles with their elbows, calling impatiently to get with it, to get down here. Straight down the quavering, feeble rope ladder, perpendicular to the sea, I kept my eyes closed as I searched with one foot, then the other, to find the next horizontal strip of rope. I am the authentic chicken of the sea.

Tandjung Pinang, the island, held about ten thousand people who didn't try to sell us everything they owned. The town had all the necessary parts: a mosque and a Chinese temple, a bank, post office, restaurants, market and a university called Hang Tuit. Not its motto, its name. Reminded me of Juan de Fuca U, which made the short list but in the end was *not* chosen as the name of a new college near Seattle.

Word spread among the dozen English-speaking travelers: Today's ferry to Singapore was fully booked. We would have to stay overnight and, by the way, all the hotels were full. But, we were told, the police would let us sleep in the police station, for a fee. One traveler bragged the next morning that he had spent the night in a brothel, but we were not impressed.

A mother of seven named Doortje came to our rescue. Doortje's husband was the harbormaster and there was a spare room to rent in their harbor-straddling home.

110

Their house sat on stilts over the water and you could look down between the gaping floorboards and see the Straits of Malacca glitter and wink in the pale sunlight. Shadows and strips of reflected light danced on the inner walls of the house. I suppose one would get used to it. The toilet was a hole squarely cut out of the floorboards in our bedroom. I couldn't stop looking down that open hole. Doortje's crawling baby was shooed out of harm's way, into the other rooms. A few small children darted through the house, but didn't come near us. We never did meet the harbormaster.

Doortje hailed from Sumatra, and she told us that before she was married she used to roll cigars. She asked me to give her some warm clothes. I was already down to the basics by now, and had nothing to give away. I felt greedy and mean-spirited but promised myself, for what it was worth, that next time I came through this way I would bring as many sweaters as I could pack.

The ferry ticket said the boat would leave at noon, and by eleven we had carried our luggage to the end of the dock. The ferry, which turned out to be a fifty-foot launch, was anchored about a hundred yards out. At noon the launch was still out there, very still, and the rainy season began. The wind whipped the rain horizontally across the dock and I wondered if our suitcases were waterproof. A young American traveler, ashen and sweating, rocked on his heels and hugged his backpack for comfort as he dealt with the pain of appendicitis. He was on this trip by himself. We offered encouragement, but we had nothing else. The storm blew for an hour, was gone, and there was some action by the ferry. The crew began unloading the mail, which someone complained should have been done last night. We sat on the pier and read our books some more and tried to ignore the local people who had gathered at the dock to stare at us, and sometimes to touch us. Responding with a smile made these shy people nervously back away.

Around two our ferry pulled up to the dock, we boarded, and were quickly under way. The sky had cleared, the sun shone, and hundreds of tiny tropical islands, some big enough for only two or three palm trees, glided past. Flying fish played leapfrog across the water. It was lovely. Crew members handed out banana leaves folded around rice and fish, a boiled egg, and cans of warm 7-Up. I was tired of rice. Whatever happened to the humble potato?

Then a worrisome rumor made the rounds. If we were not in Singapore by seven we would have to spend the night on the boat. Customs closed at seven and we wouldn't be allowed ashore.

The little boat couldn't move very fast and it was forty or fifty miles yet to Singapore, we were told. The launch had rows of slatted seats, not quite wide enough for two Western adults to sit comfortably, and anyway, all the seats were occupied. Couldn't hunker down on the deck either; many of the passengers had been seasick. The young man with the angry appendix squatted helplessly in a corner, looking more and more miserable.

Then a police boat, with a machine gun mounted on its impudent nose, pulled up alongside. Our pilot gave it a good scrape and bump as we met, which I feared would only made them mad. There was some scrambling back and forth between the two boats. An inspection would take hours.

Our captain went aboard the police boat with a briefcase, and returned later with a smile. "They wanted to come aboard to see if anyone was taking Indonesian currency out of the country, but I gave them a little tip, five thousand rupiahs, so they won't bother us," he boasted. Five thousand rupiahs was worth about twelve dollars U.S. Yet it represented a month's pay for Doortje's harbormaster husband.

The incident took only about half an hour, but when we sailed there was a lot of antsy checking of watches and squinting at the horizon.

Then, just before sunset, we could see Singapore ahead. The city had a massive port, ships from Japan and London, Sydney and Africa, and the United States Navy. It was the most beautiful sight in the world right then, aglow with tall buildings and bright-colored lights along the foreshore.

Our fellow passenger with the ominous appendix got himself into a taxi immediately, and headed to a hospital. It was six thirty. If there had been a Statue of Liberty I would have wept.

§

In January 1981 I read a short news item about a ship disaster near Jakarta, with hundreds of deaths. A fuel leak in the engine room, ignited by a cigarette butt tossed down the ship's vents, triggered a fire aboard the *Tampomas*, our old ship.

Meanwhile, a torrential storm was tossing the *Tampomas* around in the sea. The inspectors found that the ship had no smoke alarms, and the fire extinguishers weren't working. Passengers had been ordered to climb to the top deck, where the lifeboats—all six of them—were located. There was only one door to the top deck, and panicked passengers pushed and shoved to get through, although many didn't make it.

Some crew members filled one of the lifeboats and got an early start to escape the disaster, although the captain went down with the ship. As the fire spread, an explosion blew, seawater flooded into the ship, and it toppled over and sank.

There were 1,442 people aboard, and 753 were saved. Rest in peace, *Tampomas.*

§

You can observe a lot just by
watching.

Yogi Berra

PENANG, MALAYSIA
1972

From Singapore, we took a northbound train past endless miles of rubber tree plantations, the good-soldier trees lined up in neat rows, with taps impaled in their sides. The faucets' stems acted as handles for buckets to collect the dripping rubber juice, like collecting maple syrup back in the old country. We got off on Penang, the island home of the Chor Soo Kong temple.

There is only one snake temple in the world, and that is the good news. Otherwise there might be a lot fewer Buddhists. Chor Soo Kong's temple is crawling with hundreds of Wagler's Pit Vipers, coiling around the candelabra, squirming up the altar, lying in wait under tables and blossoming like stems of orchids on the tops of cupboards. At your own risk, as the sign says, come in and look around.

This particular little viper is not your everyday household garter snake. It is indeed venomous. If the snake's tolerance is tested, it may coil into an S, open its mouth wide, showing long fangs and gray-white gums. It can strike quickly and successively. Its venom is toxic and potentially deadly but usually doesn't kill its victim. Instead, the sting causes swelling, a burning sensation and

115

possibly necrosis of tissue. Stay calm, lie down on the ground, don't get all worked up. Someone will take you to a hospital.

The day before Tim and I arrived in Penang, a tourist foolishly picked up one of the snakes and was bitten. I believe he lived. Hey, you don't have to go there.

The snakes are not kept in the temple like some zoo critters, behind bars or glass walls. The doors are open, the free-range vipers are welcome to come in on their own, and they are free to go as they please back into the surrounding jungle. Sort of like having a flapping pet door for your cat.

The temple is an ordinary, everyday, dragon-studded, gaudily painted red and chrome yellow Chinese Buddhist temple. Visitors are advised beforehand that there are deadly snakes slithering free on the premises, but I can't imagine that any visitor is prepared for the onslaught just inside the shadow of the front door. Smoke from burning incense hit us inside the entrance, even before we saw the donations box attached to the wall. The pamphlet said that the smoke is a narcotic to the snakes, and leaves them groggy, even stupefied. The snakes are benign, the warnings continued, though stoned is a more appropriate description. We were further warned not to pick them up, and especially cautioned against snuggling them close to our hearts for a snapshot. The temple's promoters say it is the star appeal of Chor Soo Kong himself that draws the vipers to the temple. Others suggest the ceremonial eggs placed around the rooms are attraction enough.

Chor Soo Kong was a tenth-century Buddhist monk, a healer with supernatural powers, and a friend of the snakes of the jungle, which he sheltered and protected. A man who had been healed of a mysterious disease by praying to the monk donated a parcel of jungle land in 1850 for a new temple, which was dedicated to

Chor Soo Kong. As soon as the temple was built, the snakes moved in, according to legend, and they just kept coming. It was said the snakes arrive in greater numbers on Chor's birthday, the sixth day of the second moon.

As my eyes became accustomed to the low light inside the temple, there was a sprouting bouquet of vipers, all within arm's reach. Adjusting to the light, I saw more black, green and yellow striped fellows, the size of walking sticks, uncurl into view. I looked behind me and there at jugular height were a half-dozen more, dangling from an icon. I may have casually stroked my throat.

No staff or volunteers emerged while we visited. There were no guides to greet a non-existent tour bus. I suppose if someone had needed to scream in terror or pain, a responsible person would have emerged and attended.

Something deep in our natures made us whisper and tiptoe as we walked around the sanctuary. A handful of visitors quietly toured the temple that day, looking alert, clutching their handbags to their hearts. Tim and I walked stealthily from room to room to niches in the building, keeping watch above our heads, heeding any movement under tables and behind ornamental objects. A few of these vipers clung to a hanging ceiling light, turning it into a chandelier extending candelabra branches that might reach out to touch your hair. We peeked inside the storage room where we saw a living game of Snakes and Ladders—vipers resting on the rungs of the stepladder leaning against the wall. I took a picture for my own amusement, to remind myself of the cheap thrill of living dangerously.

Signs every few feet reminded us that we were there at our own peril. We scooped out a few more coins for the donation boxes. A new supply of eggs had to be provided regularly.

Thailand is safe. If you see anybody wearing camouflage, holding a machete, don't be scared; they're just selling coconuts.

Bobby Lee

THAILAND
1972

On advice from travelers going in the opposite direction, we checked into the Atlanta Hotel, in the verdant landscaped heart of the foreign embassy sector of Bangkok.

The neighborhood was elegant and the hotel may have been handsome in the early 1950s, when it was new. While we were there, the spacious lobby had scuffed black and beige checkerboard-tiled floors with dust bunnies in the corners. A curved grand staircase rose behind the length of the check-in counter. It was a sweeping curve but it needed to be swept. And glass display cases that had not exhibited any merchandise for a long time cried out for a squirt of Windex. The place wasn't squalid, but the Atlanta could have used a good scrub. Let's just say my mother wouldn't have approved.

An unsanitary-looking swimming pool in back was choked with jungle growth and green algae scum. Everything disintegrates quickly in the tropics. A mere twenty years after it opened, the Atlanta was the disreputable member of the diplomats' milieu—a blot of structural jungle rot in their midst.

When we were there, the hotel was headquarters for backpackers, hippies and world travelers from the West. A lot of people milled around the place, coming and going and hanging around night and day. Many of its guests stayed for a few weeks at a time, and we got to know a number of them. It was like going to summer camp, age about twelve. Here at the Atlanta was the largest number of alternate-travelers of all sorts we met in one place. Many of them were coming from or going to India. One told us, earnestly, that India was his goal because he was "into suffering and spiritual enlightenment." We nodded.

We noticed that, in some circles, social ranking was involved, with status based on endurance and poverty. "Hey man, how long have you been into traveling?" The questioner was American, gaunt, yellow-eyed, gray-skinned, with matted long hair, patched jeans, transparent Indian shirt, sandals, small knapsack, embroidered purse, less than ten pounds of baggage, at least twenty pounds underweight. He was lounging around the lobby.

"Yeah well, man, I've been going almost three years. My brother's been into it seven years and we're, like, really trying to see who can cut it the longest."

"Don't you run out of money? I had to ask, since he had obviously crossed an ocean or two.

"Ah, money just isn't in my world, man. We stay with local people in the villages and they're really nice to us, man. I stayed with one family in a village in Java for, like, almost a year when the police came and said I had to split. The woman cried when I left. Wow, that was really heavy."

"You mean you just moved in and they gave you food and a bed without anything in return?"

"Sure, man. They're really cool, these natives. They're not into capitalism or anything."

"How long are you staying here in Bangkok?"

"Oh, I'm not staying. I'm splitting, hitching to Algeria and then down into the desert. I want to hitch up with some of the wandering Bedouins. I hear that's really cool, man. But hey, this is a really cool hotel, the Atlanta. This is where all the freaks stay. Take it easy, man," and he loped away.

These travelers were off to see the world, much like us, only a little grungier, a little younger, a little skinnier, a little more anesthetized by drugs. In Asia, India, Africa and elsewhere, a number of these folks insisted "I've got it made, man," and I wonder what became of them all.

We made friends with a German named Klaus, a civilian who had been working in Vietnam and was now soaking up some R and R and considering his next move. He was clean-shaven, neatly dressed, with sharp creases down his pant legs, looking oddly out of place. A sweet young Thai woman who worked at the hotel was named Toy Hemingway. How could I forget that poetic name? She had married an American GI and was waiting for her visa so she could join him in California. She spent her days walking around with books on her head to improve her perfectly healthy posture, to make herself a more beautiful American bride. She had big, soft, trusting brown eyes, and I hope all her dreams have come true.

An English couple, Bert and Daphne, argued endlessly about splitting their money. "I'm not paying half the bill. You had two cups of tea and I only had one." Because we sometimes had lengthy conversations with people we hung out with, we learned later that when Bert and Daphne made their way to Los Angeles, they tracked down and phoned Tim's sister Sandra, and asked if they could stay with her and her husband Dee, and would Sandy pay for a taxi from the airport to her house in Brentwood. We were as mortified as Sandra.

Then we heard that a recent hotel guest, a young German dirtbag who was probably stoned, had been fooling around with a kayak paddle in the swimming pool, and somehow accidentally killed a landscape worker, a hotel staff member. He was hustled off to a Bangkok jail, charged with murder. A phone call was made to his parents at home, a sum of money was transmitted, the young man was free to go, and he left. How do you say ". . . and don't come back" in Thai?

Just speculating, but it may have been this horrendous incident, or another similar event, that caused the tattered hotel to tidy up its business plan. Plus, there may have been some stern warnings from the Thai authorities.

The budget hotel, I see on the web, and to my surprise, is still standing and still operating. A photo of that checkerboard tile floor and the sweeping staircase highlight its webpage. The Atlanta has been disinfected, modernized and reborn as "a conservative, no-nonsense bastion of wholesome, culturally sensitive tourism, untouched by pop culture," according to its entry in Wikipedia. The scrubbed-up hotel has "no tolerance for trouble makers," is very clear about its policy regarding sex tourism and drug use, and promises to call the police the instant that trouble threatens to start. The ad is also clear about children, who are welcome "only if they are under control."

The warning continues, welcoming "sleaze-free tourists, but not undomesticated people who don't know how to sit on a chair or at table . . . whose appearance and manner are so disgraceful . . . they should stay home." I love the Internet.

I'm sure this was a typo, but in a testimonial on the website praising the hotel, a 2017 guest wrote of the pleasures of "the gardens and the swilling pool."

Now, as well, the hotel has become a sanctuary for rescue animals, home to thirty or forty cats at any given time, one dog and twenty-six turtles, as of this web posting. "If you don't like dogs and cats, stay elsewhere." It goes on to say that an earlier rescue dog was able to sniff out undesirables. If the dog barked at prospective guests, they were turned away from the Atlanta.

The hotel was a good-enough temporary home for us—shabby but remarkably cheap, a shelter that felt safe, the room and the bedding clean enough. We could walk from there to many of the city's exquisite sights, the golden Buddhas, royal palaces and temples, silk shops, *wats* (temples) and *klongs* (canals). We were impressed with the wild traffic on the main streets, where city buses rushed along carrying full loads of passengers on the inside, and more clinging to the roofs and the exterior sides and ends. Often in Asia's most crowded cities, we felt that people had little regard for human life, including their own.

We remained registered at the Atlanta while venturing on a side trip. We boarded a piloted long boat, with seating like a bus, heading upstream on the Chao Phraya River. This was not a sightseeing boat, but public transportation for local people. We were sitting low in the water, when a breeze blew off my venerated Southeast Asian hat. The hat was a shallow cone, like the hats you see in pictures of rice paddy workers, but mine had artsy figures painted on it. It was both cool and a great sun-shield. I considered asking the boat's pilot, in my sweetest girlie voice, if he wouldn't mind, please sir, backing up just a little to retrieve my hat, as I watched it drift away downstream. I decided against it. I imagined all those almond eyes rolling. Besides, Tim and I seemed to be the only people on board who spoke English. I never found a replacement for that hat.

We moved upstream most of the day, half submerged in our fully loaded vessel, cruising through dense jungle that hugged the narrow river. The boat pulled up to a dock and we got off with the rest of the passengers, in what we assumed was Ayutthaya, the ancient capital of Siam. It was just about dusk and we were tired. We were on the edge of a field and couldn't see where to go. A taxi met the boat, hoping for a fare, and with us he got lucky.

We needed a hotel. I tried and failed with English and failed again with a louder one-word shout: "HOTEL!" Why do people holler when they're trying to be understood in another language? I put my palms together, lifted them to one shoulder, lowered my tilted cheek to my hands, and imitated sleep. I probably closed my eyes.

The taxi driver's face brightened. Off we drove, heading away from the river, away from the main traffic. We drove on and on through acres of agricultural fields. A faint smell of marijuana drifted in the breeze. In the middle of a clearing, with nothing around but more open space, our driver stopped with a "Ta-da" kind of salute.

There he was, an enormous sleeping Buddha, all by himself, sacked out on his side, looming above the plain. No sheltering temple nearby, no ticket booth, he was just out there in the elements. If he had awoken and stood upright, he would have measured around thirty feet tall. There was no sign of human activity. It was getting dark. We walked around it, touched it here and there, would have admired it longer, but feared that the taxi might leave us stranded. So we hired him again to take us into town and there, at last, was a hotel.

There didn't seem to be any restaurants, but we were near an outdoor market with vivid displays of fruit and mystery entrees. A young man roaming the aisles convinced us to buy a bronze figure the size of a potato that he had cupped in his hand. He swore the piece was an authentically ancient casting of Ganesh, the lovable Hindu god who looks like a pot-bellied little man with the head of an elephant. This little guy is seated in the lotus position, looking peaceful, and currently adorns our bathroom, though the bronze of his backside is starting to turn green, a chemical event that doesn't reveal his age.

At the edge of the market, we joined a dozen or so men and boys who stood watching a black-and-white TV set. The show was *Gunsmoke.* James Arness was Matt Dillon, struggling to keep the peace in Dodge, speaking sternly in Thai to the desperados. Something about the time and place, the tropical heat and steamy air, the jungly smells, the wafts of pot, the old Wild West, Ganesh in my pocket, the big reclining Buddha all alone out there, messed with my head. We bought some fruit and some inscrutable edibles to take to our room and hunker down. My dinner was a handful of chewy rubber balls boiled in Arpege by Lanvin. It had smelled so pleasant at the market.

We had thought our boat tickets that morning were meant to take us to Ayutthaya, the ancient royal city, and I suspect we had boarded the wrong boat, and got off with everyone else in a village or an Ayutthaya suburb along the river. No golden bell-shaped temples here, no royal palace. We didn't know where we were, but it didn't matter. The next morning I felt like an authentic explorer, especially after having seen the giant lonesome Buddha. Getting lost was as good as knowing where we were.

§

*Chinese culture in general is not
very religious. Ancestor worship is a
way for parents to control you even
after they're dead.*

David Henry Hwang

HONG KONG

1972-1973

Our pilot announced we were flying over Cambodia, South Vietnam, then China. This was not a good time, if ever there was one, to cross overland from Bangkok to Hong Kong. Looking down, we saw some green, some cloud, sometimes a bit of blue sky, nothing out of the ordinary, but there was a twinge of excitement I never felt flying over Manitoba. As I looked out, I half expected to see a counter-ideological dog fight, or at least a Sikorsky Black Hawk go whirring by, but nothing like that happened. We were above and beyond the fray.

Then the landscape began to reappear, brown rocks jutting out of gray water, a great many ships tied up in the harbor. One big ship was flopped on her side, halfway under like a dead fish. It turned out to be the *Queen Elizabeth*, still where she had burned to death earlier in the year. The luxury liner had been sold to a Hong Kong businessman who planned to use it as a college campus. Its refitting was incomplete when the ship was destroyed by fire. Accusations of lax security and probable arson delayed its removal. Later, in 1974, the recumbent *QE* was used as a backdrop for the James Bond movie *Man with the Golden Gun.*

Our plane landed at Kai Tak Airport, famous for its white-knuckle arrivals, through a narrow corridor between rows of tall apartment buildings. As we descended we could see people watching television in their living rooms. Modern high-rises bordered the runways on both sides, creating a slender channel for incoming and outgoing flights. Kai Tak Airport had scored twelve botched landings, with 270 deaths, before a new airport was built outside the city.

My dear old friend Kayce White met us at the airport and took us to her apartment in Wan Chai. She had already arranged for us to rent our own apartment in her building. It was a joy to see her again and gratifying to have a home with a stove, a fridge, a kitchen sink and our own bathroom with a tub. We longed to be civilized, safe from the perils of the open road. We were going to be here for a while. Though we had been on the circuit only a few months, we were ready for a break. I was eager to cook something to go with the potatoes I intended to mash, and to luxuriate in a bubble bath. To get started on these quests, I needed to close my eyes, say a prayer and strike a match to the formidably explosive-looking gas geyser mounted above the kitchen sink. The scary water heater made it possible to brew our morning tea and prepare for a warm soak in the tub.

The building had a gatekeeper, a concierge who recommended good restaurants while at the same time discouraged would-be intruders who had no business there. He seemed to be on duty all day, all evening. We gave him his first-ever pizza; he didn't seem to like it. He taught us how to say a few words in Cantonese, including our address—*ng subsay go see dah doe*—which we needed for taxi drivers. *Go see dah doe* means Gloucester Road. *Ng subsay* means fifty-one. We also had a friend living on Victoria Peak. He lived on Park Drive, or to a taxi driver, Pock Doe. I'm sure my inflection was askew but our cabs never got lost.

Tim and I were both reading Kurt Vonnegut at the time, and we asked our concierge how to say "And so it goes ..." The translation sounded like *Poot lee-ow lee-ow chi*, in case you find that useful. Why is it I can remember such trivia when I can't remember my best friend's phone number?

Our Hong Kong neighborhood, the Wan Chai District in Central, was smack in the center of this densely populated city. Wan Chai resembled any big city's Chinatown, except that its mass seemed to be compressed somehow into a psychedelic maze, each flashing image squashed on top of the last one. Shops, streets, Chinese people of all sorts and sizes, trams, neon and strobe lights, Japanese cars and American servicemen on leave. Blinking signs overlapped and merged, the fake Playboy Club inches from the imitation Crazy Horse Saloon. Throughout the compacted city, homes for Chinese squatters were piled high on top of the flat roofs of apartment buildings. Sheets of tin and cardboard were erected into houses of cards, and decorated on the outside with flapping laundry and potted plants, as many earthenware planters as could fit along a ledge. Someone told us the fire department did not have ladders tall enough to reach the high floors of these buildings.

The smells of Szechuan peppercorns, soy sauce, gasoline fumes, fennel seed, outdoor cooking, construction equipment fumes, cinnamon, cloves and tobacco smoke, ginger and XO sauce, created a surprisingly agreeable odor that matched the kaleidoscopic scenes. To this level of chaos, add the clacking of mah jongg tiles, beeping horns, drills and jackhammers from the constant construction, rattling tram cars, the chatter of people and the high-pitched whine of Cantonese opera seeping out of a nearby radio. Then mix in the close-up visual jolt of seeing ducks, snakes, chickens and sometimes monkeys in cages, fresh and alive for your dining pleasure, among the vegetable displays along the sidewalks in front of mom-and-pop grocery stores. And, for dessert, buttercream-slathered cakes in the bakeshop windows, gooey treats brought here by the northern Chinese.

We hung out at the Foreign Correspondents Club, thanks to Kayce, and met some authentic foreign correspondents, many taking a break from covering the war in Vietnam, grateful for the respite and brimming with good stories. One friend we met at the club was a Brit reputed to be a spy. He spoke accentless Cantonese, we were told. I wish I knew what and how he did what he did, so that I could write a ripping good book. Kayce was working for a public relations firm, along with a local young man named Benny Wong. They talked about going into business together as White & Wong Ltd. It never happened, but you've got to love the name. We also hung out with another old Vancouver friend, Jack Moore, who wrote for the *South China Morning Post*, one of the best newspaper names around, if you find such things romantic. One piece he wrote was a profile of the filmmaker Run Run Shaw, who produced fifty feature films a year. The title of his article was "What Makes Run Run Run?"

What I hadn't anticipated was the need to switch from scruffy hippie traveler to urban professional, or at least a well-groomed tourist. I doubt that a scruffy hippie traveler could stay for long in Hong Kong. Somehow the island was all business, too crowded, and all the bargains were relative. The pace and urbanity of our lives accelerated in tune with this vibrant metropolis. It seems, in retrospect, that we were on the go all day and into the night, with citified dining, shopping, working, socializing, bustling in lockstep with the hectic pedestrian traffic.

I found freelance employment in the territory, writing travel articles for the Hong Kong Tourist Board. It was an ideal way to familiarize myself with the colony, and be paid for the pleasure. I met and wrote about the boat people who lived, worked and intermarried solely on their junks, and whose lifestyles were shunned by the land-based Chinese. There were few of these people still fishing the South China Sea at the time, and no doubt fewer now. I wrote about an art exhibit at the City Hall, copies of paintings by Edgar Degas. At the exhibit, the painter's name on the information cards was consistently spelled Degar. Hong Kong was new at the business of city-government-sponsored art. I wrote about upcoming events such as a festival concert to be conducted by Seiji Ozawa. And tourism travel articles about riding around the city on the top of a double-decker bus, or the horse race track named Happy Valley, that sort of thing.

Tim was hired to dub a Chinese action movie into English, one of those one-dimensional kung fu films that were churned out in Hong Kong studios in the early 1970s. That decade was prime time for the martial arts film genre, especially in Asia. At his job, Tim and other dubbers watched the film together, grunting or roaring into microphones most of the time, sometimes calling out English background words as they appeared on the screen. This was not, in truth, a speaking part.

The film he worked on told the story of a beautiful guileless princess who could vault over tall buildings, and who was menaced by a jealous older woman, who was quite a tough cookie herself. The plot included poisoned lipstick, which one of the women wore to kiss and thereby dispatch the other. Tim can't remember now which was which. The thriller also had two nasty male villains. One rammed his arm through the belly of his rival, while the victim reached around his back with a sword and severed the protruding arm of the other guy. Then they both keeled over dead, having bled to death. Tim didn't stay on the set long enough to see how it all turned out. He never knew the title of the movie, nor did he get paid.

We spent Christmas there in our apartment, our second Christmas on this journey. We found some glass ornaments—no surprise, as this was the world capital of manufacturing small cheap ornamentation. We did not find a tree, but at the Post Office construction site across the street, we picked a tall weed. It was green and alive, and stood up straight despite the weight of the decorations we festooned on it. We celebrated the holiday with Kayce and other Western travelers we met en route, and found familiar holiday music on BBC World Service. It was so sweet to have a living room and kitchen to live in and cook in like regular people, at least for a while. I can't remember what we ate, but the menu included mashed potatoes.

We attempted to travel into real China, which had been strictly forbidden, although a few Western visitors were now being granted visas. We found out that Chinese Hong Kong people could get permission to enter China by applying at the Star Travel Agency, and it gave us a smidgeon of hope. We showed up at the travel service office and said we wanted to visit China. "But you are already in China," the woman explained. We said we wanted to see Canton and Peking. "But that is another country. You cannot go there," she replied. We said, if we are already in China, why can we not visit China. "You have to apply for visas from your own country." "But we are already here," we said. No matter. "You must apply for visas from your own country," she reiterated, patiently, sweetly. We hadn't really expected to get anywhere.

We took the fast ferry to Macau, which was still a Portuguese colony, and a mecca for gamblers. We admired the dazzling lit-up casinos, reminding us again of Christmas. One was built out over the water, offering a doubly radiant illumination in its reflection. Our hotel room had a view down a rock cliff and over the South China Sea. From there, you wouldn't know that Macau was the most densely populated region of the world, with more than six hundred thousand people living in twelve square miles. We walked a lot, admiring the roofless facade of an old Portuguese Catholic church, a fireworks factory, and then the border into real China. We watched local people crossing back and forth on foot across the frontier and, having been denied access ourselves, envied their privileged status.

Tim's cousin Alex arrived in Hong Kong from San Francisco, lured no doubt by Tim's letters. Alex also planned to travel around the globe. He found his own apartment, and followed his own itinerary, but we three spent a lot of time together, running into one another, by design or by accident, for most of the next year and across a couple more continents.

Alex was tall and slim, a few years younger than his cousin, with a face that always looked innocent. He enjoyed dressing well, and Hong Kong was one of the few places on our journey where he could live the life. He almost immediately found a tailor and ordered a bespoke white linen suit. Though he was a quiet and self-effacing Californian, Alex had a touch of show biz in his demeanor. In a small group, he might don a hat, and with a Fred

Astaire flair of body language, tumble it down his outstretched arm with a flourish of a finish.

Sometimes we four—Tim in his best, Kayce and I all tarted up, Alex in his new suit—went somewhere extravagant for dinner. At the Peninsula Hotel, the grand dame in Kowloon, we were advised to spend a little time in the bar and have ourselves paged. Then a man in a uniform and red pillbox hat would walk through the room summoning us by name. It added a little sway to the event, a little extra attention from the maître d'. But Tim and I didn't have the chops for it, and we only ate at the Peninsula one time. We felt too freshly jungle-bound to mingle boldly with the nabobs. Or for me, wherever and whenever I got all dressed up, I felt like it was "maid's night out."

Our three-month visa was about to expire. We could have renewed it and stayed, but it was time to move on. Back to Bangkok for a second round at the Atlanta Hotel before heading west again. The region's war appeared to be winding down, so we applied at the South Vietnamese embassy for visitor visas. Tim and Alex were allowed to go. They wouldn't let me in because from my former life I had a communist country—Czechoslovakia—stamped in my passport. I guess that stamp made me look suspicious. I didn't argue; I stayed behind, lounged around and read books.

When Tim and his cousin returned, Tim and I enjoyed a semi-familiar excursion around Bangkok. This time we shopped, buying yards of Thai silk, a pair of low-grade silver elephants shaped like plump loaves of bread and, from a similar mold, a silver pig, all from Cambodia. At an outdoor market in the city, Tim bought an old brass gong, about eighteen inches in diameter. It was so black it looked like a tire. The gong came equipped with a padded lollipop at the end of a stick, to strike the sound. The gong was bulkier than the usual spoils of our journey, and a nuisance to transport. But we, meaning Tim, carried it all the way to India, along with our luggage, because the former British colony held a reputation for reliable shipping, unlike many of its neighbors.

And so we were on the trail again, and wouldn't have the luxury of a household to keep for more than another year. But no matter, we were a lot younger then. Alex stayed behind at the Atlanta, but thanks to the invisible messenger system employed by the traveling wanderers, we all caught up again in India.

§

My perfect last meal would be shrimp cocktail, lasagna, steak, creamed spinach, salad with bleu cheese dressing, onion rings, garlic bread and a dessert of strawberry shortcake.

Joan Rivers

RANGOON, BURMA
1973

China wouldn't let us in, but we hit upon a brief opening through the mangrove curtain when visitors were allowed into Burma. The country had been closed by the military-socialist government, then opened a crack between coups, then slammed shut again not long after we were there, and Burma remained isolated for decades.

In Rangoon, there were few hotels and very little food: good reasons for refusing visitors. We stayed at the youth hostel. The only alternative in the city, according to the hostel guests, was a modern concrete high-rise known informally as the commie hotel. It was probably the newest and tallest building in the city. We could see it from several parts of town, its brutalist Soviet architecture rising above the rest. We never heard its formal name, and we certainly couldn't read the Burmese script, spelled out in interlocking rings and C-hooks.

We ate rice and fish; there was nothing else. We were also aware that we dined better and more often than ninety-nine percent of the Burmese people. So we decided it wouldn't make a difference, ethically, whether or not we dined in a luxury restaurant; it might even help the economy. Trickle down, right? We went to the commie hotel one evening. The menu was written in English. And what a menu! My eyes lit up and I salivated as I read it. It was printed on oversized slabs of heavyweight cardboard. I can't recall if it had tassels in the fold. The list was long—everything from oysters Rockefeller to beef Wellington to strawberry shortcake. We soon found out that nothing was available except fish and rice. That was the kind of disappointment that made me feel virtuous. It didn't taste any different from the fish and rice we ate in more modest establishments but it was served with linen napkins, it cost quite a bit more and we didn't have to wrestle with our consciences later that evening.

It wasn't just the food. There wasn't much traffic on the roads. The streets and the gutters were clean. Trash was recycled until it became dust. Most cars would have passed muster as antiques, but not passed inspection. The magazines on the newsstands were older, by a decade, than the ones tied up in bundles in your grandmother's basement. Yet they were displayed for sale on racks in stores.

Not many people seemed to be around either. We chatted on the street with an elderly gentleman who spoke very good English. He told us that his name translated to Mr. Silver. We met him near the hostel, in front of a bakery whose bright lights reflected rows of empty white-painted shelves, not a crumb in the place.

The official People's Stores were empty of almost everything, because there was nothing to be had. Mr. Silver told us that someone could buy a new lightbulb only by bringing in the burned-out bulb to the People's Stores. No hoarding. The black markets thrived and were essential if anyone wanted canned milk, soap or clothing, he told us. The black market was the only place to buy antibiotics, British or American cigarettes, Scotch whisky, watches or canned goods. Burmese people sold off their family treasures to the black market, often in order to provide medicine they needed for a loved one who was ill.

Around the time we visited, the government was desperate to collect foreign currency, which was probably why we were suddenly allowed to visit the country.

Black markets weren't legal, of course, but were tolerated by the Revolutionary Council because there was no alternative to these men hanging around the sidewalks with their merchandise, some of it life-saving, essential. In many parts of Asia, we were approached on the street by men who wanted to trade their country's currency for American dollars, at much higher rates than the official markets allowed. Because we never knew when someone might grab us by the upper arm and lead us off to meet the magistrate, or meet our maker, Tim and I didn't dabble in the illicit exchange of hard cash.

There were plenty of lovely things to see, friendly and curious people, but little to eat, few places to sleep, nothing at all to buy—and this traveler was a hard-wired shopper. Rangoon itself was pretty, tree-lined and peaceful; not a lot of there there. We hoped to go to Mandalay to see the magnificent temples and maybe some flying fishes at play, but we weren't allowed to travel outside of Rangoon. We admired the many glittering bell-shaped pagodas around the city, but our visas didn't allow for a long visit, and it didn't take much time to cross off an itinerary. Ironically, we didn't have many opportunities to distribute our precious dollars.

§

BURMA TO CALCUTTA
April 1973

We landed at or near Calcutta's Dum Dum Airport, as it was called, with a rousing series of thumps to end our flight out of Rangoon. I mean a butt-spanking, teeth-rattling succession of thwacks. I was truly grateful for the seat belts preventing us from being tossed around in the cabin. Still, plenty of gasps, whimpers, a few screams and a "What the . . ." As far as I could tell, all the passengers were upright and locked in our seats. Thank you, mister steely-nerved pilot of the old clunker, probably a DC-6, or possibly a senile De Havilland left over from the British postwar occupation. This was Burma's official airline.

But there was more to worry about. Explosions and fire, apparently. We were directed to exit the plane through an emergency door. "Quickly! Quickly!" crew members barked at us, clapping their hands. At the emergency door, we were confronted with a wobbling rope ladder and a longer-than-expected transit back to solid earth. I was grateful I didn't have to jump.

We were in the middle of a field, a good hike from the tarmac and the terminal building. It was a flat treeless field, suitable for unexpected arrivals. We were told the landing wheels had failed to dislodge from the plane, and our splashdown was a hefty plop on the aircraft's underbelly.

While we waited for buses to come and take us to the terminal, I realized my brain had gone into its crisis mode, a default base of numbness. I may gasp in surprise, but I won't wail. Stupor is my defense against yelping, shaking, weeping, collapsing. My robotic self just follows instructions, if there are any, and later I can recall how lucky I was. Tim and I and all the passengers waited calmly, some huddled in pairs, some alone. A few sniffles, but no sobbing and no hysterics. I needed a hug.

After we were bused to the terminal building, immigration and customs officials stared at us with their jaws hanging open, I suppose because we were expected to burst into flame and die. They looked at us as if we had risen. I was more rattled by all that eye contact, all that gaping wonder, than by the aircraft's delinquency.

§

"I used to give to beggars when I first came here," Mike said. *"But then I realized it's hopeless. It never stops."* *"Jesus said you should give to whoever asks you,"* Mitchell said. *"Yeah, well,"* Mike said, *"obviously Jesus was never in Calcutta."*

Jeffrey Eugenides

CALCUTTA
1973

We registered at another oddball backpacker hotel, one which had no hallways. The top of the stairs led into someone's bedroom, which exited across the room into another bedroom, then another, until finally we reached our own room. We were, thankfully, in the last room, with privacy and a window just for ourselves. In the mornings, the other bedrooms in the maze were occupied by sleepers as we tiptoed through to the stairs, then down to the front door. We never encountered anyone awake or otherwise active in bed.

Outdoors, early in the day, more dormant figures lay in lumps all over the streets, there in the heart of the city. The poor souls were coiled in fetal positions, sound asleep. We walked through carefully, trying to avoid waking anyone, or kicking anyone, or tripping over anyone. We were also fearful of discovering someone who could no longer be awakened.

I read that the street cleaners pick up a horrifying number of people who have died overnight on the city's streets. Most of the victims would be recognized and mourned, but Calcutta's police said more than three thousand unidentifiable bodies are registered every year, piled on top of one another in an overloaded mortuary. Their identity is unknown, their bodies unclaimed.

Out among the sleepers those early mornings, the streets began to bustle with ragged adults and children waking up for the day, all the beggars, the lepers, the blind, the disfigured and disabled people. Some squatted at water pipes, pumping out gushes of drinking water. Some attended cooking fires. Others bathed, lathering and scrubbing all over with soap while crouched beside spurting pumps.

Not just mornings, but all day and evening, the city streets were plugged with cattle. According to Hindu belief, cows cannot be killed, but it's okay to neglect them. They may be venerated as much as human mothers, with whom they are often compared, but like so many people in this part of the world, the cows have to pick through the garbage for their daily nourishment. I knew there were lots of free-range cows in India, but I figured they lived out in the country, where they belong. The urban cows were nowhere near grass or pasture to keep them going. Cows crowded outside and inside Calcutta's concrete-floored central railway station, on the steps of the banks, obstructing entry into shops, hotels and restaurants, blocking the sidewalks and the avenues themselves, interspersed with automobile and foot traffic. Some cows nimbly wove their way through the streets while horns blared, rickshaws and pedestrians scurried out of the way.

Confession: I am phobic about cows. Once, when I was in high school, a cow cornered me in the barn while I was visiting my friend Ann's uncle and aunt on their farm. A few years later I was chased by a cow while picnicking in a field near Vancouver. She came straight at me and I'd never had to run so fast in my life. Now our West Tisbury back yard borders on a farm that used to have cows, which sometimes broke through the fence and lumbered into our yard. Mind you, they just stood there and stared, wondering what the hell happened. I pretended to be cool, and artfully slipped back into the house. One time I had to dash out and snatch up my baby daughter who was sitting on the lawn. I thought I was in a Meryl Streep movie.

Tim has been working on my angst for years, bringing me small *objet d'art* cows that he has made or assembled from a blend of gizmos. Among others, I have a Holstein that bows down to a Jersey holy cow he crafted for me. Another believer has blue dots on her pink cowhide. The holy cow wears a ruby crown on her head and a cross on a chain around her neck. I run a distinguished herd.

From Calcutta's cattle-infested main post office, Tim mailed home his antique brass gong, my bundles of Thai silk, and other treasures we had collected. The gong hangs above the open doorway to our kitchen, and has been well beaten by small children sitting on Tim's shoulders, notably our daughter Chloe and our granddaughter Annabelle. Some of the Thai silk was spirited into a wedding dress for me; some of it is still uncut, folded and stashed in a cupboard, awaiting an occasion.

We ate in some restaurants which were alien to our expectations, nice-looking places where flatware was not included on the white cotton tablecloths. Like everyone else in the room, we ate with our bare hands, even the mushiest rice and curry dishes. The India-born actress Rosemary Harris said that eating with your hands is like swimming in the nude. On our way out of one restaurant, we washed up at the mosaic-tiled basin, an ornate shrine there in the middle of the dining room. I didn't see anyone wash their hands on their way in, I peevishly noted. Then I remembered I hadn't either, just a quick brush against my jeans.

We went to a more nonchalant restaurant near our hotel, patronized by the grubbiest of the Western travelers who hung out in the neighborhood. It was recommended for its low prices, and once inside, we discovered that the establishment had a caring as well as an unceremonious attitude. The walls of the dining room were lined with Indian men, no women, no Westerners, who were allowed to stand there, waiting. When a seated guest finished eating with his hands, he generally had leftovers. The standees had a regimented system whereby the next in line tapped the departing diner on the shoulder and asked politely if he could have the slop left on the plate. Since the food wasn't very good, these patiently waiting men were given generous portions of second-hand man-handled food. We didn't eat there twice, or well, but we remember the ambiance, and were brought closer to the reality of hunger. I tried to think of it as an extension of our own doggy-bag culture, but I couldn't embrace the image. You think you know something about a place until you get there. But traveling third world, at ground level, offered up unnerving revelations not generally included in organized tours.

When I emerged from the bathroom, Tim asked me "How was it?" I asked him the same question shortly afterwards.

Of all places to be when it comes time to update your immunization shots, I don't recommend Calcutta. In order to keep moving we needed to be re-injected to prevent yellow fever, hepatitis, typhoid, malaria, cholera, even plague for some of the more interesting countries. Some of our protections were about to expire and we had to reshoot for one or more of these maladies before we could travel to another country, so we tracked down a clinic and lined up early.

We were almost at the front of the line and I've seldom been more grateful. The nurse had four needles. Tim and I were numbers three and four in line with dozens behind us. We were injected with the last two cellophane-wrapped needles and we watched as the same four hypodermics rotated down through the crowd, following a quick swipe in a bowl of alcohol between customers. In other countries people are given new needles and the used ones are tossed in the bin meant for hazardous waste. Calcutta, it appeared, was much more relaxed about the germ theory.

§

*The mountains were so wild and so
stark and so very beautiful that I
wanted to cry. I breathed another
wonderful moment to keep safe in
my heart.*

Jane Wilson-Howarth

DARJEELING
1973

From Calcutta we boarded a train heading north to Siliguri, near the Bangladeshi border, where we switched to a narrow-gauge railway that climbed up a Himalayan mountain to Darjeeling. A leper seated across from us on the train stared intently at Tim's orange, the snack he'd brought along for the trip. It was as if the man were trying to hypnotize the orange, to will it into his own hand. Tim peeled his orange, then handed it to the man. The whole thing disappeared into his mouth in one gulp. He stared straight past us, never looked at Tim, didn't smile, never said a word. I think he hated us for having that orange in the first place.

During the days of the British Raj, Darjeeling became a hill station for those English expats desperate to escape the heat of the plains. These same genteel Brits who settled the community started the well-known tea plantations. The town maintained an impression of Edwardian colonialism, a real-life *Masterpiece Theatre*.

We stayed in a charming little hotel, which had a library stuffed with dog-eared paperback mysteries by Rex Stout and Ngaio Marsh. The hotel manager was the twenty-something son of the man who owned the Oberoi Hotels, one of the biggest and brightest hotel chains in India. He ran a fine establishment. Tim had sent his jeans out for laundering, and they were returned with his rolled-up money still in his front pocket, just as he had left it. I would happily stay there again.

After the initial shock of Calcutta's mean main streets, we began to see the beauty of the country. There is a splendor in the life of the place, the vitality of the people, the animals, the colors, the birds, the flowers. The Himalayas speak for themselves and don't need my superlatives. The air was wonderfully fresh and cool here in the foothills. I wanted to swallow great gulps of it and bottle some more for the trip back down into the steamy country. This jaunt felt so invigorating that I ordered and ate liver (I don't know what kind of animal donor was involved) and thumped my chest like Wonder Woman until we left the mountain. The town is built into the steep mountainside, so to get anywhere, you need to climb. Up and down, up and down—I couldn't do it now.

On a fairly clear day you could see Kanchenjunga, the world's third-highest mountain. On an exceptionally clear day you could see Everest itself. A photograph of a well-defined Everest hung over our bed in the hotel as consolation for those many days when the weather was murky. No matter; Kanchenjunga was spectacular enough, and usually visible.

A nearby national park is home to rhinos, elephants and leopards, as well as Bengal tigers, those still in existence. During our visit, we played, carefully, with a Bengal tiger cub that someone had brought into town on a leash. Man and beast were loitering on the street. The young cub, heavy for his size, warmer than he looked, with fur that was wiry and prickly, didn't mind being handled. I could feel the wildness in this little guy. I petted him

146

though it didn't feel like the right thing to do. I massaged him around with my hands, but gently. I decided not to encourage this kitten to play by tickling his tummy and making him kick. The man with him remained mum. I wondered why the cub was tamed and where he would end up.

The buildings were a curious mix of typical Indian bungalows with ample covered porches, interspersed with mock Tudor residences, Gothic churches and, predictably, the Planters Club, for members only. I felt like I was rereading Rudyard Kipling, maybe his poem "The White Man's Burden." If you don't know the theme, take a guess. Tea plantations lined the mountainside along the main road into town. I bought some ridiculously overpriced tea to send home to my parents, but they were unimpressed. Two decades later, I found the unopened package in the high cupboard above my mother's stove.

We spent time and money in the Tibetan Refugee Centre, and bought a larger-than-life pig mask with green curly hair and a dirty face. The ground-in dirt proved he is either quite old, or was made that way to look authentic. He hangs above the bathroom door. We bought masks and paintings, and small sculpted figures in just about every country we visited, and they remain good and faithful companions in our home, the spoils of our adventures.

After catching our breath and regaining our strength in Darjeeling, we took another train to Patna, a rather desolate city, ancient, hot and humid with little for tourists to admire. We were there just for a day, then on a flight to Kathmandu in Nepal. On this flight, we had a clear view of Everest bursting through the clouds. An incomparable sight, arguably the most spectacular of them all.

§

The obstacle is the path.

Zen aphorism

NEPAL
1973

We heard these blood-curdling shrieks from a couple of blocks away as we walked through the streets of Kathmandu one sunny afternoon. We headed in that direction to see what was making such a grisly sound, only to discover an exotic religious rite, the slaughtering of a goat, there on the sidewalk. I don't believe these men were thinking heavenly thoughts. A messy business. This wasn't what I expected of an official sacrificial ceremony. It was just a bunch of guys in street clothes hunched over their victim in front of ordinary buildings. There was no audience, no temple in sight, no officiating priest that we could see. We chose to walk around the red puddles and cross the street to save our shoes. And to save our sensibilities, we kept moving; we didn't stick around to watch the ritual's finale. You can tell Tim and I were not farm-raised.

We encountered a parade one day, to celebrate a more formal religious ceremony. Musicians played unfamiliar music in minor key chants, with voices, drums and cymbals, while troops of young men swayed and staggered from one side of the street to the other. They reeled in a forward direction down the middle of the road; it wasn't exactly marching. I suspected they were under the influence of some domestic intoxicant, but I was not one to judge.

148

As the procession drew near its end, we saw a golden chariot with no wheels, hoisted by a few of the faithful, being carried through the streets of the city, a grand climax to the parade. Their precious cargo was handled more steadily and carefully than the opening performers could have done. People on the street rushed at the carriage for a glimpse. Fans and paparazzi jostled for the best view. Inside the glinting chariot was a young goddess called Kumari, wearing a golden crown and too much makeup for her age. Kumari is chosen at age three or four, declared a living goddess, and truly worshipped by hundreds of thousands of Hindus and Buddhists. She lives in a temple, does not go to school, and her feet are never allowed to touch the ground. She may never play hopscotch or host a sleepover with her friends. The Kumari we saw was ten or eleven, didn't smile and wave; she didn't look happy about her celebrity.

The whole business is not so different from our culture's worship of pop stars, except that the Nepali version is ancient and religious, and although there are qualifying requirements, the chosen ones don't win because of pretty dimples or perky personalities. Instead, the applicants must have a full set of teeth, a "neck like a conch shell, a body like a banyan tree, eyelashes like a cow, thighs like a deer, the chest of a lion and a voice as soft and clear as a duck's." A duck's? Her initiation process includes proof of her fearlessness. She must remain calm during a theatrical performance featuring men in masks and the severed heads of slaughtered goats and buffalo. Then she has to spend the night alone with the severed heads.

Kumari is retired, released you might think, when she hits puberty. Then these girls become demoted to ordinary female citizen status, which is not much of a status. Although being chosen is truly an honor, life as a has-been is not much fun. It is a struggle to get used to the real world, as you can imagine. It is difficult to learn as a teenager how to walk again, and nobody wants to date or marry a former goddess who might insist on being carried over the threshold daily. Or who might demand bonbons while vegetating on the chaise.

And then there is pot. Long before we were there, marijuana was legal and available in many forms, and Nepal was the hippiest place to go. Just down the street from our hotel was the Eden Hashish Centre, "wholesale and retail" in its ad, and the Hashish Ganja Shop next door. The scene was quite exotic in 1973, if not so much now as the culture has shifted westward. On the main counter inside the shop, screw-top mason jars meant for preserving peaches were filled with various grades of weed. From the left, the row began with the cheapest display, chopped and dried plant stalks; the most expensive, on the far right, contained flower tops, small brown dried blossoms. Other varieties of leaves and mixtures were staged in order of price, and in order of natural placement along the stems of the plants.

Speaking of weed and this country's recent inclination to legalize it, the *Denver Post*'s pot critic, Jake Browne, writes about the plant using the same vocabulary that wine critics employ. "Clean with a note of citrus" headed an article. Mr. Browne checks the merchandise for bugs and pesticides, smokes a joint to describe its flavor and its heat quotient, and relates the effects of the drug. He cites the medical benefits and deficits, if it clears or aggravates a pain, aids sleep or keeps you awake, and of course he rates the potency of the wallop.

Kathmandu had a restaurant that advertised three square meals a day with marijuana (optional) cooked in the food. The downside was the building, with ceilings so low you couldn't stand fully erect, you had to hunch over and stoop like a bird of prey toward your table. The breakfast menu offered hashish oatmeal and hashish Ovaltine, to start your day with a smile. The menu listed familiar lunch and dinner dishes with or without hashish in the entrees, and for those who wished, a dessert of tarted-up brownies. Watch your head when you stand up.

But the most seductive of Nepalese food came from the pie restaurant—apple, pumpkin, lemon meringue, pecan—capitalizing on the leitmotif of the city. The pies tasted as good as Thanksgiving at home. The place was packed all day, all evening, with mostly young homesick Americans. Someone near our hotel room continually and loudly played John Denver's "Take Me Home, Country Roads." I realized how mournful the song could sound. Some of these kids had been in Nepal too long.

Our hotel room was divided from the other rooms by flimsy panels that didn't quite touch the floor. Our room had two single beds with nothing but floor in between. One night, too exhausted to go out to eat after climbing up and down the hilly city, I bought a sandwich and placed it on a napkin on the floor next to my bed. Before long, in the dark, I noticed that something was trying to eat my sandwich. It was a plump sleek rat. I gasped and startled the rat, which jumped on Tim's bed. I choked again and woke Tim. The rat leapt from his bed to mine and I sucked in my breath a third time. The rat hopped down on the floor and scampered under the partition into the next room.

Every night thereafter we could hear him and his pals tearing down the length of the building, under the partitions, racing from room to room, in search of another abandoned sandwich.

§

*Om is that god of love. Like a loving
mother Om clears us of our clutters
collected through many
incarnations.*

Banani Ray

VARANASI

1973

We drifted in circles in a slow boat carrying a dozen or so tourists.
My hand dangled over the side, dipping into the placid water of
the Ganges, and it felt refreshing. The gentleness of the scene
slowed the sense of frantic energy that seemed to dominate India's
atmosphere. Still, this was India, there always was the possibility of
an impending collision. Plenty of other boats looped around this
shallow part of the river, among people swimming or worshipping
in the same spot. Some Hindus swam casually, slowly, just as older
people elsewhere loll about, luxuriating in calm water. Others
stood submerged to their waists, and in a personal ceremony,
collected Ganges water in their cupped hands, lifted their palms
and let the water fall back into the river, a way to honor their
ancestors and their gods.

Varanasi is where believers come to cremate their dead or to
bathe in the Ganges, to wash away their sins—some believe ten
lifetimes' worth of sins. The crowds along the shore were silent,
respectful, middle-aged or better. No picnics, no splashing, no
sunbathing or annoying music. Young people did not cannonball
into the river. In fact, we didn't see any young people here.

Cows, of course, wandered along the ghats, sandstone platforms that were built a thousand years ago, horizontal steps that divided the seventy-foot cliffs seven times above the water's edge. Clusters of wet people stood around the swimming ghats at the bottom along the riverbank, the women's saris dripping and clinging, men sopping in unsightly diaper-like loincloths, dragged down by the weight of the water. They chatted quietly with each other, moving in slow motion, or so my memory tells me. There was no organized prayer going on, no communal activity happening. It was a sociable but personal occasion.

On the higher tiers of the embankments, men dressed in white gathered in loose circles around cremation ceremonies. Bonfires blazed, aggravating the mourners' grief in the tropical heat. High above, streams of wood smoke broke through the blue sky. Near each of the designated pyres, firewood was stacked in neat geometric stockpiles, ready for the next funeral. By custom, the mourners, men only, stayed at the burning ghats until the last of the fires died out. We didn't try to get near the cremations; like the worshippers by the water, these too were private.

Varanasi, once known as Benares, is the holiest city in the country, and the oldest continuously inhabited city in the world, dating back to the twelfth century BCE. That's a lot of centuries. A custom first recorded in the fourth century BCE had dutiful new widows joining their late husbands on their funeral pyres, voluntarily immolating themselves. Queen Victoria, bless her heart, put a stop to the practice in 1829.

For Tim and me, the most blessed aspect of staying in Varanasi was our bargain hotel, a former mint where rupees had been manufactured. The stone building looked like a fortress with high ceilings, our room was deliciously dark, cool, and—glory be! —our private shower had hot water.

§

India is not an underdeveloped country, but rather in the context of its historical and cultural heritage, a highly developed one in an advanced state of decay.

Shashi Tharoon

DELHI
1973

It wasn't far from Varanasi to Delhi, but our social status soared way up. Tim knew a family in New Delhi who had a summer home on Chappaquiddick on Martha's Vineyard. Andy was an urban planner for the Ford Foundation. His wife, Winann, was a longtime family friend and the sister of a neighbor in West Tisbury.

We reconnected with Tim's cousin Alex and began to travel together once more. We three were invited to stay with Tim's Vineyard friends in their stylish modern home, in a gated community within the heart of New Delhi. They had servants who had their own house in back, and those servants had other, lower-caste servants who cleaned up after the first set of household staff. We never saw most of the help. Our hosts had a big American car and a full-time driver who was also their night watchman. We were not accustomed to this degree of comfort. We were, needless to say, well served, well fed, well cooled by central air conditioning, and well chauffeured. It was very pleasant.

Getting lost on unfamiliar streets was a given. I think I have a better sense of direction than Tim, but then I liked to look at maps, especially street maps, to figure out where to go. But whenever he was right and I was wrong, he would chide me with "If it wasn't for me, you'd be in Guam." I heard that a lot, relatively, and the sad truth is, I still do.

I had to go to a bank branch in Old Delhi to collect some money sent from home. We expected to get there on our own but our hosts insisted we use their car and driver. We accepted, with gratitude. Riding through the old walled city meant a slow but wild trip through cars, cows, bicycle rickshaws, people in all manners of dress, camels, buses, children, elephants, pedestrians and more cows clogging the narrow winding streets of the original capital. We might never have found the little bank branch without our driver. And luckily, we didn't need to cross any streets on foot. Did you know that camels make a loud, mournful, wailing noise when they're stuck in traffic?

The bank had ceiling fans set on high, blowing on flapping documents trying to flee from under their paperweights. This visit predated computers, of course, and the reams of paper fluttered so desperately, it was like a room full of trapped white birds frantic to be free. With a lot of shuffling, lifting of paperweights, and chasing after escaped sheets of paper, our bank clerk finally held down the forms and documents we needed to complete our business. Our chauffeured car was waiting right outside, its American motor purring.

Our hostess told us about a snake charmer who came to their door one day when her young children were playing outside in the garden. The snake charmer told her that there was a cobra in her flower beds, and for a fee, he would entice it away, dispose of it elsewhere. She had no choice, she said, but to bring the children indoors, pay the man, and watch out the window as he lured a big, slithering cobra out from the rhododendrons and into his basket. Whether the snake arrived by itself or was brought to the yard, she had no way of knowing, but the cobra had to go. There was no arguing with the man.

We saw the historic Red Fort, the temples, all the sights of New Delhi. We were taken to dine at a genuine Tandoori restaurant in Old Delhi, where the meal differs from the Tandoori chicken you can buy from Trader Joe's freezer. The authentic way to do it is this: Dig a hole in the ground. Make a blazing fire in the hole. Rub the chicken with annatto seeds and saffron. Then marinate the bird for several hours in a mixture of yogurt with ginger, garlic, coriander, cayenne and garam masala, which itself is cardamom, cumin, cinnamon, cloves, nutmeg and black pepper. Bury the covered clay dish in hole in the ground, roast in an intense fire, around 450 to 500 degrees. A small Indian chicken takes about half an hour in its little inferno. Lip-smacking good.

We took a northbound train for a few days' visit to Chandigarh, near the wedged borders of Pakistan and China. The planned city was designed by the Swiss-French architect Le Corbusier, one of the founders of modern design. After the war, in the late 1940s, the British government granted independence to India and Pakistan. When their borders were rearranged in a messy act called partition, India lost the city of Lahore to Pakistan. In its place, India needed a new capital for the states of Punjab and Haryana. Le Corbusier was thrilled to be asked to design a whole city, and Chandigarh was the result. It was all midcentury modern, much like a neatly laid-out college campus for a million people, all done in squares and rectangles and other clean straight lines.

Our hotel was in one of the residential sections. One thing about the residential area that struck me was the orderly housing units with little yards, carports and flat roofs. You might think you were in a suburb of Phoenix, hazy mountains in the background. No slums, no sense of chaotic grungy India. I don't remember seeing any cows. But the heat was brutal, and we noticed that some of the residents slept on their flat roofs. We watched them rise from their beds in the morning in their pajamas before heading downstairs to the main part of their houses, to change their pajamas into streetwear pajamas.

My other off-kilter observation took place while touring the sleek light-filled government buildings. The project seemed to run out of money when it came time to furnish the offices. Inside these shiny spaces were beat-up old oak desks and dented metal filing cabinets that had barely survived several wars. It was a striking contrast. Where was Herman Miller's Aeron chair? Where were Mies van der Rohe's Barcelona chair and Nogushi's free-form dining table?

Another tidbit of culture clashes: I like to read English-language newspapers in unfamiliar places. I happened to look through New Delhi's biggest paper, *The Times of India*, on a day when recipes were published. I was delighted to see the instructions "Take two cigarette tins of flour . . ."—a measuring cup for the people.

Getting ready to leave New Delhi we were informed that it is customary to tip the household help. It was a jolt to learn that the suggested daily tip was more than a day's cost of living in our alternative travel world. Next: back to our real world.

Advocates of slow travel savor the journey; traveling by train or boat or bicycle, or even on foot, rather than crammed into an airplane. They take time to plug into the local culture instead of racing through a list of tourist traps.

Carl Honoré

AGRA
1973

Of course we had to see the Taj Mahal. At the Delhi train station, the clerk behind the window grate offered us a listing of trains to carry us to Agra, which was 130 miles away. We could choose from a roster of 58 trains that regularly ran this route, all with names like UPSmprk Krnti and the Chennai Rajdhni. The clerk was neither patient nor helpful as he rattled off their names. Then we heard him say the words "passenger train." We three figured that we were on the right track, so to speak. There are half a million villages in India. For the convenience of the passengers, our train stopped at all of them. We left early in the morning, got to Agra in the evening.

The trip was harrowing not only because of its slow pace, but because we were being harassed by a couple of high-strung young men who had nothing better to do than pester us. Pester me.

There are passenger cars on Indian trains that carry only women. Most of them run in the cities where women make up a large portion of the workforce. The common term for this common problem, sexual harassment, is "Eve teasing." Traveling with Tim and Alex may have saved my virtue, though both these good guys are non-confrontational and it was not in their nature—nor mine—to punch out Indian men for being irritating. My two companions sat opposite me and were engrossed in their books, which shielded their faces. The Indian creeps didn't pounce on me, but they sat next to me, three of us in a space meant for two. They talked and laughed too much, too loud, with too many jumpy little touches accompanied by soprano giggles, one unsettling grab of my unwilling hand to tickle my palm. I wanted to look out the window, read my book. No conductor came around, no authority showed up to hear my complaints. My snarling and snapping only made these guys laugh all the more.

And yes, we saw and admired the Taj Mahal. It was lovely, worth the journey. But I'm sorry that we didn't buy tickets for the Jamma Tawi Nanded Special.

§

Panem et circenses.

Juvenal

BOMBAY
1973

Next stop was Bombay, which we had not expected to be so charming. Our hotel was on a side street a few blocks from the Gateway of India monument, built by the British Raj a century ago as a symbol of British power and majesty. It was and is the heart of the Bombay waterfront on the Arabian Sea, the welcoming portal for King George V and members of the aristocracy, British and Indian. It has also been the port of entry for three different terrorist attacks in the twenty-first century. While we were there a Bollywood film was being shot at the arch, and we watched a while from the sidelines. Lots of offers here from pedestrians suggesting we exchange money, rupees for dollars, black market rates. One day a man stopped us on the sidewalk in front of the Taj Palace Hotel and offered to sell us a suitcase with a false bottom. We both burst out laughing. The man looked quite shocked and quickly scrambled down the street, suitcase in hand.

We stood on the same street after Jim, one of our traveler friends, developed abdominal pains in a nearby restaurant. The restaurant called for medical help, Jim was loaded on a stretcher and carted out to the sidewalk by half a dozen bearers who speed-walked several blocks to the nearest hospital. Luckily Jim wasn't seriously ill and was sent home to his hotel. Unluckily, he was wide

161

awake on the ride and had an expression of horror and embarrassment as passersby—Tim and I included—watched him being hustled along the crowded sidewalk in full public view.

Our shady side street had its own entertainment, plenty of it every evening, while we sat on the balcony of our room and enjoyed the shows. The entertainers were usually young men who already looked old, who often had small children or trained dogs with them, all of them doing tricks out there in the middle of the street. The opening act might have been a juggler. A dog may have balanced on a ball, or a man walked on his hands, or they performed together, a team. More thrillingly, the snake charmer had a basket full of slithery helpers who responded to a recorded Indian song sounding suspiciously like "My Darling Clementine." A monkey on a leash could run in circles around his master while jumping over a stick. Dogs walked on their hind legs. One man held his little girl's hands and swung her around and around, over and over. Someone set up a rigging of poles to hold a tightrope for the star of the family to balance-walk along its length.

Hotel guests in the balconies which lined the row of hostelries on our street cheered them on, applauded and threw coins down to the street. There may have been more professional forms of entertainment in the city, but this had the advantage of folksy charm and spontaneity.

We toured and shopped and we loved the shaded green streets of this beautiful city in this vibrant country. So much of India is appealing, teeming with life. Not only people-life, but all the flora and fauna; monkeys on trees lining the railroad tracks, waving at us as the train rolled by. The spectacle of the mountains, the charm of the red stone buildings, especially the old crumbling structures, the sheer number of birds overhead, the dazzle of lovely women in silk saris, the density and pulse of life, all of it.

One hot day we decided to go to the beach for a swim. We took a city bus to Juhu Beach, a vast spread of sandy shore on the Indian Ocean. The beach was empty, the water was the warmest I've encountered anywhere outside of my own tub. Tim and Alex hated it, they wanted to be refreshed, not mollycoddled in a bathtub. I could have floated happily and drifted around in that water all day, like those languorous Hindus in the Ganges. As we were leaving the beach, someone told us that the beach was empty that day because of warnings of poisonous water snakes milling around in the shallows. Now you tell me.

On leaving Bombay, we needed a taxi to take us to our ship. We hopelessly waved at the traffic for a while, until a leper came along on foot and volunteered to hail one for us. We were thankful for his help and his easy success. I tried to tip the leper, to push some money into his outstretched hand, which had no fingers. The palm of his hand formed a shallow cup, but the money kept slipping off the edges. I said to myself, "I'm touching a leper, I'm touching a leper," as I pushed deeper into his palm. But he smiled, looking pleased with his unexpected earnings, and we smiled back, happy to be on our way, ready to end our stay in India.

§

*I don't know who named them
swells. They should have been
named awfuls.*

Hugo Vihlen

WESTWARD TO EAST AFRICA
June 1973

It's not in my nature to choose first class. But there are times, alas, when such luck is foisted upon one. When I decided to leave Vancouver to sail to Australia, only one bed was available, and it happened to be in first class, so I booked it. When Tim and I and Alex were ready to leave Bombay and sail across the Indian Ocean to Tanzania, we were told we couldn't travel on any other level of the ship.

Our boat was the SS *Karanja*, the British Indian Steam Navigation Company cargo and passenger liner that crisscrossed the Indian Ocean, north from Bombay to Karachi, across to Mombasa and down the African coast as far as Capetown, then back again.

The line was an offshoot of the P&O Orient Lines, which had taken Tim and me to Australia in the first place. Like our P&O voyage, this was not a vacation/cruise ship, but was meant to transport its passengers one way only.

The vessel was a 1948 model with 1948 rules where, despite our recent choices of humble lodgings, it was made clear the lower deck, known as the Intermediate Class, was out of bounds. We were instructed to register as Saloon passengers, on the uppermost deck, with accommodations for sixty.

We were so accustomed to lamentable lodgings I felt a bit insulted when we were directed upstairs. Maybe they thought I wasn't tough enough. Don't get me wrong: We found it enjoyable to sleep in a comfortable stateroom, eat good food, breathe fresh sea air and watch the flying fish race alongside. I'm told that afternoon tea was served with violin recitals on these voyages, but I don't remember participating. Except for the price, I wasn't uncomfortable about traveling first class when I left Canada. But then, all levels of passengers were first world, mostly white people, and I was put there only because I booked too late to get a berth further down. Same with Tim.

Now, many months after beginning our world tour, I discovered that we weren't allowed to choose because mingling with Asian or African passengers was simply not done. I was made aware of my pampered privilege; it wasn't fair.

We were on our way from India to Africa, ready to find new cultures and traditions, tribes and their customs, and our route was taking us on one last fling through the defunct British Empire. In more than one way, we were riding the last remnants of Victoria's vast kingdom. Though the queen herself was not so stuffy, her latter-day subjects certainly were.

Tim and I were also informed that we were not allowed to book a cabin together because we weren't married. So Tim and Alex bunked in together, and my space was shared with a English bride-to-be who was traveling with her fiancé to Capetown, where they would marry and start life together. She tossed and turned at night in our cabin: it was because of nervous excitement about the wedding and her future in Africa. The poor girl couldn't stop dreaming out loud about her hopes and wishes. The only other passenger we befriended was a pleasant British barrister our own age, the cabinmate of the bridegroom. He was heading to Rhodesia to practice law. He wore a suit and tie.

Intermediate Class, we were told, was one big room directly below us with about 180 bunks, mostly occupied by Pakistani and Indian men. The space was not air-cooled. The portholes had to be kept closed because they almost touched the waterline, and odors were trapped in the room. The company never advertised or mentioned if there was another deck, even lower, true steerage class for unluckier people. But there must have been; why else was this level called Intermediate?

More recently I discovered a newsletter written by travel writer Kit Herring, who sailed on the *Karanja* a year or two after us. He insisted on traveling in Intermediate, and had finally been allowed, with caveats. Then he accused the boat line of prejudice because of the wording of a document the company required him to sign. The agreement asked the passenger to swear as follows:

"It has been explained to me that I shall be in close proximity to numerous passengers whose language, customs and habits will be alien to my experiences and that I will not be permitted to seek solitude or alternative company in parts of the ship reserved for saloon passengers and ship's officers.

"I appreciate that the toilet and ablution facilities conform to the needs and customs of Asian passengers."

I understood now why the restrictions applied in particular to women. The writer suggested that the ship, sailing under the South African flag, was upholding the apartheid policy of that nation. Mr. Herring represented a handful of first worlders like us—only more so—who traveled on the cheap, and who'd been sleeping in the land-based equivalent of steerage for some time.

Some traveling Westerners were in a new kind of mindset by the 1970s and the boat line wasn't ready or able to deal with these people. Tim and I had spent almost a year by now in offbeat corners of Asia, so I can understand why Kit Herring preferred to ride with the locals and save money, rather than spend more money to hobnob with people like those at home.

I suspect that the British Indian Steam Navigation Company, known familiarly as BI, crafted its agreement document after incidents where passengers freaked out upon seeing the reality of sailing in the undeveloped world. We heard of one first world passenger who was so intolerant of the people whose countries he was visiting that he ranted his opinions and objections all the way across the Indian Ocean, and when the ship arrived in his final port he deliberately dumped a bucket of dirty water from the deck down onto an innocent dockworker on shore, cursing racial insults as he did so.

When Tim and Alex and I bought our tickets, the captain and officers knew the monsoons were due, and that many people in this part of the world had delicate stomachs, just to make the voyage belowdecks more deplorable. I'm glad that BI insisted.

After sailing north from Bombay we docked in Karachi, and were stuck there for five or six days. This was apparently a common breakdown of the schedule. Cargo loading and unloading were done by camels, known for their persnickety work ethics and for seldom meeting their deadlines. Tim and Alex toured the city while I languished on the open top deck, queasy from some minor Bombay malaise. I went ashore briefly in Karachi, but I didn't go far and I didn't stay long. I have no keepsakes or souvenirs of Pakistan, no sense of the place.

The monsoons arrived on schedule, shortly after the ship left the Pakistani coast. When the *Karanja* turned westward, the wind and rain began to lash at her sides. One of the officers told us the lower decks were awash with seasickness, "even worse than usual." I was quite relieved to be confined by the 1948 rules, to be designated Saloon material.

Through much of the journey I enjoyed sitting out on the top deck and rolling with the punches of the agitated ocean. The rain had stopped but the wind remained active.

I was engrossed in a novel about a shipwreck. From my damp deck chair, I felt the bow of the *Karanja* slap the ocean as it dipped and fell forward; it rolled back and up and smacked again. I kept telling myself, "It's only fiction," as I was happily sprayed by the occasional splash under a hot sky. I decided the rocking, dipping, groaning, splattering and thumping of the old girl only added to the excitement of the story I was reading, like a movie shown in 3D.

We spent a lovely blue-sky day in Mombasa, Kenya. We ate lunch at a sidewalk café downtown and, before we reboarded the ship, went for a swim in a private pool.

I can't remember whose pool and how we got past the locked gate, but I have photographs of us and the Rhodesia-bound lawyer, whom we never saw again, so it must have happened. Other than our little group of passengers, there were no other people in or around the pool. Another moment of white privilege.

§

Travelers never think that they are the foreigners.

Mason Cooley

MOUNT KILIMANJARO
1973

The main attraction of Tanzania for us was Mount Kilimanjaro. To get there, we rode a bus from Dar es Salaam through the rolling savannas, arching acacia trees spaced here and there, making blots of shade across the open grasslands. There should have been lions in this picture, I thought.

Instead, we shared the bus ride with people who seemed to have come from the MGM studio lot. At the start of the bus trip in the city, our fellow passengers wore jeans and T-shirts. As we moved through the countryside, the city people disembarked and were replaced by surprisingly old-fashioned travelers. Within a couple of hours, the majority of passengers appeared to be Maasai. We knew this was a nomadic tribe, but we didn't expect them to take the bus or to dress like extras. The fashion became sarongs and sandals or bare feet, with an overkill of jewelry, including heavily beaded bibs the size of manhole covers. Most tantalizing in the seats right in front of us were those earlobes, pierced and stretched to their shoulders, the holes filled with heavy beaded jewelry or bones to pull the flaps of skin down even farther. They didn't seem interested in our presence. But in my image of world order, this was out of sync. African tribal members may wear their traditional costumes for ceremonies, tourism promotions and photo ops. They looked misplaced on public transportation, all dressed up on an ordinary day. It was, honestly, a little unnerving— too many memories of seeing *King Solomon's Mines* in the 1950s. I was relieved to note that these men and women carried gadgets from the more typical world of bus-riding; most of them wore a wristwatch or sunglasses, carried a flashlight or a transistor radio. My anxieties could relax.

Our pretty little hotel at the foot of Kilimanjaro came with a screened sun porch where I lounged around all day. Tim and Alex had signed up to climb the mountain, I stayed at the bottom. I still smoked heavily in those days, and I knew I'd never make it past first base, you might say. The guys were in a group of six or eight trekkers, along with a guide and a number of bearers who carried the camping equipment, set up the huts at each base camp and cooked the meals. Tim and Alex rented warm winter clothing and boots and were good to go, four days to the top and one day back down.

The men were muddy, sweaty, blistered and exhausted when they returned to the bottom, but exhilarated at having climbed the beast. It was, as they said, "a walk," not a climb with ropes, harnesses and crampons. Still, it was a walk that went up and up and up, crossing scree that wanted to slide down the mountain and take the climbers with it. The group ran into armies of millions of ants crossing the trail, with their guide warning everyone, "Don't step on them or all hell will break loose." The ants had the right of way. If these numbers were agitated they would swarm and bite, inflicting great pain or worse.

The climb started at the border with Kenya, at the equator, where the air was more than warm, and rose up into glaciers and wind, ice and snow and thin air at nearly twenty thousand feet, still at the equator. In the snapshots we saw later, the men looked bitterly cold, with wool scarves wrapped around their faces, only frozen eyeballs exposed. Displayed in Tim's study, there is a green and white poster that says "I have climbed Mount Kilimanjaro. Have you?" He earned the poster, but to me, that "Have you?" is unnecessary.

§

A lion never loses sleep over the
opinions of sheep.

Unknown

TANZANIA TO KENYA
1973

When I was about twelve I spent many Saturday afternoons at the Odeon or the Roxy. In the 1950s, the movie industry was running scared, as television appeared to be a successful threat to Hollywood. So the movie people came up with plans to draw people back into the theaters. One idea was 3D, a technology that had been around for decades but not successfully used until *Bwana Devil*, a feature film whose posters offered "a lion in your lap, a lover in your arms." The movie's original name, for you collectors, was *The Lions of Gulu.*

I went to see it, and a stream of other movies in 3D: *House of Wax, Creature from the Black Lagoon*, outer space movies, ghost stories, cowboys and Indians, gorillas, even the musical *Kiss Me Kate*, originally called *The Taming of the Shrew*, which was written by that misogynist William Shakespeare. The 3D fad petered out until recently. Too many people found it a nuisance to wear cardboard glasses with one red cellophane lens and one green. Or was it blue? The only good 3D movies needed to have wild beasts or monsters lunging at you so that you would duck and scream if you were twelve, or maybe have a heart attack if you were any older. Otherwise, what's the use?

So *Bwana Devil* was famous for being first. And *Bwana Devil* was based on the true story of the building of the railroad that Tim and I rode from Tanzania to Kenya, though we didn't know it until years later. Our route took us through Tsavo National Park, one of the biggest and best-known wildlife parks in Africa. On our journey the one eventful part of the trip was the joy of watching elephants reach up to nibble leaves off the tree limbs as the train rattled along. They were having their lunch as we enjoyed our own. We didn't see any lions, though from what I've since learned, the lions owed us a little face-time.

This was the countryside where man-eating lions dined on human flesh during the construction of the railroad at the end of the nineteenth century. The territory was rugged: mountains, jungle, swamps, plains, cliffs and raging rivers. The train was called the Lunatic Express. I don't suppose that insulting adjective applied to any one individual, but to the thousands involved in building the railroad. A book called *The Lunatic Express* claims that the line was named for the "turbulent race for the mastery of East Africa." The construction took six years and cost five million English pounds. More than four thousand workmen, mostly from India, were killed on the job. Death came from derailments, collisions, everyday accidents, drowning, disease, tribal raids. and lions. Considering the conditions of the work area, most of the causes were not exceptional. But killed and eaten by lions? That's big.

Dozens were dragged out of their beds at night, out of their tents, and devoured by the man-eaters. Many of the survivors fled the scene and work was halted on the project. The horror took place at the construction site of a complex bridge crossing the Tsavo River.

In March 1898 two male lions began to stalk the campsite, snatching workers while they slept. Efforts were made to scare them off with bonfires and fences made of thorns around the tent areas, but nothing dissuaded the beasts. Lieutenant Colonel John Henry Patterson led the construction project, and he personally took on the job of destroying the ferocious animals. He set traps and tried to ambush them from a tree, but month after month, he was unable to outwit them. Finally, on December 9, he killed the first lion. Twenty days later he shot and killed the second lion. The first lion was almost ten feet long, and it took eight men to carry the carcass back to camp. Each lion sustained numerous wounds from high-caliber rifles before they were brought down. After they were first shot, they spent days fighting back, full of bullet holes and determination to get even. Patterson said that the second lion died while gnawing on a tree branch, still trying to reach Patterson eleven days after he was first shot, but the fatally injured lion refused to give up pursuing his killer. The lions' skins spent twenty-five years as Patterson's floor rugs, then were sold to Chicago's Field Museum in 1924. The pelts and their skulls were restored and are now on permanent display.

We knew none of this when we boarded the old train. Patterson wrote a popular book in 1907 called *The Man Eaters of Tsavo*. His story inspired a half-dozen other books and some movies, including *The Ghost and the Darkness*, with Michael Douglas and Val Kilmer, made in 1996. And way back in 1952, *Bwana Devil*. I remember jumping out of my skin that day at the Odeon, and I'm glad to learn that there was an actual backstory. The incident also inspired a number of scientific studies and at least three video games.

So we had a pleasant, innocent train ride on a sunny day and admired a number of elephants. Elephants live a long time and have long memories, but I doubt any of these animals were old enough to remember the incident of the man-eating lions in their neighborhood.

Nairobi itself was a big city with tall buildings surrounded by asphalt. We weren't about to spring for a high-priced safari but chose to spend a day in Nairobi National Park, four miles from the city center, with its high-rise skyline off in the haze. And there we saw plenty of African critters; giraffes, zebras, hippos, gazelles, and almost every animal you hope to see in an African wildlife park. The main event took place when our Jeep stopped and we watched a cheetah as it crept up, crouched, then sprinted after her quarry, to pull down some innocent little fur ball, and haul it away for her own private midday meal.

Between the train ride and the suburban wildlife park, we experienced a surprisingly affordable, violent, gory, blood-letting safari. No lions. So be it.

§

*Along the border to Ethiopia and
Somalia anarchy reigns. The police
and military have retreated quite
some distance.*

Richard Leakey

ETHIOPIA
1973

We could see trouble brewing in Addis Ababa, the capital. Anger simmered and sometimes boiled over among the people in the city. More than once, we saw men brawling like schoolboys up and down the streets. Not armed soldiers or police in uniform, just regular local folk swinging their fists in frustration, a prelude to a revolution. Cousin Alex was sitting peacefully by himself in a bar one evening when, out of nowhere, he was threatened by a group of men who palpably intended to do him harm. Lucky for Alex, he could run fast, and he made it inside his hotel with no time to spare, the angry pack close behind. Maybe he said something to set them off, but he had no idea what triggered the threat. He was still quite shaken when he told us about the incident the next day.

We had gone from Nairobi to Addis Ababa by air. We had heard that tribal skirmishes were flaring in isolated hot spots around this part of Africa and it seemed wisest to fly. I'm not sure there were any other ways to get there. Signs at the Addis airport warned against taking photographs, and immigration officials were keenly alert, standing up straight and looking deep into our eyes and our baggage. Everyone was a suspect.

We knew Ethiopia was suffering from a severe drought, and we were careful not to waste water. Our hotel room had a sink, but no water came out of its taps. A nearby native restaurant prepared tasty mysterious meals, plates heaped with good food, but the faucets in the ladies' room produced no water. A boy about eight, dressed like Aladdin, stood next to the lavatory. He held a wine bottle with an ounce or two of water in it, which he gently poured on my hands over the sink. It was a sweet gesture, and came with an adorable smile, something we didn't often get to exchange in this country. We slinked past the Hilton Hotel after noticing the outdoor fenced-in swimming pool shimmering full of turquoise water, and nobody using the pool. It must have infuriated the Ethiopians. I felt embarrassed for my own culture's profligacy, as well as for my own intervals between showers.

We didn't peek into the Hilton. There were no signs of activity around the place, and few hints of visitors of any sort, anywhere. We had lost the trail of our fellow travelers, the backpackers and adventure-seekers, once we arrived in Africa. Most of that crew, so helpful with information and advice, must have kept going from Bombay up through Pakistan, Afghanistan and beyond.

I hadn't imagined so many varieties of facial features under one ancient flag. This is not a country of immigrants, as we call ourselves. We saw people in the city with filed-down sharp-pointed canine teeth or with symmetrical scarred skin but they were exceptions, not the norm. There are more than eighty ethnic groups in this country and it showed. Many were strikingly beautiful and some became international fashion models or super-athletes.

Emperor Haile Selassie claimed to be a direct descendant of King Solomon and the Queen of Sheba. He had big brown puppy-dog eyes and fine features, like so many of his people. He was a popular leader for most of his reign, but we were hearing rumors of his crumbling majesty. His subjects were certainly mad at somebody. We behaved, kept a low profile. Tim and I blithely ate well, unaware of the famine in northeast Ethiopia that was killing tens of thousands, maybe more. There were no beggars on the streets, only amateur pugilists. If we had known about the famine, should we have stayed away? Eaten less? Am I too wishy-washy liberal? The emperor also claimed he was unaware that his people were starving, but he presumably had more access to information, and to sources of aid.

Haile Selassie's reign was teetering, but he was still hanging on in 1973 when we visited his kingdom. He wasn't making public appearances any more, and his opulent palace looked both well-guarded and abandoned the day we walked past it. A few months later the country faced what was called a "creeping coup" by the military, followed shortly after, in 1974, by a revolution. The emperor was deposed, his friends and family incarcerated, and he died, either of natural causes or assassination, depending on your sources, in August 1975.

While Britain and other European countries collected colonies well before the First World War, Italy had a late start. But in the period called the scramble for Africa, Italy acquired a sizable chunk of northeast Africa, including Ethiopia.

The Italians, who technically lost control of their colony in the early 1940s, were encouraged by Haile Selassie to remain in place. During the Italian colonization of Ethiopia, from 1936 to 1941, the country's infrastructure was stabilized and modernized, and the emperor, pleased with the results, declared his approval, inviting the Italians to stick around.

The influence of Italy was conspicuous in the number of restaurants we found on the streets of Addis. I thought I could read an Italian menu—you know, "spaghetti, lasagna, pizza"—until I read one here. The lists were long, offering choices in detailed Italian-language descriptions and served up in generous heaps. Until that day, I didn't know that "chicken" was "pollo," and that was the easiest one to decode. Famine? Not around here.

Evelyn Waugh, doing some research before heading to Ethiopia for Haile Selassie's coronation in 1930, found an obscure encyclopedia item about the people. "Though nominally Christian, the Abyssinians are deplorably lax in their morals, polygamy and drunkenness being common even among the highest classes and in the monasteries," the encyclopedia said. In his book *Remote People*, Waugh responded with "Everything I heard added to the glamour of this astonishing country," as he eagerly packed his bags to go there.

Midway through our stay, Tim and I took a trip from Addis to the city of Djibouti, a French outpost where the Gulf of Aden meets the Red Sea. Alex left in another direction and we caught up with him again a month or so later. Djibouti is a major port for ship traffic squeezing around the Horn of Africa, bordered by Eritrea to the north, Somalia to the southeast, and Ethiopia all around the rest. The outpost had a long-standing relationship with France, but today it is an independent country. When we were there the area was called the French Territory of the Afars and the Issas. Too much to say. Now it's less of a mouthful—it's just called Djibouti.

We went by train, an overnight trip. The countryside on the way was the bleakest I have seen. It is called a desert, but it doesn't have any pretty swells of golden sand, just flat gray dirt, blowing with fine gray dust, devoid somehow of any sign of life. With all the world's variety, and all the wondrous photography we see, we expect that, one way or another, all the world is beautiful. Not so. Not here. It was as alien, inhospitable and grim as Pluto. Probably.

The people we saw from the train were long and lean, draped in sarongs and robes, barefoot, holding wooden staffs like shepherds from the Bible. Some carried spears with metal tips forged from bits of steel snitched from the railroad tracks. They stood lined up next to the tracks to see the train go by. The train watchers we saw, men and women alike, had formidable scarring scratched into their arms and faces, cheeks and foreheads. They looked as though they'd been carved up with knives by a butcher with a sense of symmetry. Nobody waved at us. Their canine teeth had been filed down and sharpened to points, as if some dentist had a powerful pencil sharpener, a look that doesn't flatter anybody. We sometimes saw a person in Addis who must have come from this tribe but here they all looked that way. Their hair was mostly matted with butter and mud. The train, I'm glad to say, kept chugging along.

Early the next morning we were awakened in our sleeping car by two friendly border guards standing over us, speaking bits of French, as in "bon jour," wearing their French Foreign Legion pillbox hats with the little curtains hanging down the sides and back. The train had stopped at the border. I was surprised to see these guys. We thought we were dreaming, seeing some old clunker of a movie. Whether we were hallucinating about the Abbott and Costello comedy, or a Ronald Coleman stiff-upper-lip drama, the scene was a wake-up treat. In the past, the unit had the reputation of being a refuge for any grown-up male, from any part of the world, who needed to run away from home. But the legion is more strict and decorous these days, thanks to deep background checks and hardcore military training. The unit has been militarily involved in virtually every contentious action from the colonial concerns of the 1830s to ongoing operations in Afghanistan.

Djibouti is an important lookout post for all sorts of military interests, including the U.S. There has been talk for years about building a bridge to span the eighteen-mile stretch across the Mandab Strait, which separates Djibouti from Yemen on the Arabian peninsula. The bridge plan has been postponed a number of times, as Yemen is a country with a great many troubles, including civil war, a cholera epidemic, starvation, and nests of terrorists.

In Djibouti city itself we were charmed by the postcard image of outdoor restaurants with little round café tables under umbrellas advertising aperitifs and digestifs. French-looking people nibbled on flaky croissants and dark café, speaking French, or doing *le shopping* on the boulevards, looking elegantly Parisian. We knew, Toto, that we weren't in Ethiopia any more.

On our way back to Addis Ababa, the border guards were no longer those suave French Foreign Legionnaires. Now we had Ethiopian officials, armed with wooden cudgels, intent on beating up on Ethiopians who tried to smuggle a few items home from their trip. The man behind us on the train was wearing several dress shirts, each collar folded on top of the other, not at all hidden. I don't know what he expected but he was beaten senseless in front of us for his crime. Another man was hunched down on the cinders in front of the train's door. He curled up in a ball, being pounded with sticks by several officials at once for having too many cartons of Gauloises. A kind of helpless fear overtook us in the presence of these beatings, and Tim and I scurried away, unable to witness any more violence.

Heading back on the train to Addis, we noticed that savvy passengers were leaping up to close their windows. There was no sense of impending rain, the sky above was clear and bright blue, but when I looked to the southwest, a wall of caramel brown was heading toward us, and would soon blank everything in our view. A sandstorm was coming our way. All the windows in our car were tightly closed. Just as our modern world is smothered in a blanket of white fluff when our airplane dives into a cloud bank, we were enveloped in an opaque brindle mud bath. Amazingly, I could still breathe. But I kept my eyes shut; I had my contacts on and didn't want to risk getting any of that grit in my face. Imagine, if you will, the claustrophobic sensation of speeding along through a tunnel of solid brown.

At the Ethiopian Airlines office, pretty young women in aerodynamic uniforms manned the counter. Crisp and professional as they looked, they had that facial scarring, the knife wounds, on their faces, necks and hands. We were a little skittish about air travel in developing countries; this didn't help. Someone said the best way to see Ethiopia was a travel film shown at the airport. So we could have flown through, watched the movie on our stopover, and been better informed. Or differently informed.

The flight out to Khartoum was smooth and uneventful, as we had hoped.

§

How do men act on a sinking ship?
Do they hold each other? Do they
pass around the whiskey? Do they
cry?

Sebastian Junger

KHARTOUM, SUDAN
1973

Our hotel's Italian manager appeared to be single and lonely, glad to have company, somebody to talk to. During one of our conversations with him, we asked how to find the spot where the White Nile meets the Blue, and he eagerly offered to drive us there. We accepted, and saw the place where the river water, blue from one stream, meets with the dominant white stream, and stays white for the rest of the trip all the way north to the Mediterranean. Tim and I had just read two histories by Alan Moorehead, one called *The White Nile*, and its companion, *The Blue Nile*. Excellent books; we both remember them all these decades later. Mystery and wonder accompany these waterways, as I thought again about their sources and their journeys so deep in this forbidding continent. There were no stone monuments or bronze markers at the site to designate the confluence. Just some mud and weeds at the juncture. We would not have found it on our own.

The city sprawled around us, low-rise buildings of stone or brick in shades of sand and gray. Minarets pierced the skyline here and there, as did the swollen bulbous roofs of other mosques. For a desert community, there were a lot of trees along the wide streets.

Just as interesting after all was seeing the Sudanese people. Sudanese men, I should say. I don't think we saw a grown woman in the city, even in the markets, the souks, certainly not in a restaurant. The men were uniformly big and very black, dressed in graceful robes, and generally in the company of other men, who looked the same. We dined in the candle-lit courtyard at the rear of the hotel, a feast of barbecued meat, probably beef, juicy delicious slabs whatever it was, medium-rare, served in the dark and presented to the restaurant's full capacity of large men, who applauded every few minutes. I don't know why—maybe in praise of the food or maybe we had horned in on a Rotary Club meeting.

We got up one morning in the wee hours to beat the rush for seats on the northbound train that follows the Nile downstream. The route out of Khartoum was an S-curved rail line through the Nubian Desert to the Egyptian border at Wadi Halfa. It was another all-day and overnight excursion. Even though we had learned by now how to elbow our way toward a seat on a train, we were definitely outshoved and outwitted by the expert locals. We were among the earliest, we thought, to arrive at the platform, but once we got pushed aboard, the seats were all occupied, some by earlier birds, mostly by soldiers with rifles, saving the seats for their friends. Khartoum was not a crowded city. Now I know why. The people were all at the train station waiting to board this particular coach. Filling the train looked like that rush-hour photograph you've seen of people being jammed into subway cars in Tokyo by white-gloved officials who are on the platform to squeeze in every last body. And so we stood, jammed in, rebreathing someone else's breath, smothering in someone's else's loose clothing, unable to move, no room to sit on the filthy floor. No way to get down there, even if you didn't mind the dirt.

Out the window the desert was bleakly empty. Once in a while we passed a village of round windowless mud huts with straw roofs like upside-down sparrow's nests, built close together and sheltered by a handful of date palms all around, often a donkey standing patiently out front in the desert heat. Then miles of plain desert, another little clustered village, more desert, another village.

When I worked in Vancouver, I once interviewed a woman from Sudan. I don't remember why she was good subject material, but I do remember her tears, telling me how much she missed her home in the Nubian Desert. At the time I thought maybe it was the winter, or Vancouver's rainy season that turned her off. After seeing this landscape I wondered all the more about her longings. But as the train rolled along, I now knew it wasn't for the aesthetic attraction of the village, nor the comforts of the little hut, but rather the yearning for the love of the family she had left behind, the safety of familiar faces, a handful of dates from the trees, even the old donkey waiting out there so loyally.

Standing in that tight spot on the train for so many hours, that many miles, exacted an absolute weariness. As darkness fell, our feet hurt first, then the rest of our bodies began to cry for a change of position, a good shake. The train stopped in the middle of nowhere, and stayed that way for a long time. Finally we were told that the tracks were flooded with sand and grit after a sandstorm, and would have to be dug out.

The doors opened and people began to spill into the black night air. We took deep breaths. Tim and I joined the spread-out crowd, lay on the sand and slept, just plain slept—all that air, and horizontal too. Gravity never felt so good. Supine had never been so rewarding. After several hours of this, word came to board again. We stood for a few more hours, rolling right along, when suddenly, in the darkness, with nothing out there, the train stopped again, and began to empty out.

We grabbed seats—we chose upholstered seats—and snuggled in for a little comfort. It was almost morning. The train was unloading in the middle of nowhere, no railroad station, no roads, no buildings. No cars parked out there or driving past. No message from a loudspeaker. Just a muted dawn light in the wide open sky and desert all around us. Then we realized the train was empty except for the two of us. We decided this must be the end of the line. This had to be Wadi Halfa.

A wadi means an oasis but we didn't see any sanctuary here, just sand and sky. The train's passengers scattered in every direction. We had no clue which way to go. We just stood there, vulnerable. Finally we saw a heavy truck with wooden slats around the open bed carrying a few standees. The truck drove toward us in the faint dawn, headlights on, over the unmarked earth. The driver signaled us to hop in the back. Despite not knowing where we were going or who our companions might have been, we climbed in, numb with fearful ignorance. What choice did we have.

This, it turned out, was the right thing to do, our ride to the Nile, to a boat that promised to take us further downstream to Aswan in Egypt. I can't imagine how the truck driver knew where to go. There were no indications. We were along for the ride. I don't think he could see the train tracks from his angled route. No road, no signposts, no trees, no ruts in the sand. Maybe he navigated by the fading stars as the sun began to rise.

The morning was as clear and pure as air can be, pale tawny expanses of sand in every direction, intense unblemished blue sky above, smelling like pure oxygen. You know how the world is absolutely round when you're standing in a wide open space or sailing the open sea? This was Wadi Halfa at the start of the day, and we were at the dead center of the curving earth, happily standing in the back of a half-ton truck as it thumped across the Nubian Desert at daybreak. I felt like Florence of Arabia.

The dock was a rickety wooden pier between the bulrushes edging the Nile. It reminded me of the baby Moses bobbing around in his little basket in the current.

The steamship, called the *Tenth of Ramadan,* looked tattered, probably held a few hundred passengers, mostly men, many of whom dressed in sky-blue jalabiyyas, long loose cotton robes. We had places to sit and soak up the desert sun as we sailed merrily along Lake Nasser. We had a fine view of Abu Simbal, the majestic temple of the sixty-seven-foot-tall Ramesses seated on his throne, his favorite wife Nefertari, and another couple, all looking out over the manmade lake like vacationers on their cottage porch. We had pre-booked a cabin with a mattress, thank God, and had a measure of comfort and privacy at night, drifting along the ancient river. After the train and truck ride, this was all a body could ask for.

§

A decade later, in 1983, *The New York Times* reported that the *Tenth of Ramadan* was on a routine trip between Wadi Halfa and Aswan when the steamer, carrying 627 people, caught fire and sank in the lake behind the Aswan Dam.

Some 325 people were rescued, though a number of them were badly injured; at least one had been stung by a scorpion after swimming to shore, and was in critical condition.

Later reports said that 350 people had died.

§

The Internet is like Ancient Egypt.
People write on walls and worship
cats.

Unknown

EGYPT
1973

I don't know how King Tut, Solomon or Jesus could walk around the desert with just flip-flops on their bare feet. They probably would have worn socks if socks had been available at the time. After our first day in Egypt, Tim and I learned to start our daily tours of Luxor and Karnak at the crack of daylight, as the temperature hit forty-plus degrees Centigrade—well over a hundred Fahrenheit—shortly after breakfast. My toes and the exposed parts of my feet in their sandals were smote with hot sand and throbbed from being incinerated. In submission and desperation, we spent the afternoons in an air-conditioned hotel bar, watching the large thermometer on the wall climb toward the boiling point. The centrally placed thermometer was the focal point of the room, and it got a lot of attention. Meanwhile, we kept cool sipping drinks with ice until the sun slipped behind the dunes.

Our first night in Luxor, fresh off the Nile boat, we slept in a bargain hotel room with no air conditioning and only one window, opened as wide as possible. The still air was torrid, downright feverish, and sleep wasn't possible. We took the hotel's big towels, saturated them from the cold water faucet (as if there was any other kind) and draped them, still dripping, over our naked bodies in the bed. The air was so dry, we got up in the night to replenish the wetness. The next day we upgraded, checked into "the nicest hotel since Ipoh," according to a journal Tim was keeping.

Luxor and Karnak are side-by-side cities, like Minneapolis and St. Paul. There was no shortage of sights to see. We hired an elderly gentleman as our private tour guide to show us the tombs in Karnak, in the Valley of the Kings. He told us he was present at the scene in 1921 when Howard Carter walked down the now-exposed sand-sprinkled steps and broke through the door to King Tut's well-concealed tomb. The discovery was fifty-some years before our visit, and our venerable guide recalled many details of that exciting time. The young king, after all, had rested undisturbed for more than three thousand years. The big whitewashed space was emptied of all its great treasures, including, so I've read, 145 pairs of royal underwear. Our guide in his cornflower blue caftan was well versed in the drama and history of Tutankhamun's short life and long death. He was also a little peeved and scolded us because we hadn't done much homework before showing up at the famous Karnak site. We didn't try to excuse ourselves, to explain our recent activities and distractions. "Yours wasn't the only magnificent, splendiferous, awe-inspiring wonder of the world on our itinerary," I didn't say out loud.

We entered and examined other tombs. Most of their treasures and mummies had been moved to museums, but still-visible artwork and hieroglyphics appeared faintly on the clean, off-white walls. We walked between the pillars of Karnak, whose height and majesty intimidated us as much as it must have done to everyone else for the past three thousand years. Only a small portion of the monumental city of Thebes, now called Luxor, was open to the public. It is so vast it took the reigns and slaves of some thirty pharaohs to complete it. Many pharaohs died young, but still, that's a lot of pharaohs.

We were now fully embedded in the Muslim world and only vaguely familiar with proper appearance and behavior. I knew I mustn't wear shorts but didn't think twice about a short sleeveless top exposing two inches of bare midriff. Cool. I didn't cover my head except for a hat with a brim to keep the sun out. Neither did I know I should keep my upper arms covered.

§

The train took us into Cairo, where we were greeted by a cluster of touts who were well versed in a singsong version of "Welcome to Cairo." We allowed the most brazen of them to take us to a hotel on a quiet street around the corner from the luxury hotels.

This was not the sort of low-budget backpacker hotel we had been patronizing for most of the past ten months. This was a nice, middle-of-the road hotel. Our room was in the crotch of another wing of the building, looking diagonally across and into the adjoining bedroom. And there, through the window, we saw our neighboring occupant and—what do you know—he was Cousin Alex. These things happen. Alex would have spotted us sooner or later, as Tim had placed a dikdik skull on our windowsill to dry it out a little. He bought the skull somewhere in Africa and Alex surely would have recognized it. Who else in Cairo would put a dikdik skull on the window ledge? We expressed our surprise at the coincidence, and we all walked over to the nearby Hilton and exchanged catch-up stories over dinner.

Our urban outings began at the Cairo National Museum. The first large object we saw inside the museum's entrance was an oversized pharaoh couple carved from Lebanese cedar, seated on cedar thrones. The ancient paint and gold leaf had faded and flaked, but their shiny glass eyes followed us around the room. Yikes. The story goes that the laborers who first dug up the figures fled in fear when they saw those realistic staring eyes. I'm sure I saw this in a scary movie in the fifties.

The sculpture was a startling introduction to Egypt's national treasures, though the collection's home was sadly in need of attention and maintenance. The air was thick with ancient dust, the light was dim, the display rooms doubled as storage space. Relics were stacked in crates in corners of the exhibition spaces, while mummies and more sculpted figures with realistic watchful eyes made for goose-pimply touring in the long dark corridors and spacious rooms. Many of the life-sized or bigger statues guarded the passageways with stiff arms and clenched fists, looking furious. In a room of his own, Tut and his worldly goods were spread out for display, except for the pieces that were on tour elsewhere around the world. And all that underwear must be stashed away in there somewhere.

One of the mummies looked a lot like Robert Stanfield, a Canadian Conservative politician who lost the federal election to Pierre Trudeau in the late 1960s. Amazing resemblance—I couldn't stop staring at his Roman nose and hollow cheeks.

Tim and I delighted in shopping in the old market, which didn't feel like a tourist market. The vendors got a kick out of dickering with us; we were such babes. We came away with an armful of brass and copper pots and vessels, dented, dinged and worn at the edges, pre-owned many times, just what we wanted.

And we weren't unhappy about the prices we paid. Everyone was happy.

I took my travel-worn typewriter in for a tune-up at a repair and rental shop near the hotel. The shopkeeper was friendly and curious, and as we chatted he offered to show me how to write in Arabic script. After a few false starts I was fascinated to be able to write my name backwards, right to left, in a cursive script that was much more elegant than my usual chicken-scratch signature. I'm sorry that I've forgotten how to do it; I may have wanted to sign a few documents over the years. I wonder if that's legal.

A short distance from the city are the Giza pyramids and the Great Sphinx. Miscellaneous camels, hoping we would hire them to pose with us for photographs, milled around the site on the sun-bleached day we visited. Since we had begun traveling in camel countries, I'd learned to dislike them. They were resentful of human contact, they made terrible screechy noises and they spit. Rude.

We waited briefly in line to enter the largest and most-photographed pyramid. We had to duck and crawl through a kind of pet door, a deliberately low opening in the stone blocks, made that way to enforce a gesture of respect for the pharaoh who built it, whoever he was.

Plenty of tourists here, as we were moving north and seeing more people with skin colors closer to our own. I noted, with quizzical interest, women with bright red lips, blue eyelids, swaths of pink on their cheeks. I hadn't seen makeup like this since we left Australia. The female fellow travelers we had met so far on this route wore their faces plain.

The Great Sphinx is at the same locale, pummeled by erosion and having had his nose shot off by the invading Turks centuries

193

ago. While we were there the critter was undergoing major repairs and restoration, and was barely visible through a support system of scaffolding. We weren't able to get a close look at his fifty-foot paws or his wounded haunches. But that noble battered head rose proudly above the tumult of braying camels, touts, postcard vendors, tour guides and tourists, ourselves included.

§

The night sky of Egypt is a swirling
mass of stars so bright and
numerous the sky seems to tremble
with the ice-blue weight of them.

Rosemary Mahoney

ALEXANDRIA

1973

Lawrence Durrell reported in one of his *Alexandria Quartet* stories that the Alexandria sky was a hot nude pearl. But that must have been on an off day: Alexandria's sky was flawless azure blue the whole time we were there in the late summer of 1973.

Downtown curled along the Mediterranean shore, a crescent of broad beachfront reminding us of a worn and faded summer resort, the kind that has outlived its notoriety. Our hotel, across the street from the waterfront, had an old-fashioned softness to it, breezes blowing the filmy curtains through the unmet edges of the sagging windows and doors.

The streets, especially at night, were tricked out in a carnival atmosphere, jugglers and fire-eaters along the sidewalks, food and souvenir vendors in a string of little shops selling toys and trinkets made in Japan and Taiwan.

This is where we failed to finish eating the world's worst pizza, an orange-colored disc so slick with oil you could see your face in it. Music and magic saturated the Mediterranean air, and wily con artists tried to sell tourists like us pilfered bottles of Johnnie Walker Scotch ("fell right off the ship") which actually held tea.

Someone went to some trouble to seal it so craftily. And yes, we bought one, and were relieved it was only tea.

§

There comes a time in a man's life when he hears the call of the sea. If the man has a brain in his head, he will hang up the phone immediately.

Dave Barry

THE EASTERN MEDITERRANEAN
1973

One evening we boarded a freighter sailing from Alexandria to Beirut and were shown to our sleeping quarters belowdecks. We were directed to a pair of loopy hammocks among the thirty or forty strung up in one big space, berths meant for the crew and anyone else who showed up. I tried to make myself fit inside my sack even though the drape of the hammock curled me against my will into a fetal position. My discomfort was amplified by the stares and the unmistakable imaginations of the work crew—the men— who were now arriving and settling themselves into their own slings. I felt as though I had been delivered into an animal cage filled with captured wildlife at feeding time. So I whined at Tim, who didn't feel so comfortable himself, and we agreed to go up on the deck and lie down there where it was flat and almost empty.

The broad steel deck, smelling faintly oily, already housed a young German couple, stretched out with some of their clothing wrapped around them, their other possessions carefully tucked away. Tim and I lined up next to them, creating a row of four mummies on the floor. We exchanged pleasantries without anyone bothering to sit up, and we lay in a row on our backs to watch the sky.

It was a lovely starlit late August night on the Mediterranean. With the wattage of millions of stars glittering away up there, I wondered how the sky in the background could be so black. We felt just enough of a breeze to cool the summer air and to make the ship rock like a baby's cradle. We hoped to catch a glimpse of the comet Kohoutek, which was scheduled to pass through these skies any time now. Comet collectors know that Kohoutek was a bust, over-promised and under-delivered. It barely showed up anywhere; it was the laughingstock of the heavenly bodies.

Eventually we gave up watching the night and easily fell asleep. My handbag, which held my passport and wallet and my whole life, was carefully wrapped inside my jacket, serving as a pillow. I was awakened abruptly about three o'clock by a tug on a corner of my purse strap. My eyes popped open and right there I was surprised to see, nose to nose, the close-up of an old fellow in a blue robe and cap, crouching over me with his hand on the corner of my purse with all my valuables. I was now wide awake. I hollered at him—this was an appropriate place to use salty language—and before I could shed the sweater wrapping me in place and hoist myself upright, he disappeared into the night, running with the awkward little steps that some old men acquire in their later years. He was no pro: his thieving hand was too clumsy, his escape too ungainly. Yet he skittered off into the dark like a sprite. He must have stayed on board the ship, as we were out there at sea and there were no in-between stops. I kept looking deeply into one set of dark brown eyes and flowing blue robes after another, but I never saw him again. The old goat, I hope he fell overboard.

§

LEBANON
1973

A snapshot of Beirut's decadent milieu took place early one
Sunday morning when Tim and I were riding in a taxi up the coast
from the city to see the Phoenician ruins at Byblos. A gambling
casino nestled along the Mediterranean shoreline road, at our left.
There, standing at the edge of the casino's driveway, facing the
southbound traffic, was a man in a tuxedo with his bow tie loose
and dangling, and an overnight growth of beard years before it
became stylish—the antithesis of James Bond. Next to him, a
pretty young woman wore a fetching evening gown hanging
bedraggled after a long and sorrowful night on the town. Their
thumbs were out, hitchhiking back to the city. It seemed a good
guess that they had gambled away all their money, and couldn't
afford a taxi to town. One of those images, frozen in our
memories, a keepsake to illustrate a cautionary tale.

Before Lebanon's civil war began in 1975, Beirut was the
bridge between traders in the European and the Arab markets, a
commercial and banking haven with all the attendant vices that
can be assembled in a Middle Eastern setting. On the city's west
side, the Paris/Vegas big-spender sector of the city, we sat on stools
overlooking a lighted glass wall, behind which a number of lightly

clad, mermaid-finned women dived and soared through a deep turquoise pool of water to amuse us lunch patrons. This was the glitzy neighborhood of glass towers and shops like Balenciaga, Hermès, Louis Vuitton, Dior, Yves Saint Laurent and Chanel. If I had a gazillion dollars I wouldn't patronize shops like these. Well, maybe for a Hermès scarf.

Because of its fluid financial atmosphere, Tim and I chose Beirut as a drop-off point in requesting more money from our savings at home. The transactions required the use of old-style mail and forms to be filled out, so we waited in Beirut longer than seemed necessary for our funds to arrive. We stayed in a part of the city where the buildings were shuttered at night with stretchable iron grates and the signs were written in flowing Arabic script. All the structures were in shades of Middle Eastern sand, unlike the glass and steel towers a few blocks away. We faced Martyrs Square, a short walk uphill from the dock where we had disembarked. And where parades took place, not jolly upbeat parades, but political, religious or funereal; it was hard to tell which was which. All of them at once, I think. When protesters gathered here outside our balcony, it was with sadness and resolve, rather than imminent fury. That was two years away.

We were not thinking about revolutions. For weeks or months now, we had been reminiscing about various food items that we missed. We both yearned, for example, for mashed potatoes. Rice and french fries dominated the world's starchy side dishes; we seldom saw other choices. We frequently asked, just in case, for mashed. Finally, in a café near our hotel, the waiter nodded yes when we inquired. In celebration we ordered T-bones to go with the long-contemplated humble spuds. Our meal was delivered with a flourish. They looked like mashed potatoes. We dug in. The potatoes were ice-cold, straight from the refrigerator.

While we waited for our money to arrive, we adopted a female marmalade cat and named her Audrey Hepburn because she was so skinny. We were staying in a '50s-modern hotel, second floor, with a little balcony overlooking the square. Our first day there, this exceedingly thin little cat arrived at our sliding glass door. It was obvious she was a new mother. Audrey may have recognized that we were the types who always had food on hand. In fact, we had some ham and cheese, and happily shared them with her. Audrey returned alone the next day, just to be sure we were sincere. On the third day, she came with three small kittens, and we had a party. They showed up every day for several weeks while we were in Beirut, and left through the slider after dark. We could only hope that the next occupants of the room were similarly indulgent. Maybe they would be Egyptians with traditional values.

I felt torn about feeding and nurturing these little cats, knowing we would be moving on, but hoped we were buying Audrey and her kittens some time to grow and fatten up. I worried about her again when the civil war began two years later. My first thought when hearing that the war had started was "Oh Audrey, I hope you're safe." Why is it that people—or at least this one—can be empathetic toward a small animal in harm's way, but so unconcerned about all the human beings in the same sinking boat? In this case, we hadn't adopted any humans. Mea culpa.

§

Walking is a virtue, tourism is a deadly sin.

Bruce Chatwin

SYRIA
1973

We were unable to locate train or bus service from Beirut to Damascus, and so we went in a shared taxi. It wasn't far, but it was a long ride, considering the forlorn frontier and the sourpuss company of our fellow passenger, an elderly Arab woman who refused to smile or make eye contact. I decided to watch out the window for shepherds tending their flocks, but the aspect was bleak and dull all the way to the boundary.

The Syrian official at the isolated border crossing didn't seem glad to see us either. He wasn't busy. Our taxi was the only vehicle to arrive at the crossing, and no one else was waiting on foot. Our fellow passenger sailed through and disappeared into a waiting car on the other side. At our turn, the functionary in his brown uniform and duly authorized scowl inspected our documents, opened our suitcases and hand baggage and dumped everything out on a table. He rifled through our clothes with his hands, flipping things around, digging into pockets. Then he turned and left, leaving a messy mound for us to repack. As he walked away he looked both angry and disappointed by our failure to commit an international crime.

We were driven into town on the road to Damascus, or at least a wide road into Damascus, which may have been the most monumental site on this leg of our trip, if it was *that* road. We had no way to find out. We rented a room in a quasi-residential neighborhood, could not find anyone who would tell us about the history, the culture, the archeology, the hot spots of Damascus.

We walked around the city streets, hopped on buses that looked promising, and toured various commercial, industrial and residential districts, but saw nothing more than one handsome old mosque with a bulbous top and no apparent way to find out if it had any significance. Tourism wasn't part of Damascus's business plan.

But we did see a memorable people scene. We happened to be walking on a downtown street when a bus full of people from Denmark began to unload in front of a big hotel. The visitors were attractive fair-haired women, dressed in bikini tops and shorts so short they exposed pink globules of buttocks. Maybe they were athletes of some sort, probably not dancing girls. They looked strong and fit. The women were unmindful of the numbers of Syrian men who had collected on the sidewalk at the entrance to the hotel. The men stood in a cluster, gawking back and forth between each other and the disembarking passengers, eyebrows raised, jaws agog. I expected one of them to walk into a telephone pole. The bus driver stooped over the baggage hold, intent on unloading luggage, not looking at either group, not taking sides.

In the same neighborhood, the Syrian women we saw were covered from crown to toenails in black cloaks and niqabs, veils that covered their faces. Even their eyes were hidden behind opaque patches of loosely woven black cotton the size of a cigarette pack, sewn into their head coverings.

At night, in the peace and dark of our room, we could hear distant thundering noises coming from far away. I awoke fearing another Mideastern war had started, but was told next morning that no, it was just customary noises coming from the airport.

§

*I wanted to become a policeman
because I wanted to be in a business
where the customer is always wrong.*

Arlene Heath

JORDAN
1973

Another taxi took us to Jordan, which was our gateway to Israel. We had chosen to make Israel the last stop on this circuit, as the Islamic countries were denying entry to people who had Israel stamped in their passports.

Our hotel room in Amman was next to a bathroom with a shower that noisily splat and dripped but provided no running water when the faucet was turned on. It was a hot night and we both longed for a shower and a drink, even a tepid rusty one. There were no stores nearby. Our only recourse was to hold a cup under the dribbling tap until we collected enough drops of water for a good gulp. Never mind how it tasted.

Late that same night we were awakened by a loud knock on the door, a midnight visit from two Jordanian policemen. I don't remember if they waited for us to open the door or barged in without an invitation. We had been sound asleep. The hotel desk clerk who checked us in and withheld our passports tagged along —reluctantly, we could tell. The poor clerk trembled in the doorway, afraid he had committed a terrible mistake. I was both baffled and frightened, with no sense of the trouble we may have caused, only a fear of dreaded jackboots intruding in the dark of night. Their charge was that we were unmarried and sharing a room. We lied and insisted we were married. Tim pointed out that our passports, which one of the policemen was holding, showed we had been traveling together for almost a year now. The police didn't know what to do next; they probably just wanted to go for coffee, so they shrugged and left, thank you, Allah. The desk clerk may have decided to look into a new career.

The longer we stayed away from home, the more we succumbed to what Tim called Giddison's disease—outbursts of hysterical laughter that had no justifiable provocation. It was caused by too much travel. With Giddison's, something serious or something silly would set us off, like our late-night police visit, and we would start to laugh and not be able to stop—like a pair of thirteen-year-olds.

In daylight, we went to the government offices to apply for visas and travel permits to cross the Jordan River by way of the Allenby Bridge into Israel. To Jordanians, the bridge is the King Hussein Bridge. To Palestinians it's the Al-Karemeh bridge. On the Israeli side it crosses into the West Bank; this is the only border location where Palestinians were allowed to cross. An interesting mixed group of people gathered at the Allenby Bridge on the Jordanian side waiting for the bus to carry us across. One man asked me to carry a package for him. "Just some photographs," he promised. "No thank you, please," I said. He smiled, I smiled. He didn't get on the bus; he was still looking for a messenger as our bus drove away.

§

It ain't those parts of the Bible that I can't understand that bother me; it's the parts that I do understand.

Mark Twain

ISRAEL
1973

Our hotel was in the Arab Quarter in Jerusalem, across the street from a little park that housed a certified first-century tomb in a cave where many Protestants believe Jesus was laid to rest. As a drop-out of a Lutheran Sunday school, I knew all the New Testament stories. This was a holy-moly moment. I was quite excited by the idea that we were sleeping across the street from Jesus. Jesus himself had been interred RIGHT ACROSS THE STREET. At the nearest corner, a parking lot for buses lined up against a stone cliff shaped like a skull. The word *golgotha* is Aramaic for "skull." Golgotha = skull = proof. The geology around here convinced me that this had to be the place. I very much wanted it to be. When we went inside the park, called the Garden Tomb, and walked into the opening where the stone had been rolled away, we found an empty rock cave surrounded by understated informal gardens. Tim bent over and pocketed a small pebble from the floor of the cave, a gift he later presented, along with its provenance, to his old buddy John Alley, who may or may not have had any faith in this story. A true story.

We went to the official site of Golgotha, or Calvary, built in 333 by Constantine, blocks away from the true site and inside the old city. It is called the Church of the Holy Sepulchre, a formal gilded dazzling spectacle of a cathedral choking with incense. The real Golgotha has been in question since the fourth century. I preferred the uncluttered, fresh-air cave in the garden across from our hotel. Jesus was a simple unpretentious liberal guy; that's my belief.

We joined a bus tour to see Hebron in the West Bank, where we were shown Adam and Eve's graves. A likely story. The guide casually mentioned that it had been several months since protesters had bombed a tourist bus in Hebron. A more likely likely story. We went to Bethlehem to see the manger, not a stable as I'd been given to understand, but another unadorned cave next to the suburban streets, which were lined with small shops selling olivewood figures of typical Christmas tableaux.

Inside the old walled city of Jerusalem, we walked the Via Dolorosa, where Jesus had carried his heavy cross through the ancient streets. The walk is reenacted each year by pilgrims. Walking these narrow stone streets felt hauntingly timeless. People wore the same robes from the same pattern they sewed two thousand years ago. The tiny shops were crammed with merchandise that had barely changed since New Testament times. No postcards, snow globes, T-shirts, Coke machines. Many of the women here wore tunics with exquisite embroidery circling the throat or the hem. I didn't see any shops selling them, unfortunately. A few years later I bought a similar blouse at a yard sale in West Tisbury, hosted by a woman who had lived in Afghanistan. But it didn't have the same sentiment. One near exception on the Via Dolorosa: I'd been looking for a zipper to replace one that had broken on my handbag. I asked several people how to say "zipper" in Hebrew and in Arabic. And what do you know, I found one along this spiritual path. It isn't often that you can visit such an emotionally stirring site, and at the same time find a dime-store item that you have been searching for. Not that anyone ever asked, "Hey, where did you get that zipper?"

We had moved on to Tel Aviv, and we knew that Yom Kippur would be observed the next day. Don't expect the restaurants to be open, or the evening entertainment venues up and running, we were told. It's a very quiet day here, they repeated. We brought in some food, I repaired my handbag, and we went to see *The Day of the Jackal*, playing nearby. When we entered the theater we were thoroughly scrutinized, the contents of my bag and Tim's pockets examined before we were shown a seat. The inspection was not unusual; we had been checked out at most other stops in the Middle East, but this time it seemed more intense. There weren't many people in the theater, but this was a serious time for penance and reconciliation.

We enjoyed the movie; we walked back to the hotel on quiet, dark, empty mid-city streets. It was around ten o'clock; you'd think it was four in the morning. The streetlights and building lights were turned off, which didn't seem all that odd considering we had been in plenty of places lately that had little or no electricity. Still, walking around a modern city in blackness was disquieting. There were very few pedestrians afoot. A solitary man ran toward us, screaming something we couldn't understand, his hands waving in the air. We were curious about the few cars driving by, their headlights covered with blue paper or plastic. I later learned that these shields had slotted covers to deflect the light beams downward, so they couldn't be seen by enemy aircraft. But at the time, Tim and I decided we had underestimated the depth of atonement and repentance the Israelis espoused on this most holy of days.

We returned to the hotel, we went to bed. We got up the next morning and I went down to the front desk to ask about catching the ferry to Cyprus, which was not far away, and which was about to host a festival. The man at the front desk said he didn't expect the ferries would be running. I asked, "Why not?"

"Because of the war," he said.

"What war?" I asked. He literally slapped his forehead with the heel of his hand. Oy.

While we were peacefully reading in our hotel room the previous afternoon, Egypt and Syria launched a joint attack. Egyptian forces crossed the Suez Canal unopposed and moved into the Sinai Peninsula. Meanwhile, Syrian troops entered the Golan Heights. The conflict was already being called the Yom Kippur War. The next morning, the downtown streets were lined with television sets moved outdoors and tuned to a news channel, with clusters of people gathered around watching events unfold. We tried to watch as well, but it was all in Hebrew. All we knew was there was a lot of activity on those television screens, and a rapid high-pitched male voice describing the scenes.

After breakfast Tim and I returned to our room to rearrange our plans. Scratch Cyprus. We'll get there another time. Tim, who had been a faithful blood donor for many years, went to find a Red Cross location to roll up his sleeve. I went in search of a wire service news agency that would let me file my account to *The Vancouver Sun*. On this crazy news day, the bureau chief was sternly against letting a freelancer use the service. I had to insist, although I had no recent credentials. I really didn't mind his gruffness. I was sympathetic; he'd probably been up all night. He finally reluctantly agreed to give me access. I suspect I was able to feign toughness because he was eating a sandwich and had some lettuce stuck between his front teeth. It gave me courage. So I filed my story without a thought of being censored by the Israeli military; I hadn't given away any secrets. But I got a phone call from a censor who scolded me for changing an adjective after my article had been approved. Hey, this was my first war. I promised it wouldn't happen again.

We didn't usually go anywhere with pre-planned rules, but before we decided to visit Israel we had agreed we would never fly in or out of the country, and we swore we definitely would not ever fly on El Al. Too many unpleasant incidents haunted the airline's recent history. It was time to leave Israel. Without a pause, we went directly to El Al and were advised to show up at the airport at midnight for an unscheduled flight to Athens. We went, of course. We were thoroughly examined in little curtained booths, Tim more intimately and bodily than I. Then his camera was aimed at the ceiling and clicked, just once, to make sure it wasn't an explosive device.

An older man who would be boarding with us had a panic attack in the terminal. He was shaking. He was grabbing people's clothing. He was in tears. He was afraid he wouldn't get home to Montreal. He noticed that my passport was Canadian and he latched on to me—literally, clinging to me for some kind of tribal support. He told me he had been imprisoned at Buchenwald as a child, and couldn't handle another such terrifying experience. Poor guy. One of the El Al stewardesses comforted him and helped him settle down. He was quiet once we were on the plane, although we sat there without moving most of the night.

When everyone was seated, a stewardess came by handing out pamphlets called "Drawing Near: The Lord's Prayer as Our Guide to Approaching the Almighty God." It began "Dear Lord, save us from enemy ambush . . . ," which of course didn't calm anyone's jitters. You never never want a flight attendant asking you to pray. Then she disappeared behind the little curtain, the plane sat on the ground and we waited for hours that felt like weeks. I'm happy to report it was an uneventful flight, and we got into Athens on a bright sunny morning. The customs and immigration guys at the Athens gate waved us through, with big happy smiles for us, didn't ask for any documentation, didn't look in our baggage. They knew where we had just been.

§

ATHENS
1973

We sent telegrams home, declaring our safe arrival, before we checked into a seedy hotel in the Plaka district near Syntagma Square in Athens, central to all we needed. We were installed again in a tight colony of hippie hangouts. I don't remember how we found our way, but our fellow hotel guests were a familiar looking crew, last seen somewhere in India. Winding alleyways, too narrow for vehicles, charmed us with their very cheap hotels and markets and—ahem—authenticity. (The settlement was the original Athens millennia ago.) I heard later that the government shut down the loud music and tossed out the undesirables sometime later in the '70s, but the little inner village was its own Haight Ashbury when we were there. Among the shops we were curious to patronize was a hole in the wall, a doorway wide, where retsina was sold in bulk. The bitter wine was poured from a large dented metal vat into a bring-your-own container. Retsina tastes like sucking on a hawser you found down at the dock but I suppose it could become an acquired taste. Our best sense of the Greekness of the setting was the pleasure of seeing the Acropolis itself high on a ridge above us.

We were near the main government center and presidential palace, where we watched the changing of the guard. Why is it that countries with palaces that change their guards costume them in such silly outfits? In Athens, it's red caps, white puffy sleeves, white pleated miniskirts over tights and puffball tassels attached to their shoes. Except for the rifles they carry on their shoulders, these men don't look at all dangerous.

On a corner straddling the Plaka and the more elegant Syntagma Square, home of the good hotels and American Express, was the brazenly named American Restaurant. Do Greeks say to each other, "Hey, let's go out for American food tonight?" For people like us, who'd been away for a long time, it was a treat to eat a cheeseburger with catsup and fries.

Our digestive systems had become immune to the pestilence we encountered on our journey. Our crumbling old hotel in Athens did have indoor plumbing, but I would have preferred the refreshment of the outdoors. The light bulb in the windowless communal bathroom had burned out and remained that way during most of our stay so I couldn't see the filth of the toilet and bathtub, which enclosed the shower. "Ew," I probably said when the lights came back on. The once-white fixtures crawled with microscopic life, and the floors puddled in slimy earth tones. I did my best to avoid touching anything. I wanted to wear rubber gloves while washing my hands. While the facilities we had encountered until now were generally outdoors and the running water was cold, and scorpions lined up along the ledge of a wash basin somewhere in Indonesia, at least the comfort stations were clean.

I don't know how the connection was made, but Tim's cousin Alex met up with us there. He was staying in a similar hotel a couple of winding alleys away.

Late one night, someone banged on our door and said that Alex was badly injured and had been taken to a hospital. Alex and some fellow travelers, hotel-mates, had been partying one night.

Later, when he should have gone to bed, Alex decided to get a little air and climbed out to an overhanging roof below his window. The roof was not a solid projection but a metal awning that gave way. He fell into an enclosed concrete courtyard a couple of stories down. His neighbors heard his cries, but no one was able to reach him. The ambulance crew had to track down one of the street-level merchants to come and unlock his shop in order to gain access to the courtyard through the back door.

We found the hospital, and found Alex, more than a little woozy. He had some broken bones and a concussion. This was a chilly October for Athens, and it was cold in the frenzied and careless atmosphere of the city hospital, the one where foreigners staying in the Plaka hotel district were delivered. Alex's parents, who were Tim's aunt and uncle, had a friend who was an admiral in the U.S. Navy, based in Athens. They had contacted him asking for his help with Alex's crisis. We dropped in to see the admiral, to offer our services as messengers and delivery people. The admiral looked us over and stepped forward, blocking the door into his home, in case we had thoughts of paying a visit. We must have looked like we belonged in one of those run-down hotels. And he had to be stressed by his job. The local news had reported that an American sailor was charged with murdering an Athens cab driver. The incident provoked some recurring rumbles of expulsion of the U.S. naval presence, taxi drivers were refusing to pick up U.S. servicemen in uniform, and that week our new acquaintance had to deal with problems more onerous than Alex's discomfort.

Still, the admiral arranged for Alex to be moved to a private hospital elsewhere in the city. The upscale hospital was warmer and quieter, had clean sheets on the bed and tasty-looking food on its trays. Alex gradually regained a little color in his cheeks. When he was well enough to be discharged, Alex was booked into a whole row of first-class airline seats and shipped home to southern California. He recovered his good health, and has been hale and whole ever since.

§

If one had but a single glance to give the world, one should gaze on Istanbul.

Alphonse de Lamartine

ISTANBUL
1973

While still camped out in Athens, Tim and I took a train up and around the Aegean to Istanbul. As we approached, the city looked like a big birthday cake, with dozens of minarets like candles pointing to the sky. From the minarets, the muezzin, who is the congregant with the most melodious and loudest voice, called out five times a day the Islamic message for the faithful to kneel and pray. While we traveled in the Middle East, I had grown to love the sound, especially the early morning summons, the ceremony meant to hail a new day.

We admired Topkapi Palace's jewels and treasures, and the seraglio, the village-like harem of the palace, which would be a nice place to live, if you didn't mind sharing your boyfriend with all those other girls.

We walked across a bridge that connects Europe with Asia, feeling rather smug about such a feat. (Many years later, we posed for pictures while straddling the equator in Ecuador—same feeling.)

We fell in love with the casbah, the mosques, the souk; that is, the old city and its markets. In one of them, Tim ordered a hand-tailored leather suit, jacket and pants. It was finished a week or so later, with a surprising Pepto-Bismol-pink slippery polyester lining. And the suit wasn't exactly glove leather, more like shoe leather. Despite the thick skins of the animals that gave up their lives, and the flashy lining, the suit appeared to fit pretty well. Later, as we were leaving Turkey, Tim turned his new ensemble inside out for packing purposes, and the truth revealed itself. Good grief—it was assembled with metal staples instead of thread. No sewing machine needle had been in contact with this ensemble. There were no metal detectors, luckily, when we left the country, or there would have been alarms going off.

§

*I can't think of anything that excited
a greater sense of childlike wonder
than to be in a country where you
are ignorant of almost everything.*

Bill Bryson

MALTA
1973

From a port outside Athens we boarded a ship which took us
alongside the mysterious empty Albanian coast. We didn't see any
harbors, towns, fields, beaches or people—just trees. We sailed
across the Adriatic Sea and landed in Bari in southern Italy. It was
November, but still unseasonably cold for this part of the world
and we had no warm clothes, other than Tim with his leather suit,
so we kept heading south.

We took a train to Sicily, where we were saddened to see that
Chianti wines were now sold in plastic baskets molded to resemble
the raffia baskets they replaced. *Tant pis.* Every spaghetti restaurant
back home recycled the straw baskets into candle holders for
dripping tapers, colorful centerpieces on red-checked tablecloths.
Another lost symbol of a modest but romantic first dinner date.
This was before pizza caught on—at least in Canada.

We kept heading south. Next island over was Malta, a few
hours on a ferry from the southern tip of Sicily. We were charmed
by the ancient walled city of Valletta, where you can see the
Mediterranean from almost any high street. The city is baroquely
sixteenth century, notably designed to accommodate its famous

219

knights. Marble staircases were built with shallow risers, just a few inches high. The knights clunking around in their armor couldn't lift their legs more than a mincing step, and the stairs were designed to compensate for that incapacity. (Though I'm surprised their metal suits were worn while walking around town.) The Maltese language is full of x's and z's in the most unlikely words, a combination of Arabic, Italian and Sicilian with a teaspoon of English, and is the only Semitic language in the European Union. Everyone speaks English; I never had to learn to say "Where is the ladies' room?" in Maltese.

"How was it?" Tim asked.

We celebrated American Thanksgiving in Malta, ordering turkey dinner in the local Hilton. We always seemed to aim for the local Hilton when we needed some home-style comforting. Malta, unfortunately, had serious water problems. The water there was simply not potable. Somehow our turkey got wet before it arrived at our plates and the taste was ruined. No matter—it's only a meal. Otherwise, we loved this little country.

§

Outside the sleet had gotten thicker.
It was the kind of night when you
might expect to see a skeleton flying
through the air.

Dan Chaon

NORTH AFRICA
1973

We didn't have warm clothing but we anticipated some relief from the late November chill when we ferry-hopped another leg across the Mediterranean to the ancient port of Tunis. We admired the delicate wrought-iron Juliet balcony attached to our hotel room's French doors. And a block or two down the street, I coveted the earth-toned geometric Berber carpets in a shop window, but only in an abstract sense; there was no yearning for a room to house these rugs.

By the next day it was too cold and raw to go to any of the granulated-sugar beaches, where we might have seen camels parked on the sand. Or to track down ancient Carthage, which is adjacent to the city, because it was now raining heavily. Although there is a museum, Carthage is so ruined it doesn't have any Carthaginian ruins left, no relics or souvenirs from local hero Hannibal's trek through the Alps, just bits from the conquering Roman empire days, but Roman ruins—may I say it—are everywhere.

Certainly don't go to Tunis if you are gay; executions are not unknown, then and now.

We tried to wait out the weather but gave up after a few days, and boarded a train to Algiers. It was still cold; in fact it was snowing and sleeting in Algiers. Weather was just one of our problems. Unknown to us slaphappy wanderers, a major conference of Middle Eastern heads of state was gathering in Algiers and every hotel room in the city was taken. Places like this didn't have lines of taxis waiting for customers in front of the train station. Nor did they have lockers to stash luggage or a row of phones with direct lines to hotels.

So off we went, on foot, toward the budget hotels in the slushy rain and snow, dragging our suitcases behind us. Maybe those hippie backpacks were a good idea after all. We should have known better—known that of course the heads of state and their entourages would take all the good hotel rooms. If all the crappy hotels were full, there was little point in knocking on the upscale hotel doors. But we didn't think. We slogged to the moderately priced hotels. No luck. We moved on to luxury hotels, on foot, dripping wet. All full, and not exactly welcoming as we dribbled through their lobbies. We were no longer hopeful. We had trudged around the city for hours, a pair of lost puppies. We sloshed back to the train station. There was a roof overhead but no walls, only pillars which couldn't shelter us from the sideways winds and water. We bought tickets and boarded the next train heading west. We were wet and tired, all day and into evening. We got off in Oran, still in Algeria and still soaking.

We'll never forget or forgive Oran. It was late at night and the sleet kept coming. Nobody else got off the train here. Again, no taxi stand. We checked into a scabby old hotel next to the train station. It looked haunted and dingy from the outside, but it had an electric light turned on over the front door and a room available for us.

First, we ventured next door and ordered dinner in a restaurant that had no other patrons. But we couldn't eat it; the plates and silverware had the previous diners' food stuck on them. The waiter had disappeared and I guess the dishwasher hadn't shown up for work. It was about as appealing as the restaurant in Istanbul where the rice on our plates began to get up and walk around. At least in Istanbul, we could walk out and find another restaurant down the street. Who were these people?

When we opened the door to our Oran hotel room I could feel my throat closing up. The bed reeked and we reeled from the stench of urine, a soul-destroying atmosphere. The mattress caved into a well in the middle; the slope was so steep we had to hold on to the bed frame. There was no other hotel or restaurant within sight through the blinding storm. It was dry inside, and we could lie flat, more or less. We stayed for the night, breathing as shallowly as we could, clinging to the edges of the pit.

Despite the insults of that hotel's existence, it was a relief to be under shelter and lying next to a sympathetic source of hugs with the means to get out of town at the soggy crack of dawn.

In my current life, Oran frequently shows up in crossword puzzles and I grit my teeth and fill in the answer while trying to wave away my feelings.

When morning came, we were on the first train west, riding through orange groves blurred by sideways-blowing snow—looking like Saskatchewan with a soupçon of Florida. We rode on to Rabat in Morocco. On board the train we met a young man who wanted to practice his English. This was a familiar request wherever we went, and we always enjoyed talking to these eager youngsters. This man gave us a gift in return—teaching us a few words of Arabic. Unfortunately the only word I can remember is the word for "cold," which is ba-ar-d, pronounced bar-ed or bard. But the way he spoke, it was brrrrrrr, with gales of laughter, never a problem in remembering it. I'm not sure he understood why we laughed, but he laughed along with us. He may have found it funny that my tongue didn't want to make the vibrato trill, but my tongue is accustomed only to English, and we English-speakers keep it simple. No staccato, no fricative. Then the sun began to shine. The world and our outlook brightened considerably.

We ended the train ride in Rabat, and after a day and a look around for something a little more exotic and romantic than government buildings, we began to circle around the country, stopping at several cities for a couple of days at a time, hitting the outdoor markets, the casbahs and mosques in Fez and Casablanca, enjoying the artistry and history in every city. Marrakesh had become slightly tainted by the volume of visitors after the popularity of Graham Nash's song "Marrakesh Express." Too many hookahs and bongs in the casbah. We found an appealing place to stay in Tangiers. The city had the cool notoriety of hosting spies, sultans and smugglers. Before that, it was home to Berbers and Phoenicians. The casbah with its winding alleyways was straight out of Hollywood, exciting even for non-shoppers. I couldn't resist buying a mirror with a painted wooden frame, cut in an ogee arch, still on our living room wall, and a cotton Berber caftan, celery green, still in my closet and a little snug now through the armpits. I also stooped to buying a T-shirt from a restaurant claiming it produced the best hamburgers in Africa. My idea of a funny T-shirt.

We met a local man—would he be a Tangerine?—who spoke English quite well. He said his name was Benny Goodman and that was good enough for us. Benny invited us to a house party to meet his friends. Circling the living room were a number of mismatched wooden chairs, occupied by mostly men, some women, in their thirties and forties. We all had drinks and finger food. We sat around smiling brightly as nobody else spoke English. We couldn't just comment on the weather as the warmth and sun had returned, and "brrrr" would not have been appropriate. We watched people dancing. One young woman, in her twenties or younger, padded in through the front door by herself, fully covered in her burka and veil. She peeled them off, revealing a miniskirt and sweater underneath. She kicked off her shoes, lowered her gaze to her bare feet as she danced alone, rocking to the beat, looking as familiar as any American girl on any dance floor. After a couple of hours of being lost in the music, she pulled on her black cover-up and shuffled meekly out the door and into the dark street.

§

A journey is like a marriage; the certainty to be wrong is to think you control it.

John Steinbeck

SPAIN AND PORTUGAL
1973

The rain in Spain was depressing. It was also endless. We were in Seville, looking for a place to sleep. A cab driver took us away from the heart of the city to a residential neighborhood and stopped in front of a pleasant middle-class house. From her neatly mowed front lawn the woman of the house quoted an impossibly high nightly rate and we did not attempt to bargain. We didn't want to be so far from the city center anyway. So we asked the driver to take us back downtown. We hadn't even looked at the room and the señora turned to go inside.

As we climbed back in the cab, the matronly landlady stuck her head out the front window and made kindergarten monkey faces at us, spreading her hands next to her ears and waving, with her tongue out. She propped her thumb on her nose and wagged her fingers saying "Nyah nyah nyah nyah" at us, recognizable in any language. We were taken aback by the outburst from this distinguished-looking older woman who surely didn't intend to make us laugh so hard.

The cab driver remained stony-faced, ignoring the woman and his amused passengers. We were giggling at her expense and I hoped she wasn't his mother. He drove directly downtown to a little hotel filled with thriving greenhouse plants inside a skylighted courtyard.

It felt good to peel off my soaked-through corduroy sneakers and blue jeans and drape my dripping clothes over the chair to dry overnight. While it was warm under the blanket, there was no heat in the building, and our clothes were as wet in the morning as they had been the previous evening. Reminders of Oran, without the toilet smells and the dirty dishes. I was traveling light, no spare shoes or jeans. I didn't like the sensation of pulling on marinated clothing and saturated sneakers on an unheated December morning. But we had seen plenty of barefoot children playing in the wet cold streets of Seville and I didn't believe they were barefoot for fun. Awareness of these niños made me feel less twee about myself, so I shut up and got dressed.

It remained wet and cold for the next few days before we headed west to Lisbon. Here was where we celebrated our third exotic Christmas in a row. On Christmas Eve we went to a nearby restaurant which was bursting with happy local households, all the generations crowded into vinyl-clad family-sized booths, infants babbling in carriers on tabletops, gamboling youngsters pausing to stare at us and brandish their new toys, nursing mothers, solemn menfolk and grinning great-grandparents, celebrating the holiday with a festive night out. Noisy and fun, they put us in a holiday mood.

The centerpiece of our hotel room was a bidet, where we propped up some unadorned evergreen boughs we'd bought at a street market. We wrapped gifts for each other in fold-up maps we had collected while getting here. We purchased a barbecued chicken in a supermarket, along with a luxury-priced can of Ocean

Spray cranberry sauce, jellied. Some good bread and wine. Our previous two traveling Christmases had been spent with new friends. This year it was just we two. Heavenly peace.

§

*There is no night life in Spain. They
stay up late but they get up late. That
is not night life. That is delaying the
day.*

Ernest Hemingway

CANARY ISLANDS
1974

New Year's Day, 1974, we flew south from Madrid along the African coast, landing in Las Palmas, the capital of the Canary Islands. The islands belong to Spain and are clustered in the ocean opposite the southern boundary of Morocco. It wasn't raining here. It was sunny and pleasant, cooler than the semitropical getaways on the left side of the Atlantic. We indulged ourselves in the watercolor warmth, the sunshine, the busy city streets, its little restaurants serving tapas—our introduction to tapas. Las Palmas was a commercial and government city, surprisingly free of tourism. We liked what we saw and decided to explore more islands.

The archipelago was not named for little yellow birds, but for some big dogs found by early Spanish explorers. The dogs, on closer look, turned out to be seals. Oh well.

In Tenerife, we found the tourist resorts. The beaches were dotted with trashcans painted with the word "Aloha." New high-rise rental apartments and condos under construction rimmed the beaches. Workmen with barrels of cement buzzed around the

229

worksites, and the air smelled of wet plaster, mud and paint. Few people were in the chilly water or lying on the sand, some of which also looked new.

Many of the tourists were German or British. The Germans I remember were from my parents' generation, and a few we talked to said that home base now was somewhere in South America. That made my eyes pop. Most of them seemed to be elderly single males. Or if they were married they weren't taking their wives out to lunch. Rumors flew, of course, that the Canaries were a favorite haunt of old Nazis. Scuttlebutt on today's Internet tells numerous stories of the underground railways sponsored by the Vatican, South American countries, mainland Spain and various Canary Island locations where Nazi war criminals fled at the end of the war. Thousands, allegedly, lived comfortably in South America in their golden years. Heinrich Himmler began to construct a research center in the 1930s on the Canary Island of Fuertaventura; evidence of its ruins is still intact. The Ahnenerbe Institute, which had a number of branches worldwide, was founded by Himmler and funded by the SS, and its scientific goal was to prove Aryan supremacy. But the work was suspended when the Second World War began, and Himmler committed suicide in May 1945. So we digested the gossip we heard from people in Tenerife, and whenever we saw a group of Germanic codgers socializing in a restaurant or on the streets, we silently sized them up and shuddered, suspecting them of being among the worst war criminals of the twentieth century.

We moved along from this island to the next, settling on the round little island of La Gomera, where we spent the rest of the winter. We found an apartment we liked. We shopped for groceries and I cooked, an activity I hadn't practiced since Hong Kong a year earlier. We also became enamored with some local tapas made of tiny new potatoes served hot with a spicy sauce. On the face of a cliff overlooking the village center someone had painted the name FRANCO. I didn't know if it was vandalism or propaganda—disdain or praise. Dictator Francisco Franco was still alive and in charge.

We made friends at the town square, next to the harbor, at tables under the shade of some broadleaf tree limbs. Here a group of expat English-speakers met for company in the late afternoons. Among our new friends, a British Protestant missionary woman who appeared to have few converts and didn't seem to regret her poor results. It had to be tough to convert an island of devout Catholics who had no good reason to change their minds. She was not on vacation and she didn't proselytize to us during her off-hours. She was good company. Another regular was a Norwegian sailor who parked his little ketch there in the harbor and proudly showed us around inside his tight and tidy home.

The woman who ran the village bakery frequently stopped at the outdoor café. Tim called her Señorita Pan, and she laughed at our lousy Spanish whenever she heard her new nickname. On our first full day on Gomera I had gone into her bakery alone and stood there, frozen, realizing that I didn't know how to say "bread." Her products were not on display but we worked it out with hand gestures and a bit of French, laughter and patience. After that, she knew what I wanted on my visits. One of the town square regulars had a black Lab he named Satan, which he pronounced Satin. I preferred the name Satin, which suited the dog's silky coat and smooth temperament.

This little island wasn't a tourist drive-through: no tour buses, no resorts, no airport, no nightlife, no designated beaches, only one hotel. The place now has an airport and a list of hotels, and I wonder if the islanders are still as curious and friendly with visitors. When we began this trip, we talked about inhabiting these places, not just breezing through. With our limited linguistic skills and reluctance to barge in, we barely scratched those surfaces. La Gomera was the one place where we came closest to mingling. And that was just with the select group of people, few of whom were natives, who could afford to lounge around the town square in the afternoon.

One day, with another couple, we rented a Volkswagen bug to tour the island—more up and down than straight across. The road was rough, rocks kept banging into the tinny floor of the car and one of the rocks came right through a hole in the bottom. We almost ran out of gas in the hilly wilderness but luckily saw a fishing village, where we were able to buy some fuel that I believe was intended for the fishing boats. Whatever it was, it got us back to our village.

The island was a mix of forests with dense canopies, rocky coastlines, lumpy mountains and photogenic fishing villages. Gomera is the home of the unusual whistling language, where people whistle messages to friends and family on the next mountain over, across the tops of the roller-coaster hills. A local young man—one with the true blue eyes which are common among this population—demonstrated the whistle language for us, loudly whistling whole sentences, whole paragraphs and stories, as far as I could tell. I can virtually hear him whistle the three syllables of "Timothy." Curiously, some Canary Islanders' accents drop the sound of the letter S; Las Palmas sounds the same as La Palma, both important island place-names. One could get lost.

Our village was called San Sebastian. Our town's soccer team was Los Leones. The nearest village over on Tenerife, where the ferry met the boat from Gomera, had a team called Los Cristianos. When I saw the schedules posted on a bulletin board, the Lions versus the Christians, I was delighted by the waggy sentiment. We went to a game and cheered for the Lions, both to support the home team and to enjoy a mild sense of transgression. The Lions lost.

Christopher Columbus slept here. In fact, he had a house which was still standing and operating as a modest art gallery. Chris also built a silo of sorts, right outside our apartment window, where bananas and other trading goods were stashed by him and later generations who sailed the prevailing winds to the Americas.

We examined the coastline, clear and chilly. The water here was too cold for winter swimming. Latitudinally, we were nearly opposite Cape Kennedy in Florida. Warm Atlantic currents flow north along the American coastline, and arc across from the Arctic down the European and African coasts, holding on to their northern chill on their way down. The beaches and the sea were quiet and beautiful. There was never anybody around. We stumbled across a wide natural cave tucked under a rocky cliff along the beachfront. We were told that the wide-mouthed cave had been used as a restaurant in years past, and still provided a hideout from the ocean breezes, with spectacular views out to sea. Sometimes we sat there on the rocks, straining to see beyond the horizon, looking for a sign. Should we move on to South American Or not.

We had run out of warm European countries to visit. The next island over was North America. Our passports were full of stamps, and no foreign country would let us in without a blank spot in the booklet for another stamp. There were no embassies here. We'd have had to go back to mainland Spain to add more pages. We already had filled up extra sets of pages. We didn't want to go back to Spain. My bank account at home was shrinking to a warning level. Besides, it was early spring, we were frankly getting tired of living this way. South America could wait. It was time for our real lives to resume.

§

Part Three:
Finding My Way Home

The whole object of travel is not to set foot in foreign lands; it is at last to set foot in one's own country as a foreign land.

G. K. Chesterton

HOME

Late March, 1974

We were on our way home by way of New York, feeling both excited and anxious because neither of us had any idea what to do next. We hadn't talked about staying together. Although some sense of commitment was implied, or even expected, Tim couldn't say he was able to support me, let alone himself. I couldn't just show up in the U.S. and get a job; I'd tried that once before. And he didn't want to think about moving to Canada. We didn't know how we would feel about each other once we settled back in our native habitats. We had to wait and see.

We didn't know what we had missed, or if we had missed anything. Along the way, some earnest young man told me we had missed a lot of great music. Surely the music was still there.

Our plane landed in Baltimore, where it sat on the ground for several hours, as the weather in New York was stormy. The flight attendants fled, the temperature inside the aircraft was getting hotter. We would have loved a drink of water, but it was not forthcoming. Finally the aircraft took off and flew to Kennedy. It was quite late at night. We had missed our connecting flights and the airline put us up for the rest of the night in a hotel near the airport.

We were too wound up to sleep. We turned on the TV because we hadn't seen television for years. There wasn't much to watch in the middle of the night, but that didn't matter. It was a novelty for about ten minutes. We dropped a quarter in the Magic Fingers attached to the bed. It refused to jostle and we couldn't stop giggling. Our bodies were still jiggling on their own from sitting in an airplane all day. We still didn't talk about our future. We had to let it simmer for a while—we weren't that far apart. We couldn't allow ourselves to get serious and mopey.

Too early in the morning we were in the terminal again, Tim to board a flight to Boston, me to Toronto. We tenderly said good-bye. No clinging, no tears. This will all get sorted out. Meanwhile, we were both heading home to families we hadn't seen in at least two and a half years, and we expected to be greeted properly, with open arms and welcoming hugs. We hoped somebody would say "I missed you."

Tim arrived in Boston and took a cab to his parents' house in the downtown neighborhood of Bay Village. His parents were on Martha's Vineyard, and the door was opened by their longtime housekeeper, Mary. "Oh, it's you," Mary muttered. "Don't throw your jacket on the couch," as she slogged back to her vacuum cleaner.

I arrived at my parents' house in a suburb of Toronto. They seemed to recoil. They told me I looked scruffy and my hair needed washing. I needed more than shampoo. I had been living so long as a wandering vagrant that the particulate matter of the squalor was ingrained. I cleaned up as best I could. For a week or so I hung around and paced around and reported what I've been doing for the past couple of years. I wrote and phoned old friends and contacts, announcing my return, maybe sniffing around for a job, or for a clue.

I told my mom and stepfather one evening about Tim. My stepfather, known as Mac, had uncoiled into a nasty drunk in the past decade, and now he lost his temper. He was furious that I had been traveling with a man. I pointed out that I was thirty-five years old and divorced. My sarcastic mouth made things worse. "Did you think I should save myself for the second husband?" That did it. He ordered me out of the house, pointing his finger out the window at the late-season grimy snowbanks. My mother wrung her hands in the background. It was pretty late at night. Teeth clenched, Mac told me I may stay the night, but insisted I be gone before he got home from work the next day.

In the morning, my mother remained silent. Neither scolding nor kind words were offered. Mac had left for work in the city. First thing after breakfast I said good-bye and walked the few blocks to the nearby mall, where Mom had maintained my bank account; thank goodness it was close by. I closed out the account, something less than a thousand dollars, but it was enough. The mall had a couple of phone booths, and I had Tim's parents' number on the Vineyard. Luckily, he was there. I said I would fly down today and he said he would meet me in Boston tomorrow. I caught a cab to the airport and I was outta there.

At Boston's Logan Airport I stood next to a bank of telephones connected to hotels in the city. I had never been here before and had no idea where to go. A uniformed skycap noticed my anxiety and my derelict demeanor. He took one look and advised me to go to the Bradford Hotel, a budget hotel right in the heart of downtown. I went, I checked in, and I was secure for the night.

First thing I did was find a meal nearby and call Tim from the restaurant to finalize our schedules. In my room I ran a hot and relaxing bath. When I emerged, I could not find a towel anywhere. I picked up the phone to call Housekeeping, but the phone was dead and I was dripping. I didn't want to roll on the sheets and get them all wet before bed. The bedspread appeared to be water-repellent. I settled for the heavy lined draperies which hadn't been cleaned for a while, judging by the dust and cigarette smoke captured in their folds. The Bradford had seen better days.

The morning was bright and fresh. I strolled around the neighborhood waiting for Tim to arrive. A woman on Tremont Street was selling roses, one at a time, for some vague fundraiser, possibly to benefit herself. I bought one. I stood on the sidewalk sniffing my unscented rose when a policeman roughly grabbed my arm. He accused me of selling flowers without a permit. I suppose I looked the type. The woman who sold me the rose was nowhere in sight. Welcome to the US of A, I thought. The officer and I debated my intentions for a few minutes. I was relieved he didn't ask me where I lived. But then he decided to believe me or forgive me, and he walked away, on the alert for a more formidable criminal.

Just then, Tim arrived and boy, was I glad to see a friendly caring face. As it happened, the Bradford Hotel was just a couple of blocks from charming little Bay Village, which included the Maleys' city home. Since Tom and Helen, Tim's parents, were now living part of the year on the Vineyard, the three lower floors of the brick townhouse were rented to Florence, a colleague of Helen's, while the top two floors were kept as a pied-à-terre for the family.

Tim and I unloaded our stuff in the guest bedroom in the upper part of the house.

To celebrate our arrival, dear Florence hosted dinner in the downstairs dining room. Also in attendance were Mary the house cleaner and her boyfriend, whose name I no longer recall. We had a pleasant evening with lots of stories to tell. Mary and her boyfriend had gone home by the time we headed up to bed.

Next morning, just before leaving for the Vineyard, I discovered that my wallet had been emptied, not a single dollar left. I'd like to accuse Mary's sullen boyfriend, but then again I hadn't looked in my wallet since buying a rose from the nefarious woman on the street. On the other hand, the wallet was still in its place inside my handbag; just the bills were missing from their leather pocket. Only the top echelon of pickpockets on the street could have been this delicate. Much easier for a novice to withdraw the bills while my purse was out cold, lying defenseless and alone on a bed upstairs. Welcome to the USA, again. I'd just been traveling in some of the scariest countries in the world, but this was the first time I had been physically accosted by a policeman, then robbed and stripped of all I owned.

And now I was at the mercy of people I hadn't even met. "The kindness of strangers," I drawled to myself, thinking of the crumbly Blanche Dubois.

§

Fame lost its appeal when I went into a public restroom and an autograph seeker handed me a pen and paper under the stall door.

Marlo Thomas

WOODS HOLE
1974

The bus to Woods Hole left on time from its creepy old terminal, which I believed was a substance abuser's home away from home, behind Paine's Furniture on Arlington Street in downtown Boston. The southbound highway, once out of the city, was and is plain and straight, not a bit scenic. So much for first impressions.

Ornamentally, moreover, early April was not an ideal time to discover Martha's Vineyard or to appreciate the roadside views en route. Grass hadn't yet turned bright green and the forsythia and daffodils on the south shore were barely thinking of waking up. The weather that day was drab, raw and damp. The bus's long wipers ran intermittently, and the heat was on by our feet. The winds off the Atlantic were icy.

The only excitement of the highway ride was the gamble to see if the bus would meet the boat before its scheduled departure time. If not, we bus passengers could witness the heavy car-deck doors drawing shut in our faces and watch the bloated ferry slip away into Vineyard Sound. If that happened, the next boat wouldn't sail for more than an hour—but traffic was light that weekday and our bus arrived on time. Even though it was only

April, and a handful of passengers were already waiting inside the Steamship Authority terminal, a line of eager customers from the two-hour bus ride had formed outside the ladies' room.

Men never had to queue up; men weren't asked to pay.

By law, one of the women's stalls had to be free of charge. The other two required a dime for admission. Some women felt it was more sanitary or more seemly to wait for an available ten-cent opportunity; others waited for the free cubicle in the name of thrift. Both kinds held up the traffic. It was a fallacy that the pay stalls were cleaner than the free stalls. Equal amounts of dropped toilet paper collected on all parts of the wet floor.

Most people were kind enough to pay it forward and hold open the pay doors for the next in line. It was a matter of expediency and courtesy to let the next person inside. Sometimes, though, a departing bitch would slam the door shut, maybe even through the skin of your hand. My friend Binnie described how one such high-minded shrew smiled with satisfaction as Binnie's hand caught in the latch when she grabbed for the door. Binnie hollered "Get a dime! Get a dime! Get a dime!" in an effort to free her hand. The guys in the adjoining men's room must have heard her but had no idea what she was yelling about.

See, the 1970s women's movement involved a lot more than battling for equal pay and abortion rights. It involved respect and equal consideration. Every little step of the way took a fight. College students and other protesters formed the National Committee to End Pay Toilets in America, as the pay-as-you-go requirement discriminated against women. The movement was successful. By the middle of the decade a dozen states had banned pay toilets, and by the end, the Woods Hole, Martha's Vineyard and Nantucket Steamship Authority eliminated the fee.

Even worse, in the distant early '70s, the Steamship Authority's most misogynistic insult was in prohibiting women from riding on the freight boat. There you are, at or near the front of the standby line with a freight boat loading up to go to the Vineyard, and there's a female in the car and you are shunted off to the side. Or you are a female foot passenger hanging around the waiting room and there is a freight boat about to leave for Vineyard Haven and you're dying to get on, but you can't; only men are permitted to board. The *Auriga*, the boat line's first and only freight boat at the time, ran back and forth on its own schedule throughout the day, and was a perfectly safe and suitable method of transport across the same sea lanes on Vineyard Sound, whether you were on foot or in your vehicle. It was mighty handy between scheduled passenger ferries, and who cared that the ferry didn't have food service or proper lighting to read a book. But the *Auriga* did not have toilet facilities for women, so we had to wait behind for a properly equipped passenger boat. The *Auriga* was sold in 1989 and replaced with the *Katama* in 1988 and the *Gay Head* in 1989, each retrofitted with a phone-booth-sized ladies' room in a corner. Facilities now are much improved.

Much more recently, Tim and I were in Vienna with a group and a tour guide, who was telling us at length about the buildings around us. I suddenly had to interrupt her to ask where the nearest bathroom was located. She looked at me sternly and said, "I vill tell you everyzing" and went back to her architectural review. I left the group to ask around and found a nice big underground public ladies' room. The stall needed a coin. I had euros, but not parts thereof. Another block away was a money-changing place and I was able to break down my euro into suitable coinage. It seemed like a protracted ordeal for a simple task. When I rejoined the group I told Tim, "Travel sucks." He reminded me of this whenever I suggested another vacation.

§

*I have already lost touch with a
couple of people I used to be.*

Joan Didion

WEST TISBURY

1974

They were charming, worldly and gracious, Tom and Helen Maley, and they scared the hell out of me. Now that I think about it, the fears were mutual. There was a certain shell of suspicion around my arrival. Tim was unglamorous and easy, he was my whole comfort zone, but in his parents' elegant home he was their son who needed protection from predators. I was a little older than Tim. I was divorced. I was a rootless illegal alien. I'd just been thrown out by my middle-class parents. I smoked. I looked feral. I drank their liquor. And I just happened to be penniless. What was it about me that could make them nervous?

As for me, I was at their mercy. I was intimidated, tongue-tied in the presence of such attractive people, especially in front of Helen. I knew she could see through me. I tiptoed around their house, enjoying their hospitality and their generosity, but not at all sure of my place there.

Helen and I were in the kitchen when a gray striped tabby walked into the room. I picked up the cat and said to it, face to face, "You must be Thelma." Helen smiled, seemed to loosen up. Another animal lover, good. A thread of a bond sprung up between us because of that plain cat.

246

After a few days, Tim's father took me aside and diplomatically asked, not about my intentions, but more or less what attracted me to Tim, which I guess was the same thing. I talked about his kindness, his empathy, his genuine respect for women even though he often teased us almost to the point of getting slammed with a flying handbag. Tim had grizzled hair and beard, and wore mismatched socks, and still does. But his heart was compassionate, his hugs were guileless, his honesty embarrassing at times, and he was unwilling to suffer fools, blowhards or Republicans. I don't believe I said all that so eloquently, but Tom exhaled with relief.

Helen was an early childhood specialist who taught at Wheelock College in Boston. She had persuaded the college administration to allow her to create a rural teaching program on Martha's Vineyard. Her young women—at this time they were all women—spent a semester living with half a dozen fellow students in a sprawling rental house in Vineyard Haven. The off-season rent was affordable.

The students joined several private preschools on the Island, aiding the teachers, learning from the teachers, meeting with parents and other family members to establish relationships. And of course they practiced what they were learning about and from the children. Moreover, they were expected to attend community events of all sorts and get to know local residents and Island concerns. Because they came directly from home or from dorms, the student teachers also learned about sharing and managing a household, paying for groceries and divvying up the phone bill. The courses were well received. Several of Helen's students returned to the Island after graduation to teach and sometimes to marry and raise families of their own.

247

Until the day she died Helen maintained an abiding respect for children. She knew how to talk to them and listen and understand them at eye level, always down on her knees when she was with a small child. She had a higher opinion of young mothers whose jeans were worn at the knees and whose floors were slippery with spilled Cheerios, than of those whose beds were made and dishes done and kids planted in front of the TV.

Tom was more celebrated, as his work was public and accessible. Tom was an artist who loved to paint but was better known as a sculptor. When the Maleys moved permanently from Boston to West Tisbury in the early 1970s Tom had enough outdoor open space to create eight-and twelve-foot-tall figures of women dancing, leaping, frolicking, all painted white, and placed in an open field on their property, facing the State Road, smack in the heart of the village. His sculpture reflected Tom's persona— exuberance, artistry, grace, humor, a high regard for big bottoms. Like almost everybody, I was soon crazy about Tom Maley.

A short time after we arrived, I reconciled with my own parents, at least by mail. It was clear that I intended to stay on the Island, and they shipped me the big blue trunk that I'd left behind when I left Canada, as well as the trunk I'd shipped back from Australia, and the artwork I had bought along the route of my travels. Mac even crafted a solid wooden crate to ship my New Guinea mask, which was about five feet tall. I believe the crate was made so carefully as atonement for our abrasive last evening together. I had never before known him to make anything out of wood.

At the same time, Helen made it clear she wanted me to drop any complaints about the thief who raided my wallet in their

Boston house. She was loyal to Mary, her cleaning lady, and didn't want me, this newcomer, causing a fuss.

Tim and I moved into the little barn on the property, a onetime goat barn that had been expanded upward to include a one-room apartment in the new second story. The ground floor had been converted into a studio for Tom. We didn't have a phone —too much culture shock. But we did have a deck overlooking a storybook pond with Muscovy ducks, fish and otters, guinea hens, snapping turtles, blue herons; dogs and cats running around. Arched Japanese bridges connected to the far side of the oval pond at either end, and in the middle, a weeping willow dipped down to the rippling surface of the water. Once a month, weather permitting, a beefy full moon rose over the center of the pond.

At first I felt disoriented trying to find my way around the Island. But what do you expect? North Tisbury was south of Tisbury. A friend of Tim's explained to me: "Yes, but it's north of West Tisbury." Then there's up-Island. If you look at a map of Martha's Vineyard, the top part is called down-island and the lower part, along with a shift to the west, is known as up-island. Those crafty New Englanders, wanting to scramble the brains of the rest of us.

Of course Tisbury is really Vineyard Haven, and Gay Head is now Aquinnah. And if you drive up-Island just past the Grange, which used to be the Agricultural Hall, which has moved, you'll come to a sign that says Entering Chilmark. But in fact you are still in West Tisbury for another mile, on the right side of the road, but Chilmark is, yes, on the left.

More than that, roads and streets were never marked in those days, no signs on posts telling you where you are or where you're heading.

Sometimes, though, people put their names on signs facing the road, to help their visitors and their UPS drivers. One such sign was posted along the Edgartown Road (also known as the West Tisbury Road, depending on your starting point. Its proper name is the Edgartown–West Tisbury Road). One such family name sign on this road said Katzenbach. It led to the summer home of Lyndon Johnson's Attorney General Nicholas Katzenbach. Vineyard kids, as they were being driven along this long straight stretch of the Edgartown Road, used to call out from the back seat as they whizzed past, "Katzenbach, dogs in front," then burst out laughing at their own wit.

And I burst out laughing the first time I saw a sign pointing to Lobsterville. Having been here a while, I no longer think it's funny.

As spring flowered into summer, I did some freelance writing for the *Vineyard Gazette* and peddled my travel articles around the continent while Tim took over managing the Field Gallery for the short season.

As we both worked quietly and casually during the day, I was introduced to the magic of summer life in this fanciful resort. Sunny days on Lambert's Cove Beach, celebrity spotting on Main Street, Vineyard Haven. I was startled one day to see Lillian Hellman walking down the street. Like a proper newcomer I stared at her. Her evil eye scowled right back at into mine. Scary.

A week later we were seated next to Ms. Hellman and Philip Roth having lunch at Helios. We ignored each other.

Just recently a friend asked his local friends on Facebook to say who was the most important person they had ever met. On this Island the list is interminable—presidents and queens, movie stars and Muhammed Ali, intellectuals and stand-up comics. Anyone here who works with the public or goes to fundraisers can draw up long lists with details ranging from elbow rubbing to more intimate associations. Our sightings don't come up in conversations—not cool.

Evenings meant social cycles, getting together with old friends of Tim's or new-to-me friends of his parents. As Tim commented, our long trip around the world was worth about one cocktail party before our acquaintances switched the conversation back to local politics or the latest good book. Helen and Tom glided through the summer either attending cocktail parties and dinner parties or hosting their own, with Helen cooking massive amounts of gourmet food and sit-down dinners with cloth napkins and enough stemware for twenty or thirty.

In those days, at these parties, the women got all done up in their best summery frocks while the men dressed neatly but casually, no tie, no jacket, often in barn-red pants from Brickman's. Not jeans, not yet. I only remember this because, at one party we attended, a couple arrived, she in crisp cottons and good jewelry, he in a suit with jacket and tie and matching pocket hanky. When he saw how informally all the other men were attired, he had a hissy fit, fists pumping, yelling at his wife for making him get all dressed up, and loudly blaming her for ruining his evening, if not his life. If we saw a man wearing a jacket and tie in the daytime, we knew he had just gotten off the boat.

By the end of that whirlwind season, the senior Maleys reckoned they had spent only two evenings at home alone. We frequently were invited along, and we sometimes held small dinner parties, but it was not a way of life we wanted to lead for the long haul.

Each summer Tom and Helen rented out their main house and moved into the big barn, originally a genuine barn meant for

251

farm equipment and buggies, remade in the 1940s by the Maleys into a magazine-worthy summer home. Big parties fit nicely into both houses.

On my first peek inside the barn that spring, I saw that the upholstered furniture was draped in white sheets, which reminded me of the opening scene I had seen in at least one play but never before in my real life. The interior walls and ceilings, floors, rafters and beams, were rough-cut wood, the color of overdone toast, untouched since their first exposure a century before. Of course, paintings hung everywhere. The focus of the room was a classic brick fireplace, well used on chilly evenings in June and September. A Victorian round oak dining table had been cut down to coffee table height, still balanced on its jumbo pedestal. Soft couches and chairs surrounded the coffee table and the fireplace. Even if you were a new friend, you could put your feet up.

The top floor was one open dormitory space with several guest beds under the skylights and rafters, trunks of funky old clothes for kids' costume pageantry, and plenty of space for rainy-day play. Tim was not quite five years old his first season in the barn and he spent at least part of every summer there until he left for Australia when he was thirty.

A good part of the Island's conversation that summer was the filming of a movie called *Jaws*. Who had a bit part, did anyone have a speaking part? Tim's buddy and next-door neighbor John Alley had a walk-on role in the movie. John was active in local politics. He and his family ran the general store across the road.

When we first saw the film in its Vineyard premiere a year later, John was seen in an early scene carrying a fishing rod as he walked along a dock. The widespread recognition elicited great whoops of joy in the Strand Theater in Oak Bluffs.

This segment and others with familiar Vineyarders on the screen were greeted with happy hollering and cheers during the movie's debut screenings on the Island. Seeing the film in its native habitat with its hometown population made it an exceptional entertainment beyond its being the first and one of the all-time great blockbusters.

At one point John came striding across our yard to insist that we sign up for a phone. He was tired of having to deliver messages to us in person. He was right. We hadn't thought of it; we needed to domesticate ourselves, to acculturate.

Tim even went out and bought himself a used truck he named Mulciber, another name for Vulcan, the Roman god of fire, and something to do with vulcanizing rubber. Mulciber was painted a rust color, and may have been rust-colored all through its innards too. Even though we were gravitating toward civilization, it was a slow process.

§

*Art, like morality, consists of drawing
the line somewhere.*

G. K. Chesterton

THE FIELD GALLERY

One evening in August 1970 Tom and Helen were having dinner with their good friends Bob and Maggie Schwartz and the Chicago artists Max Kahn and Eleanor Coen. Tom had recently finished the first of his oversized white dancing sculptures and installed it in the field in back of their house. Its completion inspired the group of friends to imagine building an art gallery for themselves and others, there in the Maleys' extended yard, facing State Road, the town's main and only thoroughfare. The grassy meadow had once been a cornfield where West Tisbury's police chief, George Manter, told me that he and other kids used to go to smoke cigarettes they made from corn silk. He did not suggest it was a slippery slope to other kinds of inhalants.

The late-night gallery project took form before the advent of zoning rules for the town, so Bob Schwartz, an architect as well as an artist, was on the vacant field early the next morning with a tape measure, a clipboard and a pencil, to design an art gallery. On his heels came the rest of the dinner party group, their children and their house guests. They carried hammers and saws and nail aprons, newly purchased for this fresh adventure. Among the novice builders was the aging but distinguished poet and literary force Stanley Burnshaw, who happily began pounding nails into the ascending walls and sloping roof.

Soon enough other friends joined the construction crew and sometimes strangers driving along State Road enlisted, because it looked as if fun was being had. The workers' wives produced lunch, plenty of it, hams and turkeys, cheeses and roasts of beasts, salads and homemade bread and suitable condiments, laid out on picnic tables at the building site.

There's a related story that goes with this project; it captures a Vineyard motif of the era. In those days, local dogs were not policed and they had their own agendas and hangouts. The uptown regulars gathered daily in front of Alley's General Store, across the street from the gallery, and howled in unison as the town clock at the church on the corner chimed the hours. This was not only a dog-meets-dog social scene: there was always a chance that some child might exit the store and drop her ice cream on the porch just as the screen door swung closed.

One noontime, the gallery wives arrived with their copious lunch components and because of a scheduling mix-up, all the humans left the picnic setting around the same time. Moments later, the word or the scent had gotten out that the tables had been left unguarded, and every up-Island dog within sniffing or barking distance was helping himself to the ham, the turkey, the meat loaf, the mayhem.

The building project wasn't completed until the following season. Over the winter, Tom wrote a letter that noted, "Work on the gallery will have to wait until all the free labor gets out of school." The youngest of the Schwartz children, William, was fourteen when he installed the electrical wiring in the building. But the homespun plumbing, electrical work and carpentry have withstood the tests of time, and the gallery still stands upright.

In the Field Gallery's first couple of seasons, the artists or their spouses took turns minding the shop. In the summer of 1974 Tim became the official manager of the business and I took over as manager the following year. We knew somebody. The gallery was open only in July and August, a nine-week season that made those summers fly by.

Early in the spring, a committee met to plan the season and restock the bank account for the upcoming summer. Overlapping profits never once eased us into the new year. Tom and Helen, Bob and Maggie Schwartz, Timothy and I made up the jury. We sat around an antique gaming table in the elder Maleys' living room and reviewed slides submitted for our consideration by hopeful artists. This day was the annual unveiling of the roll-up movie screen. When the artists' works were seen as postage-stamp size slides, all the *oeuvres* looked wonderful. Blown up on the home-movie screen, the flaws became magnified and the art was sometimes less appealing. But every year we saw some new art and new artists whose work we all liked. We kept adding people to our lists of contributors and that was usually good, even though there were a lot fewer artists on the Island in the 1970s than there are now.

Each summer Saturday night the artists and gallery staff took down the current shows and hung new ones. Of the three rooms in the building two were set aside for one-person shows by painters, sculptors, photographers and potters. The third room was hung with a selection from the gallery's stable of artists. The four founders had first choice of dates, as well they should have. Everything was fresh and new for an opening reception the next day. I was usually impressed with the quality of the work, and how striking it all looked together those late Saturday nights.

We the jury were not thinking only about sales back then. When somebody's old friend pointed out that her nephew was a brilliant art student and needed a gallery show for his résumé, or somebody's sister-in-law was just widowed and it would give her such a boost if we showed her watercolors, we good liberals sometimes caved and offered up some of our space. Besides, in those very early years, there weren't always enough professional artist candidates to fill all the vacancies.

To wit: we once allowed a young man to stretch a cat's cradle of colored strings from one wall to another. It was sort of pretty but about as marketable as a spider's web, which it resembled. It was his entire exhibit.

Then there were the feather people. I think they were a couple. They dyed hundreds, maybe thousands of bird feathers, murky lime greens, dirty chrome yellows and muddy magentas competing for offensiveness, colors just too weird to have come from nature; attached the wisps to strings and things; and displayed them around the room. Not only did they offend our aesthetic senses, but a number of our patrons were bird lovers, insulted by the presumption.

One memorably spacey fellow was quite late to arrive and hang his work. He finally showed up moments before the Sunday opening with an armful of dog-eared loose pages of pencil sketches which he attached, crookedly and haphazardly to the white walls, using beige masking tape. I believe he was stoned. Some artists weren't invited back.

Every Sunday afternoon at five, for those nine Sundays, a crowd of devotees, freshly showered and dressed up in resort wear after a day at the beach, collected on the lawn for nibble snacks, punch and wine. We gallerists hoped they brought their checkbooks. With any luck at all, red dots appeared here, there and everywhere during the openings and throughout the week, each dot meaning another sale. Smiles were broad. Fingers were crossed.

As well as the four artist-founders of the gallery, a number of talented and appealing young artists, including Allen Whiting, Peter Simon, Alison Shaw and Doug Kent, were among the novices who showed their work in this fledgling space. A lot of the sold artworks were shipped abroad to America, and Alison Shaw, bless her heart, came into the gallery after hours to securely wrap and safely pack up her own sold photographs.

The gallery did not have a telephone. We did not have a cash register, or a proper booklet for receipts. I don't know if other galleries had a credit card machine; we did not. Cash and checks were kept in a small unlocked metal box adrift on top of the desk. If somebody bought a work of art small enough to fit into a paper bag, it was a recycled bag from the A&P in Vineyard Haven. Nobody got rich.

As the gallery grew in prestige, the lawn became a popular site in summer for politicians, federal, state and local, to host fund-raisers, meet-and-greet parties, always for Democrats. Our much-loved congressman, Gerry Studds, came every summer to catch up with local concerns and chat with his followers. One summer, the gallery was showing reverse paintings on glass by the artist Richard Lee while Mr. Studds' gathering was scheduled. Mr. Lee's paintings that season included naked leches and libertines, all prancing around, leering through the glass, fully tumescent and not a bit ambiguous. Too late, one of the gallery owners realized that the artwork might be offensive to Mr. Studds or to some of his followers. But it was not to worry. Mr. Studds did not go inside the building that day. What's more, at question time, someone in the audience asked Congressman Studds what he thought of the movie *Rambo*, which was filling the theaters that summer. Mr. Studds responded, "To my constituents, Rambo is a French poet."

§

I'm not crazy about reality but it's still the only place to get a decent meal.

Groucho Marx

YEAR-ROUND

So our Island life began in 1974 with a taste of summer people's pleasures. There were and are many layers of community here, and we first sampled one of the luckier strata—a group of Maley friends, mostly academics, writers and artists, who were able to spend the whole summer on the island. Few of the people we met that first July and August had to rush back to work after a two-week break.

Because Tim's parents bought their vacation house at the end of the Second World War, and were themselves an artist and an academic, it was a natural tribal connection for them. Tim had Vineyard friends he had played with every summer since he learned to tie his own shoes. It was easy that summer for the two of us to join several overlapping social circles. Some were the children of artists and academics. Some were the great-grandchildren of Portuguese fishermen who came here from the Azores in the nineteenth century. Others were year-round Vineyarders whose ancestry went back three hundred years, and who were bound to be related to each other. A few were members of the Wampanoag tribe who had been islanders for thousands of years. Some had moved here in the '60s or '70s. New people who stayed through the winter were granted honorary citizenship.

Island friends were different from my old pals back home. I felt as if I were still traveling, learning about other cultures. These Islanders loved slurping raw oysters, and they were nonchalant about it and can swallow them while sober. These friends either didn't swim at all, or they leapt into the ocean in May when the ice floes seemed to drift just beyond the headland. Some wrote and published poetry. Quite a few appeared to be overeducated for their career choices.

By late summer, our down-time alliances had shifted from the elders to our own age group, who often had the chops to throw some pretty lavish good times. For example, the classic New England clambake. To do it the traditional way, you needed a lot of manpower, a whole day, and a private beach on the ocean, where a number of multigenerational Islanders had access. It seems my brief collection of publishable menus all require digging a pit in the ground.

While someone dug a deep wide hole in the sand, ideally by heavy equipment, someone else gathered gobs of seaweed, then kept it fresh in a big tub of saltwater. Someone else collected several medium-sized round stones. And someone else gathered a good supply of firewood. A cloth tarp, saturated in the sea and big enough to cover the hole, was needed too.

Okay. So you place the stones and the wood in the pit and build a roaring fire, letting it burn until the stones are glowing hot. Then sweep the ashes off the tops of the stones and rake the ash between them to make an insulating bed. Place a layer of wet seaweed on the stones. Add steamers, mussels, quahogs and lobsters, especially lobsters. Alternate layers of seaweed and seafood, then include potatoes, onions and corn on the cob. When everything is tucked in just so, cover the whole with the drenched canvas tarp, and let it steam for a few hours. Dance barefoot to the Bee Gees on your cassette player, have a drink and an oyster, and spit out a mouthful of sand.

Fall on the Vineyard is a delicious season, warmer than the mainland and suddenly quiet. It was my first year when I noticed the empty streets on Labor Day. It felt like an emergency evacuation had taken place. Where'd everybody go? One time, we had houseguests who decided to come to the island at the last minute, drove directly onto the ferry that Labor Day Friday, and off again Monday morning, without booking prior reservations. But that was a long time ago.

By December, though, it wasn't so easy to live in paradise. Many friends rented old houses which were either summer camps not intended for year-round use, or farmhouses that had been occupied by hardier souls who hung out in the kitchen next to the wood-burning cook stove. There weren't many new houses, yet. Renters in these places had to cover their single-pane windows with sheets of clear plastic in winter, as well as foam-stuffed cloth tubes, called draft dodgers, which were laid along the length of the doors, keeping out the wind. The same people lived with archaic plumbing, and warned visitors not to flush. Everyone had outdoor showers. Growth—a malignant word around here by the '80s— didn't happen until the end of the '70s and throughout the next decade. Then the fields and forests of Martha's Vineyard were cut up into housing developments. Growth proceeded at an alarming rate, but at least renters eventually had a better class of winter housing, if they could find an available shelter. Many of them began to build their own houses.

As the temperature and the daylight shriveled those first winters, jobs for Tim and his buddies were scarce. Tim worked as a carpenter on a short-term project, then shucked scallops while standing all day on a wet unheated cement-floored fishing shack in Menemsha. He was paid by volume and didn't enrich the household by much. More carpentry projects sprung up and Tim remained serially employed in the trades. I managed the gallery and continued to write and peddle freelance articles, which, if you must know, paid less than the earnings of migrant pickers in the South. I was also awarded grant money from the Canada Council for the Arts to do some book-length writing, which made me feel I was contributing to the household economy.

We could feel the earth rumble beneath us when the bombs dropped on Noman's Land, the uninhabited island next door where pilots from nearby Otis Air Force Base practiced discharging their live payloads. The air force doesn't do that any more. At first I thought we were having little earthquakes. "Oh no, it's just the air force bombing Noman's." Noman's Land is now a bird sanctuary, and humans are forbidden to tread on its shores, partly because of unexploded bombs, partly because it is a bird sanctuary and partly because the military just doesn't want anyone to go there. Lately, little ads pop up on my computer trying to entice me to try to best hamburgers on Noman's Land, or meet the most attractive singles on Noman's Land. They probably say *in* Noman's Land, and I never found out who was selling what.

Back then some newly minted carpenters on the Vineyard had PhDs in philosophy. Some of the women had advanced degrees but waitressed for a living. Numbers of the sweet young adults living here, seemingly hand to mouth, were grandchildren of the titans of industry, commerce and Washington. One pair of teachers in our neighborhood had a house cleaner whose grandfather was a U.S. president. She expressed true gratitude when the teachers offered her their castoff toaster. A few had come directly here from service in the Peace Corps, hoping to live as deliberately as they had practiced on more disadvantaged continents. It was all about living on the edge of the grid, in a pre–New Age kind of way.

A number of Tim's old friends and my new acquaintances showed up at our door at Christmas bearing gifts for us. I wasn't familiar with this neighborly community custom. I was flustered that first year because I had nothing to offer in return. Not even a cookie, because I eat cookies as soon as they arrive in our kitchen. I chided Tim for not warning me but he was unaware, unfamiliar with who bestowed what gift upon whom. Different genders, different wave lengths.

Vineyard winters are not as cold as Canada's but the dampness, strong winds, early darkness and a sense of isolation can make the Island seem pretty bleak, especially when the local economy is tanking. When the northeast winds howl we are reminded that we are alone out here on a small rock in the vast North Atlantic Ocean. In this humidity, twenty-eight degrees feels like twenty-eight below on inland thermometers.

And oh, the darkness. We are the leading edge of a time zone that stretches westward to Louisville, almost to Chicago. In December the darkness arrives around four o'clock and by bedtime it feels as if we've been up all night. We ought to adopt an earlier time zone like the one we found in Maritime Canada which would give us more daylight when we need it. Or maybe just stay on Daylight Saving Time year-round. Then it wouldn't get dark until five o'clock, a much more civilized hour. Schools could operate between nine and three. Americans get up too early as it is.

The darkness here is more noticeable because this is a rural community, we don't have streetlights beaming through our windows, so we plug in little nightlights all over the house.

In the '70s and later, the majority of the dude population wore beards, chamois shirts, blue jeans and hammer holsters, drove pickup trucks with Lab mixes or retrievers on the passenger seats. I never met anyone whose job was in Accounts Receivable. These were the guys with jobs. Those decades were a time of exceptionally high unemployment, widespread poverty, hungry families, and for many, dangerous excesses of alcohol and drugs. By our second summer here, Tim was on a construction crew full-time.

It wasn't only the poverty and its attendant shame, but many people on the Island worked directly for summer residents who were rich and important, whose powers were so intimidating that their effects echoed through the generations. One friend had placed her four-year-old in a summer day camp in Chilmark, a program meant for summer kids as well as locals. The teacher, a friend of the local family, reported that she had asked the little girl if she was here for the season or if she lived here year-round. The child blithely fibbed that she was here just for the summer. The teacher asked her where she lived the rest of the year. "Las Vegas," the girl said. Then she added, "Las Vegas, Connecticut."

There wasn't much to do for fun. The one and only movie theater operating from time to time those winters showed films in the Hopalong Cassidy genre, and sometimes a reel went missing or never arrived in the first place. Television meant a gray static image from one of the Providence stations, Boston being out of reach of our tall antenna. Providence and New Bedford local news in those days never seemed as exciting as the house fires and car pile-ups in Boston.

Here on the Vineyard, most restaurants closed down, except for the faithful Black Dog in Vineyard Haven and the Red Cat, a lunch place in North Tisbury (just south of Tisbury) with very good Portuguese kale soup. The first time I ate at the Black Dog it was winter, raining hard, when the roof decided to leak over my head. My chair was directly under the stream which splattered on my hairdo and shoulders and on my plate. I politely laughed it off, feigning charm and grace, when the waitress began to yell at me for finding it funny. She let me know, loud and clear, that this was no laughing matter. And here I thought I was being generous, showing that I wasn't going to demand a free meal or threaten a lawsuit. Sheesh, some people.

One off-season evening that first year Tim and I attended a concert held in the basement of the Oak Bluffs elementary school. Low ceilings, exposed water pipes and heating ducts, occasionally an overhead drip, a vapor of cement and dampness. Folding chairs and a sold-out crowd filled the concrete floor, standees lined up against the walls. The locally connected performers were a couple of young marrieds who had made it: James Taylor and Carly Simon. The event was a fundraiser for some Vineyard cause. The program was probably the same one they had played in Carnegie Hall earlier that year, but this was off-season, and they played to an appreciative and enthralled hometown audience.

§

Home is where you can say anything you want because nobody listens to you anyway.

Joe Moore

BUYING A HOUSE
1975

We decided to buy a house. I had never owned anything grander than a black-and-white television set, and despite living on the Island for a full year, I didn't know my way around well enough to recognize a good neighborhood from a so-so. Waterfront or water-view properties belonged on another planet, well beyond my wildest aspirations.

The up-Island landscapes that became most familiar to me were haphazardly groomed, not manicured or pedicured. There were no decorative oceans or beaches visible from the front windows. West Tisbury lots were bigger than mainland suburban lots, and they generally came with a homemade lawn and flowerbeds hugging a rectangular box covered on all sides with cedar shingles. Inconspicuous consumption was the motif.

Then, scattered nearby, a garden shed, fields and weeds, woodpiles and a sunny patch for a functioning clothesline. The generic house had one of those low-down wedge-shaped cellar doors, poking out of a side wall. I never knew what it meant when I was a kid and we sang a song about playmates who slide down the cellar door. In Canada, cellar stairs were indoors; think mounds of snow.

In a corner near the kitchen door, an outdoor shower and a corral for trash cans by the compost pile. Maybe a garage/workshop, and maybe, just where the lawn turns into a field, there was a boat cocooned in a tarp and stored until spring. In another corner, unmarked graves of dogs and cats.

As for Tim's location preference, it had to be either West Tisbury or something exceptional in another town. I suppose there were professional realtors on the island at the time we were looking; it never occurred to us. Our information source was the classified ad sections.

So we checked the houses for sale in the Island's two weeklies, the *Gazette* and the *Grapevine*. We called the owners or whoever ran the ads and made appointments to look at the houses within our financial and emotional reach. We went to see one about a mile from our current home: so many junked vehicles piled up next door that we didn't get out of the car. Another shared a well with its neighbor and that made us nervous. A few were freshly maintained but stifling somehow. Too nice to fix up—doing so would seem wasteful—and otherwise bo-ring. We are both frugal by nature, couldn't bear to slap paint over somebody's upgrade even though their baby-pink living room made my teeth ache. So we kept looking.

Then we saw an ad for a house on Music Street and Tim got quite excited. For one thing, Music Street was virtually across the field from the Maley compound, and it had some charming old white clapboard houses tucked among the mature maples, oaks and chestnut trees which turned the street into a shady green tunnel in the summer. It's the only named Street in town; everything else is a Road, a Way or a Lane.

In the story we heard, prosperous times developed for the neighborhood whaling captains who celebrated their good fortune by buying pianos for their families. On summer evenings, through open windows, the music of Chopin and Brahms, even saucy Chopsticks, floated through the center of the village. Before its appealing name was adopted, long before the Vineyard became so fashionable, Music Street had been called Cow Plop Lane. I love those down-to-earth New Englanders.

People we knew from Westchester County in New York had visited the island and loved the name Music Street. Because their New York house was the first and only one built on a road in a new subdivision, they went to see their town fathers and asked if the name of their road could be changed to Music Street. The town officials took the request under advisement for a week to consider the potential consequences of such a proposal and returned with their verdict: the street name might be changed to Melody Lane. "Never mind," said our friends.

Before we had a call back from the lawyer who was running the ad for the house, we decided to walk the length of the street and try to guess which one it might be.

The street began with the First Congregational Church on one corner and the three-story mansard-roofed school building opposite. The venerable Academy, as the town's schoolhouse had once been known, was in the process of changing into the town hall, while the elementary school children had just that year begun to soak up knowledge in a sprawling new building a mile or two away on Old County Road. The town's library, a smaller mansard jewel box, was next door to the old school.

Then the houses. First came the widow Jane Brehm's house, next to the church. Jane was a true Vineyard Yankee. Her first husband had been the magazine illustrator Perc Cowen, who died in 1923 from the effects of some rough slogging through muddy France in World War One. In her last months on earth, whenever someone drove Mrs. Brehm around the corner and past the Field Gallery, she quietly said, "I see the critters are still in the field."

A Victorian clapboard with lacy cutout trimboard along its deeply peaked roof lines stood next door. Next again, the symmetrical home of Rosalee and David McCullough, the historian, author and eminent winner of many literary prizes. And all-around nice guy, nice family. One Christmas morning, when Tim and I were driving to my in-laws' house to celebrate the holiday and open our packages, one of the McCullough children was in the process of shoving a new red bicycle out through the front door. An all-American Norman Rockwell tableau. The McCullough house was one of several that was sheathed in white clapboard and had shutters on the windows, the yard surrounded by a white picket fence. What a daydream those fences conjured.

Across the street, the house and fence we most desired had been the home of Gertie Turner, recently deceased. Another tall white Victorian, with a wrap-around porch and floor-to-ceiling front windows, the house was vacant and very appealing. Surely this wouldn't be the one, not at that advertised price.

As we moved farther from the village center, the houses were farther apart, reflecting different generations, from genuine pre-Revolutionary to almost new. We looked all the way up and down. When we found out which house was on the market, it wasn't one of the graceful grand old charmers. Of course not. It was a 1950s prefab one-story shoebox tucked way in the back of the lot, with an overgrown field in front. We were told by friends that it was the first prefab to be constructed in West Tisbury, and people remembered clusters of the curious standing around to watch the work crew assemble it like a puzzle.

It wasn't put together all that well, but we didn't care. The cement block walls of the cellar were stacked neatly exactly on top of one another, where they ought to have been staggered like bricks. Who would notice? The corners weren't exactly square. Our infatuation lay with the location and the possibilities for the modest little house. Lots of room for lots of possibilities. The outside walls were black-painted plywood panels that looked like tar paper. Imitation tar paper. The big front windows were leaky single-pane glass. We didn't care.

The interior walls and vaulted ceilings were chocolate-brown plywood panels; the watery grain of the plywood seemed quite decorative to our hungry eyes, and who doesn't love chocolate. The floors were plywood covered with a plastic-coated paper in a brick design like the one used for linoleum. Imitation linoleum floors, if you will. The indoor air held a tantalizing essence of mold. The kitchen was, to put it kindly, incomplete. All the light bulbs, hanging naked, were burned out, but Tim and I were electrically charged with possibilities. We bought the house, virtually on the spot.

Some furniture came with the house, notably a wicker couch and matching chair with faded orange Naugahyde upholstery, patio furniture though there was no patio. No lawn in the right place either. The front yard had been used as a parking lot, a semicircle of plain dirt. As soon as we bought the house, we bought and planted the cheapest grass seed and grew a green lawn, but the following spring the ground was bare dirt again. Who knew there was such a thing as annual grass seed?

Winter meant we copied our neighbors by stapling sheets of plastic around all the windows. It meant wearing thick longjohns all day, all night, so we wouldn't be too stiff with cold to move around. The ancient oil burner in the cellar chugged and huffed trying to keep pace with the thermostat.

Among the treasures we found: a long-dead stuffed seagull with its moth-eaten wings outspread. It so happened that the gull had once belonged to the town's librarian Lena McNeil, and how it made the journey up Music Street is one of life's unsolvable mysteries. Mrs. McNeil was notorious for striking out offensive words in the library's books, for inspecting children's fingernails, and for bragging that the library owned a certain number of books and every single one of them was right there on the shelf where it belonged. She is also the subject of an oil portrait, sitting alongside her seagull, painted in the 1950s by Tom Maley and now owned by the new West Tisbury Library.

I don't think we knew enough to dicker about the $38,000 price tag that came with the house. We asked Jimmy Alley, the town's postmaster, John's brother, a businessman and an occasional real estate salesman, for advice. He said the location alone was worth the price. That was all the counsel we needed.

We went to see Bill Honey at the bank to apply for a mortgage. The going rate was ten percent, which looked pretty good a few years later when rates drifted upward toward twenty percent, though lately that ten percent looks like usury. We were given a twenty-five-year mortgage, to expire in the year 2000, which was a million years away. Who could imagine living until 2000. Friends of ours, also unmarried at the time, went to see Bill

Honey for a mortgage. She squirmed a little, because of the sin of living in sin. Mr. Honey responded, "It's okay, my dear. I own some real estate together with Jimmy Alley and we're not married either."

We discovered that a number of people we knew had rented our new house at one time or another. It had been a rental property for many years. Other friends, a little younger, had attended nursery school here when the owner ran a preschool in her plywood living room. Tim had fuzzy memories of the original owner and her two daughters, one of whom had been killed in her teens in a never-resolved hit-and-run car accident up the road in Chilmark. The departing tenants, the ones who hadn't replaced the burned-out light bulbs, told us that the house was haunted. Sadly, we found the teenager's aluminum grave marker tossed in the bushes behind the house. If there had been any ghosts we must have exorcised them when we respectfully salvaged the grave marker and ceremoniously disposed of it.

It was early summer when we assumed ownership. "Assumed" is the right word. I recall walking around the property, through the weedy wildflower field at the front of the lot, stamping my foot and saying "I *own* you, tree" and "I *own* you, clover, and I *own* you, Queen Anne's lace, and buttercup, flower-of-the-hour and you too sumac bush." I laughed at the very idea, as if anyone could *own* something that grows wild in a meadow.

Our first big task: the house had sprung a few leaks. Tim and a couple of friends worked on installing a new roof on the hottest days of the summer. The sun shone down on them relentlessly and reddened their naked sweating backs. I hauled ice water and lemonade. Tim and I worked together stuffing pink fluffy spun-glass insulation in between the exposed ribs of the walls. The original insulation was aluminum foil bags filled with air and sealed. When they were installed, the bags must have looked like pillows, but when they were removed, they were flat, flabby and useless. People who have restored old New England houses sometimes discover that the original insulation was corn cobs. That, at least, has romantic cachet and probably remained effective longer. The 1970s stuffing, cozy-looking candy-floss slivers of glass, turned our skin into pin cushions. It required more than one shower and a painful scrub to remove the prickles of glass.

The house needed a lot more work before it was habitable. New windows had to replace every old one. Cedar shingles on the new exterior walls doubly covered the pink insulation. We moved two interior walls back to back to expand the living room and the master bedroom, and squeeze the former third bedroom into a space just the right size for a pantry. Wide pine planks went down on all the floors. Cupboards were attached to the bare kitchen walls, and more cupboards installed under new countertops. A new kitchen sink and basic appliances moved in.

The bathroom housed a washing machine filled with cigarette butts. Assuming it didn't work, I scooped them out and called a repairman who, a tad annoyed, showed me that it worked perfectly well. He stood there and glowered at me as the tub filled with water and began to slosh back and forth. The dryer was a set of three ropes attached to two poles in the back yard—a solar model.

Tim built bookshelves in every room, bathroom and hallway included, and we consumed many gallons of paint to cover and brighten the dark plywood's watermarks. Paintings were hung over the prominent seams between the panels. I sewed curtains. Over the years we added on in three directions. It's still a small house but we don't covet anyone else's. I like to think our starter home will remain our forever home, as we have promised our rescue

274

pets, one after another. We too have a number of unmarked dog and cat graves out there on the edge of the lawn.

§

*Smoking is one of the leading
causes of statistics.*

Fletcher Knebel

QUITTING
1975

I went to see our neighbor Milton Mazer, the Vineyard's resident
psychiatrist, to beg for some kind of tranquilizer to help me quit
smoking. I knew the Mazers mostly through their dog Fred, a free-
spirited roaming Bassett hound who made his daily rounds all
over the center of town. The dog regularly slid in through the crack
in the barn's sliding glass door to monitor the supplies on the
open pantry shelves, which were low to the ground, as was Fred.
One time he broke into a box of cake mix, ate the floury particles
and left our house with telltale powder on his nose and a
meandering trail of white paw prints.

Milton and his wife Virginia were abashed. To make them feel
better I sent the dog a Saint Christopher medal which someone
had given me when I started my travels. I figured Fred needed
more protection from the perilous wide world than I did at this
point.

I had to quit smoking. I had tried and failed many times over
the years. Tim had never smoked cigarettes, although he often
enjoyed a pipe or cigar at the end of the day. He had a nice
collection of pipes. Cigarette smokers don't collect anything other

than strangulated lungs, an essence of stinkiness, and an early death. I don't know anyone who smokes any more; they're all dead.

I had started to smoke, with deliberate intent, when I was eighteen (actually after practicing a lot in the privacy of my room with the door closed—as if that kept out the smell—when I was seventeen). Any self-respecting Canadian teenager felt it necessary to look grown-up and sophisticated, and the best way to master the affectation was by smoking. My mother told me that smoking caused lung cancer. I smartly responded that lung cancer would be cured by the time I was forty. Smoking wasn't easy; it took patience and determination to toughen up my throat and lungs enough so that I didn't cough. By my twenties I was smoking a pack a day, and in my thirties I sometimes devoured two packs. Here on the Vineyard, I had begun to gasp for breath on muggy summer nights. It was time.

Doctors didn't dole out prescriptions just because somebody popped in and asked. But after a pleasant hour, including a trickle of tears, I left Dr. Mazer's office with a non-renewable prescription, a firm resolve and a plan.

Anticipating my final tobacco purchase, I consciously and ceremoniously bought my last carton at the A&P. I then rationed myself to three smokes a day; one after breakfast, one after lunch and one after dinner. Those were my rules. At first the hours between meals were interminable. But I did it. Before I half-finished the carton I tossed the remaining packs into the trash. I was healed. I was done. I threw my hands in the air. I haven't had one since.

But if you've been there, you know it isn't just about quitting; it's about staying quit. The first major trial I had to overcome was to quell the excitement of attending a glitzy party in Boston. The date of the celebration was a couple of weeks after I had stopped my disgusting habit. The party was designed to launch a new nightclub and restaurant called Whimsey's at the Copley Plaza Hotel. The hotel was owned by a gregarious bon vivant named Alan Tremain, who had visited the Island and been charmed by Tom's figures at the Field Gallery. Tremain phoned Tom and told him he wanted to order "five or six large sculptures." Tom thought it was a joke. "No private collector orders statues by the half-dozen," he said. Tremain in fact bought seven of the oversized female figures and developed the restaurant's theme around the artwork. As it turned out, two of the statues had to go back to the Vineyard. They were too tall to fit under the ceiling of the restaurant.

Tim and I were invited to come to the restaurant's opening along with Helen and Tom, as the artist was also being celebrated that evening. All the way up in the car, while the others enjoyed their own notions about the upcoming event, I kept reminding myself to be strong; smoking was very much on my mind.

The city's subways and buses were plastered with posters for Whimsey's, illustrated with one of Tom's carefree ladies pirouetting across the cardboard. Inside the restaurant there were matchbooks and coasters, menus and ashtrays animated with the same figure.

The vast restaurant space looked like a windowless auditorium. There was nothing warm and cozy about it, other than Tom's sculptures, larger than life, placed here and there among the tables, bold and bright enough to transform the cavern into a frisky play-space for all.

With plenty of advertising ahead of time, the opening party was mobbed with invitation-only guests tarted up in maxi-dresses, polyester bell-bottom leisure suits, sideburns and mustaches. In those days, anyone who could grow one had a mustache. Boston's television personalities were the only celebs recognizable to me. Lots and lot of smokers, but I resisted. "No thanks, I quit," I said a number of times, and ate too many hors d'oeuvres instead.

The restaurant didn't cater to the elitists who might have expected an ambiance and menu like the decorous Copley Plaza dining room. Whimsey's menu was basic steak, hamburgers and seafood. Whimsey's had "no tablecloths, required no ties and admitted all sorts of middle-class gaucherie," according to *The Boston Globe*'s restaurant critic Robert Nadeau.

Not quite all sorts. Not long after it opened, Whimsey's got in trouble when a group of African-Americans were turned away at the door. A short time later the restaurant was vandalized and the pretty dishes were converted into smithereens. The restaurant was closed and never reopened. The space was later used as a parking garage, which may have been the architect's intention in the first place. Tom's sculptures, some of them badly damaged in the melee, were stored in a warehouse, left to suffer in the dark silence.

Some time later one of the figures was kidnapped from its storage depository. The heist came with a ransom note, according to a brief article in *The Boston Globe*.

From the *Globe*: "The object of the kidnapping was a statue called Daphne that stood in the lobby of Whimsey's discothèque in Copley Square. The $3,000 piece of art by Martha's Vineyard artist Tom Maley disappeared two weeks ago. Folks at Whimsey's put out the word that a reward of $300 would be paid for the return of the statue—no questions asked. Then came a mysterious phone call ordering that the money be delivered to a spot outside a church on Hanover Street late Wednesday night. Whimsey's manager Chandler Atkins made the money drop and, as instructed, he went around to the back of the church a little later, and there stood the five foot, one hundred pound statue." Daphne didn't finger her abductor.

There was no further word for several years. Then just recently, we heard that the purloined art had reappeared at a gallery somewhere in New Hampshire. The statute of limitations applies.

§

FIREWOOD

When Tim sees a truck heaped with cut-to-length firewood he will stop and gaze longingly—the same wistful expression that some men display when a Ferrari 458 Spider barrels down the road. But Tim virtually salivates at the sight of harvested logs. Tim loves felled trees, cutting them into wood stove length, splitting them with wedges and sledge hammers, stacking and storing the wood for burning next year or, more likely, the winter after that.

Sometimes on this Island, a property owner will take down a tree or two, cut the wood into fourteen-inch logs, and leave it in disarray at the side of the road. No need for a sign; the message is well known: Help yourself. The forager who gets there first will collect enough free logs to keep his family warm for an extra week or two a couple of winters from now. Like makers of fine wines, wood stove connoisseurs know that logs need to be kept under cover for at least a year to dry out, better yet two years, before they are burned for heat.

Because this precious fuel is often stored outdoors, it can become a target for theft. Our friend Don noticed that his woodpile kept shrinking. He suspected the guy next door. Then one early winter morning Don saw boot tracks in the light snow, leading from the kitchen next door straight to his woodpile and back. Maybe the pilferer wanted to be caught, as in "Stop me before I steal again." Now the two no longer speak to each other and Don's firewood is better secured.

The woodstove became a member of our family some time in the late '70s. We are on our fourth stove. Our fifth if you count the bruiser that first came into our living room, an industrial-strength mean-looking brute that a friend was trying to unload from his basement. It looked as if it came from a cellar in northern Chechnya. It didn't take much complaining or whining on my part to get it out of the house and back to its original owner.

Then it became a study of the best brands: Scandinavian or American. We've stuck with American, the same prototype that is in the permanent collection of the Smithsonian as an example of American righteousness, rectitude, hard work and moral fiber. Even its name, Defiant, suggests something of the revolutionary spirit.

This model, velvety black cast iron, has glass doors with a sunburst of mullions, semi-cabriole legs, carved panels on the sides, and a curly bracket to hold the drying rods. It's a focal point which announces itself in the living room, the centerpiece of our seating arrangement, a shrine, a brawny and handsome exemplar of the noble work it does.

It's like buying a car, or maintaining one. Some people know by sight the difference between a rear suspension upper control arm and an automatic transmission control valve. My Tim, who shies away from automotive discourse, knows when you need to clean your chimney and your catalytic combustor, how to delicately adjust the damper and replace the gaskets. He can tell you why you should burn pine in spring and fall, a soupçon of locust mixed with oak on the coldest winter days, and he has several gourmet recipes for in between.

I like to warm up the stew or soup in a pot on top. They say I could, but I haven't tried, to cook from scratch on its griddle surface, whose temperature is unfathomable, unmeasurable. We dry mittens on the rods that protrude from the side like antennae.

Heat is heat, you might say. But that's not so. Heat from a woodstove soaks into the upholstered furniture and the rugs and curtains, and then deals itself back to us as cozy comfy mother-huggin' warmth. A soporific kind of heat that rises higher than you would ever set your oil burner thermostat, and the older I get, the more I savor it. Besides, if you really feel chilly, you can walk right up to it, lift your shirt and get a near toasting, something you can't do in front of the floor register. The biggest plus is gazing from the couch into the fire, feeling its primitive beauty while stroking our chins in deep thought, solving the world's problems and feeling satisfied about sticking it to Big Oil.

On summer evenings Tim pulls a lawn chair beside his outdoor woodpile next to the woodshed, and admires it until the sun fades in the west. He'll get up once in a while and place a fat stumpy log upright on another thick log base, pound a few wedges into the cut end to initiate a few cracks. Then he'll whack at the vulnerable cracks with a sledgehammer until the wood splits apart into several suitable logs, spraying them like popcorn, sort of. And then he stacks them into the mound for winters to come.

The woodstove is not my department. I never load it, strike a match, shovel out the cinders and ash. I don't fell trees, don't cut and split and stack or trudge the wood indoors. People who do these things will remind you that wood heats you twice. I merely live with it like it's a favorite house pet, and benefit from Tim's passion and the stove's reliable generosity.

§

When I was kidnapped my parents
snapped into action. They rented
out my room.

Woody Allen

LANDLORDS
1976

Tim's parents decided to retire from renting out their main house, and generously offered us their summer barn so we could move into it and collect rent on our own place. In-laws like this are rare treasures, hard to come by.

Rental housing was and is hard to come by. House swapping, aka the Vineyard Shuffle, is an entrenched fact of life on the island, generally relating to the summer months. There is a shameful lack of housing here, which has gotten much worse over the decades and become a major crisis. It's classic supply and demand. Lots of people want to come, but nobody volunteers to leave.

For Tim and me, having the renovated barn for shelter, and the opportunity to rent out our own home in summer, meant we could collect enough free money to make the bank's payments for most of the year. Many other mortgage payers were in a similar boat.

The downsides for us landlords were few: sorting, packing and moving our stuff was minor, though a heart-rending scare for the pets. Deciding what to bring, what to store and what to leave behind for tenants became a trickier mental exercise. Where is the damn teakettle?

Having to scour and swab everything from ceilings to floors was an unpleasant nuisance for me. I wished everything looked like a sparkling hotel suite. It didn't, it wouldn't: we never lived that way. But while I was scrubbing I told myself that writing a good-enough book would probably never be as lucrative as renting our house for a couple of months. Plus, the house got a thorough cleansing once a year. Another plus: we got to live in the barn, which was a delicious place to spend a summer.

The true downside was more emotional. Walking away from our beloved home, leaving it in the hands of total strangers, was something like watching your adolescent daughter head out the door with her new boyfriend, who was a dork, maybe even a rapist.

The day we moved out, when we abandoned our nest, I couldn't bear to look at our house, sanitized though it was. To set a good example, every blanket was folded neatly, corners meeting corners within a quarter inch. Toss pillows were tossed just so, and the last dead fly swept from the windowsills. But the effect on me was that the rooms had as little character as a furniture store display. No sense of living things, no personality, no humanity. We left fresh flowers, a list of the house's idiosyncrasies, and a bottle of wine for our tenants, but the rooms felt as though the house had died and was laid out for final viewing. I couldn't wait to get out of there.

Our realtor was a sweetie named Goldie Silverman. (Did she know that the inventor of the supermarket shopping cart was a guy named Sylvan Goldman? I always thought they should get together.) Goldie wore a Greek sailor's cap—on her it looked good.

They usually started arriving around early April, Goldie with a stream of prospective renters traipsing through the house, either approving of what they saw or sour in the puss with critical distaste. *Chacun à son gout,* I said to myself. This was our *gout,* and if you, dear reader, will recall, I got an A in taste at the New York School of Interior Design.

Many would-be summer renters came from New York, Washington or Philadelphia, where spring had already sprung by mid-April. Their trees were greening, ours were still wintry bare. One suspicious prospect squinted as he scanned the yard and asked, "Why are all your trees dead?"

We never did get a whole-season tenant, which would have been nice, but neither did we have anyone come just for one week. Goldie told us that whole-season tenants take over the house, move your furniture around, make it all their own. And the weeklies? You never know at the end of the summer which one made off with your grandmother's Lalique.

We rented our house by the month for seventeen summers. We had only two vexing tenants. In one case, we rented it ourselves, without Goldie to guide us, to a group of three or four young well-heeled singles, none of whom was attached to any of the others. We didn't know enough to insist that just one person sign the lease and accept responsibility for our home. The night before they left the Island, they had a blowout of a party. We came home to find candle wax stuck on every surface including soiled bed linens, spilled stinky booze and food stains on tablecloths, cigarette butts mashed into the dirty dishes.

Plus there was a little matter of some unpaid rent. We inquired about the missing rent, and learned that the perp was a woman who had moved to Hollywood to make a movie or a TV series. We inquired further and learned that to collect in small claims court, we needed to fight the battle in the city where the culprit was living. We were not about to chase her to Los Angeles for her share of the summer's rent. So we learned something: that one, just one, person signs the lease.

Our second troublemaker was a naïve young woman with two small children and her own two live-in servants. Her coming with on-site household help seemed like insurance that our house would be well cared for. *(Please!)* Just before they arrived, a moving truck stopped at our house to deliver mounds of clothing. Plus new bedding, boxed-up sets of new dishes and more cartons of new kitchen appliances, all of which we had adequately supplied. And in the truckload, a new humidifier. One thing you don't need on Martha's Vineyard in summer is imported humidity. This young woman had grown up summers on the Island; she must have known about the climate. Still, having a staff of two gave us hope. One to cook and clean, one to mind the children, right?

When we returned home that Labor Day weekend we found that the glass in our bedroom skylight had been broken. It was a homemade skylight; it had two layers of glass, an inch or so apart. The inside layer was broken, not the exterior layer. We figured a child with a good arm had tossed a rock-like object while inside the room, to see if the window was open to the sky.

We have an antique full-size folding screen, three canvas panels painted with antique-looking flowers, to separate the kitchen from the dining room. It is old. Someone (the same rotten child? or the other one?) poked a series of holes with a pen through the canvas. We had it restored. We had the skylight repaired.

We traded war stories with friends who rented out their houses. One family had to buy a new couch because the existing one oozed peanut butter when poked with a finger. One neighbor had installed wide pine plank flooring, a now-scarce soft wood, only to have it trod upon by a tenant who wore his golf cleats as he paced around the living room. One found dirty underwear under the bed. One tenant set a fire in the kitchen, leaving the house uninhabitable for several months. Others complained of breakage and missing treasures. Mostly, messes and bad habits left behind.

Our tenants screened by Goldie were thoughtful and kind, and well aware that this was our very own home—our castle—that they were occupying. One family even invited us to dinner, serving us a good meal in our dining room, with our dishes, maybe even our wine. It felt like the old TV program *This Is Your Life.* "Oh look, our plates, our salt and pepper, our table!" I almost leapt up to stir the sauce.

In 1977, after only a year of renting, one of our tenants offered to buy our house for $100,000, almost three times what we'd paid for it two years earlier. We were flattered, a little puffed up, relishing the idea, daydreaming about a water view, but no, the reality was we were firmly attached to this place.

§

Even if a snake is not poisonous, it
should pretend to be venomous.

Chanakya

WEST TISBURY WILDLIFE

I was just getting up one lovely June morning our first summer in the barn. Tim had already gone off to the Whiting farm with his friend Allen to watch the resident sheep get fleeced. This was the day an off-Island shepherd came to oversee the annual shearing. A kind of ceremonial day.

I reached into the bedroom closet to retrieve my ensemble du jour, some jeans and a T-shirt. Looking back at me from the shoulder of a shirt on a hanger inside the closet was a snake.

I can't tell you if it was an equatorial spitting cobra, a death adder or a dusky pigmy rattlesnake. It was a serpent and it was in our bedroom closet and I was barefoot. I must have sucked in my breath, hands flying in the air, and disturbed the contents of the closet. The copperhead was now on the floor and I was still barefoot.

There's something daunting about having bare feet within reach of a boa constrictor or a python on your bedroom floor. My mind quickly reviewed the many times I'd gotten up in the night for a pee or a snack, bare-footing across the unfamiliar house in the dark, not even thinking about pit vipers or asps.

I flashed back to the day in Malaysia when Tim and I visited the Chor Soo Kong temple with its hundreds of Wagler's pit vipers slithering around us, unsupervised, untamed, fully fanged and toxic. A higher dose of adrenaline exploded through me now. My blood circulated faster, my muscle and sinew tightened and flexed as if I were about to do battle. We knew what to expect at the Malay temple; that was voluntary and we had no stake in it. Today I was alone and at home. This was mano à mano. It was personal.

I quickly dressed and headed for the phone, one eye all the time on the black mamba. I watched it slither across the floor, then climb to eye level in a fold in the curtain.

I remembered that Tim was out in the middle of a field somewhere with the Whitings and their sheep, basking in the nurturing sunshine. Cell phones didn't exist yet. Who else could I call. Aha, Tom, who was Tim's father and our landlord I suppose, although we didn't pay any rent. And he lived right across the field, a minute away. He said he'd be right over.

As I waited for Tom I pretended this was a normal day, except that I didn't make our bed. I had breakfast, I did a little kitchening and waited for Tom. He didn't seem to be in a hurry to rescue me.

Losing hope, I called the police. I talked to the chief himself, George Manter, who was tall, handsome, quietly manly, tough when necessary, and widely respected. A Gary Cooper kind of guy. He said he would be right over.

I had lunch and continued with my daily tasks, ignoring the bedroom.

Finally Tom showed up carrying a golf club. He didn't play golf. The python boa was still wrapped in the curtain. Tom shook the curtain. Nothing happened; the adder hung on. Tom took a swing with his golf club and the asp rattled his rattle. Tom and I both gasped at the sound. Tom assumed the golfer stance, feet apart, elbow straight, took another swing and the pit viper flew in an arc out the bedroom's back door and was never seen again.

I asked Tom what took him so long to get here and he admitted he needed to build up his courage with a cocktail before coming over.

An hour or two later, Chief Manter showed up. I told him that Tom had dispatched the puff adder out through the bedroom door. He sighed with relief. He said he didn't much like dealing with snakes. I've been told that any self-respecting snake will make a rattling noise if it's provoked. I'm told there are no venomous snakes on the Island. I was told it was probably a garter snake. Yah, right.

§

I prefer winter and fall, when you feel the bone structure, the loneliness of it, the dead feeling of winter.

Andrew Wyeth

ON PATROL

At the crack of early morning, the air was still. The wind wouldn't begin to whistle down Music Street for another hour. Our woodstove's chimney smoke hung straight up. Tim's old dog Talon tugged on her leash to get going on our regular rounds, on patrol around the Panhandle, a couple of country roads which form a square circle past our house and embrace a portion of the town center.

There wasn't much winter traffic in those days, maybe somebody driving to work or to catch a ferry, sometimes the familiar jogger who lived a few miles from here. I wondered if she jogged from her house, trotted around the circuit and then all the way back home, or if she parked nearby and circumnavigated the three-mile lap, as Talon and I did, although our pace was much slower and we were never far from home.

I remained vigilant as we walked. Some of my neighbors were still tucked in, others had left for work or school, and it was my self-appointed role to see that all was well on the circuit. On cold mornings, Talon and I moved briskly, overseeing the seasons of the grasses, monitoring the arrival and departure of leaves, blossoms and berries, wildlife half-hidden behind stone walls. After Talon died, other dogs and I took the same route, with the same job description.

We began by walking west and then north, to avoid the blinding winter sun so low in the sky. As we walked farther away from the town center, the houses became incidental.

After the first bend in the road, piles of oak leaves softened the edges of the pavement. Talon liked to dive into the mounds and emerge nose first from the other end. She didn't need her leash; she knew the pedestrian rules. But there were wild things to excite her, deer on the asphalt sometimes, skunks, plenty of crows, rabbits too. Raptors hunted for lunch while circling overhead. Not all the sounds and movements were significant; dead leaves crunched underfoot, a single feather might have drifted by.

Across the road, segments of ancient stone walls were interrupted by scrub forest that seemed to go on forever, and did, all the way to Waskosim's Rock in Chilmark and beyond.

The walk took us all around the rear boundaries of the Whiting farm, its pastures, grazing land and forests, the open fields' contours tempered by centuries of sheep, still out there now, descendants of the woolly critters first brought here by the Island's early settlers.

Also housed on the farm in the 1970s was a herd of Scottish Highland cattle, horns out to here, squat necks, long wavy auburn fur and shoulders to die for. They all looked like bulls; even the females had those handlebar horns. They sometimes stood at the fence that divides the farm from our yard, staring rudely at me, and once or twice broke through the fence, just to scare me. I went back inside.

We turned right again, onto State Road, where the traffic is heavier and faster. Across the street was the town's main cemetery, which housed the genealogy of the community. Salty weather had blurred the storied inscriptions of sailors lost in storms, forty-niners mortally wounded on their way west to search for gold, so many of the names still carried by citizens of the community.

On a wintry day much like this one, a generation earlier, the town's handyman was assigned to dig a grave. The winter had been harsh, the frozen ground relentless. So the handyman went to find a helper, offering his friend a bottle of whiskey for sharing the task. The friend gladly accepted the offer of gainful employment and the two returned to the graveyard to begin digging. Before long the men decided that the ground was so hard, they had better fortify themselves with a little advance in salary. They took a drink and continued to dig. The warming effects were so beneficial the workmen nibbled at the bottle, between hacks at the hard ground, until the bottle was empty. The town employee felt so selfish about consuming half of his friend's pay that he retrieved his own bottle from the floor of his pickup truck, and they continued to dig.

It got dark. The handyman's wife began to worry about his whereabouts and called the police. As the officer approached the blackness of the cemetery, he heard merry singing. He found the two workmen, two shovels and two empty bottles at the bottom of a nine-foot deep hole in the ground. It seems that when the diggers reached the soft loose sand under the frozen soil, they continued to shovel with such determination they didn't realize how deep they had dug. They were unable to climb out of their pit, and the policeman had to fetch a ladder for their release.

With the farm still on our right, we saw three houses from three different generations of Whitings along State Road. The

295

farthest and oldest farmhouse, designated the oldest occupied house on the Vineyard, was built in 1668 by Josiah Standish, the son of Myles, and there are implausible rumors that the attic holds treasures that came over on the *Mayflower* with the original owners. I'd been told, as well, that the attic also housed a more recent relic, a big ball of string with the label "String too short to save." The kids called the barn Fort Moon.

The dog and I continued around Parsonage Pond, whose slopes were perfect for sledding and whose shallow surface was often suitable for ice skating. Above the bend, almost peek-a-boo from a pedestrian's viewpoint was the home of Miss Jane Newhall, who came each summer from her lovely home in Pacific Heights, San Francisco. Her home here was built by her great-great-grandfather Asa Johnson, who went west at the time of the gold rush, and did well. Her family established the town of Newhall, California. Town lore has it that Ulysses S. Grant slept here, in this West Tisbury house, on an official visit in 1874. Official history says that President Grant was here for ceremonies in Oak Bluffs, a good hike from Parsonage Pond. He got around.

We huffed up the little rise, around the bend to Alley's General Store and Post Office, where so many of the population got its sliced bread and sixpenny nails, its local news and gossip, along with the U.S. mail.

John Alley's first memory of the store was standing next to his father, learning to use the big silver cash register. "You had to add everything up first on a paper bag and push in the numbers and crank it around a couple of times, then the drawer popped open."

Across State Road, Joe Howes was ready to plant his front yard flowerbed, as he always did at the tail end of March, by poking plastic daffodils into the frozen ground. Customers coming out of the store and people driving by were startled into remembering it was April Fool's Day. People around here knew what was possible and what was a good annual joke.

Next door, visitors and locals aimed their cameras at their families and guests, bundled in quilted jackets and mittens, posing with limbs outstretched in front of the sculpture at the Field Gallery. Year-round the photo shoots were accompanied by bouts of laughter, whether the poser lost her balance or just wobbled.

Beyond the gallery, which was closed for the winter, and the Rosenthal house, also closed for the winter, was the home of John Alley and his widowed mother, Mary Alley, who also had a deep raucous laugh that carried a long distance. The barn where we spent summers was tucked between and behind the two buildings. Hearing such good sounds from both sides was, for us, one of the joys of spending our summers there.

Across State Road again was the spiritual center of town, even for non-believers, the pristine formal Yankee squared-off clapboard First Congregational Church. Its hourly chimes reminded us what time it was, and in so doing jarred the winter silence and set the neighborhood dogs to howling. A guest in the barn once complained that the church bells began to toll at eight in the morning. We assured her that they rang twenty-four hours a day. We've noticed that visitors sleep well at sea level. There still wasn't much traffic. Our walk had taken us back to Music Street, where the wind caught up with us. I turned up my collar and tightened my scarf. As usual, nothing happened that morning.

§

Second marriage is the triumph of
hope over experience.

Samuel Johnson

A WEDDING
1976

I wonder, sometimes, where I would be if Tim and I hadn't gotten married. We did it in a rush, so it seemed, because we wanted to thwart the *federales*. There I was, feeling comfortably at home in our West Tisbury retreat, infinitely settled into our sweet West Tisbury life, so it seemed natural for me to apply to the Immigration Department for permanent resident status. I was thinking, "I like it here, I'd like to call it home," as if that might impress anyone in Washington. My request was forwarded to the federal Department of Labor which took no time at all in ordering me back to wherever it was I came from.

The Department of Labor told me the United States had enough writers. What a pack of Philistines. How could any self-respecting country have too many *artistes*. One of my prospective in-laws, whose career revolved around moviemaking, commented that the government was right. "There are far too many Canadians working in Hollywood and taking jobs away from the rest of us." I sputtered inwardly. My romantic, tradition-bound Timothy responded with "Fuck 'em all, let's get married."

And so we did. The event was as informal as the proposal. The selected date was Valentine's Day, chosen because it was school vacation week and Tim's sister Sandra would be able to come east and be my maid of honor. And it fell on a Saturday. Lots of people could come. We didn't think of it beforehand, but the holiday helps us (helps Tim) remember our anniversary.

The date, a few months away, also gave us time to plan a simple wedding. We went to see Max Kapp, the Unitarian minister in Vineyard Haven. Mr. Kapp's first question was to ask why we were getting married. And Tim blurted out, "Because we have to." I jumped in to explain what he *really* meant (wife-like already) was that the shotgun wielder was the government, and to assure him I wasn't pregnant—as if he cared.

Mr. Kapp suggested we write our own vows, as people had started doing in those days when the Western world began to lose respect for authority. Being a skilled journalist, I wrote something so dry and stiff it read like a bylaw for the department of septic systems. I was a nervous wreck. My fingers froze on the typewriter keys. I didn't dare mention tenderness and sentiment, love or promise, in case the whole thing was a big mistake. The love was there, but so was the anxiety. *What am I doing?*

Joyfully and optimistically I sewed a long simple wedding dress from a swath of silk I bought in Thailand, shimmery turquoise shot with raspberry pink. I didn't have enough material to cover my shoes, my best shoes were a little cloddish, and it seemed extravagant to buy new ones. But my face was glowing, the shoes only show in a few photographs, and as it turned out, the room was so crowded nobody could look down.

I needed a coach for all this, though I don't think that job description had been invented yet. I was never the kind of girl who played a bride, or paid attention to rituals and ceremonies. Marriage, sure; wedding, not so much. I couldn't define the word "nuptial." I could only envision, as a joke, a train that dragged around the block and a chorus line of bridesmaids in matching pink costumes. I looked in the mirror and knew I couldn't do this artificial princess thing. I was lost. Yet for all those months, my excitement drove my nervous system into such a spin I couldn't believe my feet were staying attached to the ground.

The antsy and excited pair of us went to Oak Bluffs to buy a wedding ring. We found the world's only cynical jeweler. He didn't care a whit about our thrilling news. He was unmoved by our starry eyes. Here comes another couple, yawn, like the ones who pop in all day long in the winter to buy wedding rings on Circuit Avenue. I wasn't surprised later to see that his business had folded. The simple gold ring that Tim bought that day still works.

My happy future father-in-law drew an announcement card illustration for us, a variation of Michelangelo's Sistine Chapel ceiling painting of two hands reaching across the cosmos toward each other. At the same time, without our knowledge, Tom made a cartoon drawing of us with photographs of our faces glued onto our cardboard necks, to use as a topper on our traditional tiered wedding cake. The artwork is kept in our wedding photo album.

My prospective mother-in-law organized potluck food and a cake, bouquets of daffodils and tulips from Farmer Green's greenhouse. Perfect.

The officiating took place with a few friends and family in Tom and Helen's living room, Max Kapp conducting. Sandra was maid of honor, John Alley was best man. My parents chose not to attend. My sisters Linda and Lorna came from Toronto for the weekend; sister Tyrie wasn't able to get the time off work. Friends came from New York, Boston and Philadelphia.

We intended to adorn the scene with Vivaldi's Four Seasons on the record player, but we forgot to turn it on. I hoped nobody was paying attention when our strident marriage vows were quietly repeated.

It was done in a minute. We hugged and kissed each other, bundled up and walked across the frosty yard to the Field Gallery for a party. I think everyone we knew was already there and so were some mystery guests whom nobody recognized when the snapshots came back from Mosher's. It was mid-February after all; some people hadn't been out to play since New Year's Eve, and were ready to explode with celebratory enthusiasm.

I was reminded to do the traditional bouquet tossing, when a guest from Boston took an unexpected flying leap to the front of the gathering. Helen's housekeeper, Mary, snatched my airborne bridal bouquet from on high, bruising the daffodils and tulips and a few female guests, then hoisted the flowers up for a victory lap around our more ladylike friends. I never expected to see such speed, such sheer will. Mary never did marry and she died too young.

I remember the spirit, not many specifics of those few days. We ate and drank and frolicked and laughed and continued to enjoy the company of all the guests who had piled into the gallery, then to our house and my in-laws' house and other friends' houses for a weekend of goodwill and good wishes. After more than forty years, it still seems pretty wonderful, as a properly sanctified marriage, a solemnly sworn covenant, ought to feel.

§

You get old and you realize there are
no answers, just stories.

Garrison Keillor

WEST TISBURY
2018

We have a book around here somewhere that lists the life expectancy of almost everything—refrigerators, raspberries, faucets, mattresses, light bulbs, tea bags, goldfish—but not of people and their relationships. That aspect of our lives is cruising along nicely, no expiration date in sight.

In all those in-between years, we've raised a daughter, Chloe; added a fully grown daughter, Stephanie; and experienced the joy of a grandchild, Annabelle. We've had a number of jobs, mourned the deaths of beloved family, friends and pets, and traveled to more countries and to South America, our sixth continent, though our post-marriage travel was mostly in two-week segments to fit in with our employers' expectations.

But now we've lost the desire to go anywhere. Whenever a travel brochure lands in our mailbox and I feel a flutter of interest, I remind myself of the following:

Modern American hotel rooms have nice big beds, but the pillows won't punch into the right shape, the room is overheated and the window doesn't open. If the curtains are fully drawn, the room is pitch-black. If the curtains are open a crack, a bright light beams into my eyes. If it's totally dark, I can't find my way to the bathroom. The shower is impossible to adjust, the carpet smells like chemicals, the TV doesn't carry the right channels. How can we sleep without the dog and the cat on the bed with us?

I don't have the energy for touring. No more reverent hushed visits to gold-lined cathedrals, no more temples or mosques for me. No more churches, synagogues, pagodas, ashrams, shrines, naos, dagobas, ziggurats, stupas, not a single sanctum sanctorum. I don't want to get lost on unfamiliar streets, or struggle with languages that nobody understands, or figure out how much that costs in dollars. No more taking off my shoes to stand in airport lines. No more renewing passports with increasingly ghoulish pictures—"too sick to travel" photographs. No more rides along stony Andean roads too narrow to accommodate a chicken-filled bus that was certain to tumble over the edge and kill us all, feathers everywhere.

No more wondering where the public bathroom is, and will it be plumbed, and will they charge a coin that I don't have on me. No more modern tour buses that think it's a good idea to cover seven hundred miles in a day. I've climbed to enough mountaintops to see inside castles, even though the last mountaintop castle we ascended to outside of Prague contained an ancient master suite with the skull of a dragon on a table next to the curtained bed. Actually it was a crocodile skull that somebody brought north, a gift for the twelfth century king who prized it jealously, as did his descendants. After all, none of the other kings in Eastern Europe had a dragon skull. That relic, kept next to the canopied royal bed, gave the place a human, egotistical, braggadocio touch and I appreciated it. But the climb was brutal.

No more passenger ships filled with seasick travelers crossing the Indian Ocean in a monsoon. No more standing in a long line waiting for the bathroom in a little restaurant which we hadn't patronized and where everybody else from the tour bus lined up and the innkeeper arrived and scolded the lot of us in the line for unethically using his plumbing even though there was no other WC in sight in this charming Alpine village, and our bus driver/guide had disappeared around the corner after lighting his cigarette.

I don't want to cancel the newspaper for two weeks, or break the heart of our old dog who has known since birth what a suitcase means. No more eating unrecognizable food. "What is it?" I once asked a waiter. "It's meat," he shrugged, and left the dining room.

The excitement and the fun of travel have dissipated with age, I guess, but there is bliss and simple comfort in their place. There's private pleasure in the knowledge that I've actually done things I never dreamed of as a child.

But that's me, probably not you. I recently visited with a ninety-three-year-old friend who longs to go to China some day, although she's not sure it will ever happen. I hope she gets there.

I'm staying in place for the duration, but I wouldn't have traded it for the world. Oh wait: it was the world.

§ § §

Acknowledgments

Many thanks to all those who helped me pull these stories out of my memory bank, especially the Sunday Writers Group; our hostess Cynthia Riggs; Shirley Mayhew, Paul Magid; Susanna Sturgis, Andrea Rogers, Everett Spees, the late Alan Janger, and Dan Sharkovitz. Special thanks to my editor Susanna Sturgis and production editor Amelia Smith.

Some of the travel stories have appeared in The Vancouver Sun and other newspapers. 'West Tisbury Wildlife' and 'Firewood' were published in the Vineyard Gazette, and a version of 'On Patrol' was printed in Peter Simon's book 'On the Vineyard II.' Harper's Monthly published an adaptation of the story 'Khartoum, Sudan,' and a twelfth grade textbook called 'Language Matters' ran a variant of the snake temple article 'Penang, Malaysia.'

Made in the USA
Middletown, DE
01 October 2018